OH,
SAN
LORENZO

OH, SAN LORENZO

A JOURNEY THROUGH ARGENTINE FOOTBALL CULTURE

WILL DALTON

First published by Pitch Publishing, 2025

Pitch Publishing
9 Donnington Park,
85 Birdham Road,
Chichester, West Sussex,
PO20 7AJ
www.pitchpublishing.co.uk
info@pitchpublishing.co.uk

ISBN 978 1 83680 199 3

Printed and bound on FSC® certified paper in line with
our continuing commitment to ethical business practices,
sustainability and the environment.

Typesetting and origination by Pitch Publishing
Printed and bound in India by Replika Press Pvt. Ltd.

Contents

Introduction

I WAS 13 years old when I realised that football could teach me more than just the trivial matters of the game itself. In a year nine politics class, Mr Nelson was outlining the history of Spain when he paused to ask us what we knew of the country and its regions. The room was quiet. Even those on the eager front row looked down sheepishly at their desks. For once, it was my hand in the air.

Without much thought, I blurted out something about Catalan independence, the different language and identity of the Basque Country, and the importance of Madrid as an economic centre. It didn't amount to a very profound analysis, but I was the only one in the class who had any meaningful reference points for the country. Mr Nelson looked impressed by my rare contribution but, of course, I hadn't engaged with any extra reading before the class. I simply knew that Catalan flags were waved at Camp Nou during Barcelona matches, that Athletic Club in Bilbao only signed players with ties to the Basque region, and that Real Madrid's *Galácticos* project was symbolic of the city's power and prestige. I didn't yet know what football culture was, but I was already being influenced by it.

About ten years later, the game's capacity to teach me about nations and society came into sharper focus when I lived abroad for the first time, spending six months in Argentina. Approaching my mid-20s, I was finally ready to learn a new language and discover a different culture. Most of my peers had felt this curiosity long before me, throwing themselves into French exchange trips, Erasmus programmes and overseas adventures each summer. With the ignorance of youth, I had taken little interest. At home I had my friends, my family and Charlton Athletic. Why did I need to travel?

By the time the urge struck, most of the people I knew were building successful careers in London. Meanwhile, I was sitting in an airless classroom in Buenos Aires, sweating over Spanish textbooks with backpacking school graduates six years my junior. But I enjoyed the routine of those weeks at the Spanish school. Crucially, classes only ran for half the day. In the mornings I could study the language, and in the afternoons I could study the people.

Porteños (those from Buenos Aires, hence the reference to the port) were instantly fascinating. Hours that were intended for reviewing my Spanish notes in cafés and plazas were lost to people-watching. Everything about their style of communicating was so different to my British compatriots: the way they whistled and waved at each other, their tactile greetings, the exaggerated hand gestures as they spoke.

I soon found out that putting these people in football stadiums sent their expressive ways into overdrive. In public spaces, people are generally restrained by inhibitions and social norms – even Argentines, who are hardly famed for their reticence. But on the terraces, the unwritten rules that kept people in check seemed to flutter away with the ticker tape as soon as the players entered the pitch. An inner being was unleashed from the people around me. To this day, I find myself watching the supporters almost as much as the match itself when I'm in Argentina.

Anyone with a passing interest in football knows about the passion of Argentine fans, but being among them offers a peek inside their world that you cannot get from videos on social media. Woven through the bombastic rituals and, at times, feral behaviour are people expressing their love, hopes and fears; their anger and dismay at the world, and the joy they defiantly carve out within it. Every game feels like an anthropological study – and the people's culture reveals itself too. Matchdays are an exhibition of street food, street slang, music, politics and local traditions.

Nearly all of my experiences on the Argentinian terraces have come watching Club Atlético San Lorenzo de Almagro. Curiously, it was Charlton who led me to *El Cuervo* – 'The Crow' – due to some striking parallels in the clubs' histories, which are mentioned in Chapter 3. San Lorenzo and their fanbase sucked me in, and I became more than just an observer. Following the club has never supplanted my support for Charlton – which takes up an embarrassingly large part of my identity – but my desire to watch San Lorenzo home, away and on a laptop screen in the early hours of the morning has grown steadily over the years.

Osvaldo Soriano, the legendary Argentine writer, famously supported the club and often discussed his relationship with fandom. 'Being a San Lorenzo supporter is to live with interminable suspense,' he wrote. 'It's a burden you drag through life with the same mix of pride and bewilderment that you have as being an Argentine.'

The statement struck a chord with fellow *cuervos* – San Lorenzo fans – who still quote Soriano nearly 30 years after his death. His words encapsulated San Lorenzo's turbulent past and the club's habit of intertwining itself with Argentina's journey as a nation.

Football fans are prone to overplaying the drama and jeopardy around their own team. However, as I stood in the kitchen of my London flat at 3am one night, hands on head and panting in shock after San Lorenzo snatched a last-gasp winner against Flamengo to stay in the Copa Libertadores, I couldn't help but think Soriano had a point. *El Cuervo* seemed to attract these moments more than most. The Argentine commentator Mariano Closs, who has no affiliation with the club, agreed. 'What a team this is, *por favor*,' he said in a hoarse voice through my laptop speakers

9

as the players piled on top of each other and the supporters celebrated wildly in the stands. 'Miracle after miracle after miracle. San Lorenzo de Almagro, ladies and gentlemen, live by these heroic feats!'

Off the pitch, the club's existence has been even more dramatic, and as Soriano inferred, it has reflected the ups and downs of Argentina as a nation. As the population boomed and the country prospered, so did San Lorenzo. When the military dictatorship seized power and embarked on its reign of terror, the club nearly disappeared. The resilient Argentine people fought back to reclaim democracy, and San Lorenzo rose from the ashes.

All the while, *El Ciclón* – 'The Cyclone', another one of the club's many nicknames – maintained a reputation at the vanguard of Argentinian football culture, from the emergence of organised fan groups on the terraces to creating songs that travel around the world, press archives and football folklore repeatedly point to the influence of *cuervos*. This irresistible fanbase, battle-scarred but inspired by their club's tumultuous history, kept me coming back for more. After my initial six-month stay in 2014, I returned to Buenos Aires every year before the Covid pandemic, including a one-year spell living in the city. When borders reopened, I compensated for lost time with two more extended visits in 2023 and 2024. Every single trip back was planned around San Lorenzo fixtures.

Despite my addiction to one particular club, an appreciation of Argentina's wider football culture has taken me to 18 different stadiums across the country, spanning four tiers of their domestic game. All of these clubs and places have helped me make (some) sense of Argentina, its people, and how they experience football like no other population in the world. As such, I have included several non-San Lorenzo experiences in this book. Drawing on terrace songs, my handwritten diaries, a swiftly abandoned Tumblr blog, press archives, interviews and countless conversations with the talkative locals, the following chapters tell stories that typically begin on the streets of Buenos Aires, but sometimes travel hundreds or thousands of miles.

Flying on the wings of The Crow, this is a journey through the greatest football culture on earth.

Will Dalton

Chapter 1

A la cancha

Voy a dejarlo todo	I'm going to drop everything
Para ver al Ciclón	To go and watch *El Ciclón*
Yo pienso que esta noche	I think that tonight
Vamos a festejar	We're going to celebrate

AS I closed the door at the foot of the towering apartment block in Caballito, Buenos Aires, I could already feel the sun beating against my back. Softened by an early spring breeze, it was a pleasant warmth. The streets were quiet with a distinctly 'Sunday' feel. It was Mother's Day in Argentina, which made it quieter still. The faint smell of *asado* – Argentina's national dish of barbecued meat – drifted on to the street, suggesting how most people were spending the afternoon.

The relative hush was punctured by the beep of a horn as a car rolled through the dappled sunlight. '*¡Vamos San Lorenzooo!*' the beaming middle-aged driver shouted at me, flicking his hand back and forth through the window in that trademark gesture so particular to football fans of these parts. The mere sight of my blue-and-red-striped shirt was enough to provoke the commotion behind the wheel. One stranger greeting another with the kind of enthusiasm that only a matchday can give you.

Kick-off between San Lorenzo and Barracas Central was still five hours away, but the pre-match build-up starts early in Argentina. For a nation of momma's boys and football fanatics, *el Día de la Madre* was a problematic item on the agenda, with fans torn between their mother and their team. Thankfully, smart diary management from my San Lorenzo-supporting friends Gonzalo and Eduardo had seen their family duties wrapped up by 2pm, so cold beers could be flowing within the hour.

I began my journey to Gonza's place in Villa Devoto, on the western edge of the city. It was the opposite direction to San Lorenzo's Estadio Pedro Bidegaín, known as El Nuevo Gasómetro, but the allure of drinks on his spacious terrace was too strong on a sunny day. After some refreshment, we would catch a fan-organised minibus to the game.

A year had passed since my last trip to Buenos Aires. Walking past Río Café Bar, a favourite spot from previous stays, I was relieved to see that the waiters in shirt and tie, the old wooden furniture and faded pink walls had not changed over the previous 12 months. In truth, they probably hadn't changed in the last 30-odd years, but in the places you love there's always a strange paranoia that things won't be as you left them.

My journey to Gonza's had got off to a slow start, with four failed attempts at topping up my SUBE transport card offering more reassurance that Argentina wasn't changing too much. In one corner shop, the friendly owner said the SUBE machine often ran slow or stopped working on Sundays. I wasn't sure about the technological validity of such a claim, but I liked the idea that the machine was just another worn-out worker who needed a day off.

Eventually I found a machine that worked and headed towards Villa Devoto on the number 105 bus, hurtling down narrow streets, accelerating into bends and screeching to an abrupt halt that jolted me out of my seat at every stop. If there is another way of driving a Buenos Aires bus, I'm yet to experience it.

An upbeat, shirtless Gonza greeted me at the door, where Edu had also just arrived. On my last visit, he'd loudly announced to his cats that 'the English pirate' had turned up, but I was spared the nod to my colonial ancestors on this occasion. Customary male-to-male cheek kisses were exchanged and we headed up to the terrace where the beers were opened. The hiss and crack of the can sent a wave of bliss through my body as I settled into a deck chair with the sun on my face and Argentinian *rock nacional* drifting from the speakers.

Gonza and Eduardo have been around the world and speak nearly ten languages between them, but as our conversation switched to football, any worldly sensibilities they may have picked up on their travels stayed well hidden. The pair embodied the cliche of the Argentine male: hairy chests exposed to the sun, one hand holding a beer and the other gesturing wildly as they despaired over their team.

'Today we have to win, *si o si*,' was Gonza's verdict given San Lorenzo's worrying position near the relegation zone. Three points was the only option on the table.

And 2024 was proving to be another tumultuous year for San Lorenzo on and off the pitch. A few days previously, a group of the club's *barra brava* hardmen (similar to hooligans – but we'll get to that) had invaded the training pitch to lecture the players on their unacceptable recent performances. Experienced centre-back Gastón Campi had tried to interject but was told to 'shut up and listen', as the *barra* and the players came close to blows. On the same day, the club's third manager in six months was appointed. It was now up to the 68-year-old Miguel Ángel Russo to steer *El Ciclón* away from trouble in his second spell at the club.

But Gonza was just as concerned with the journey to the ground as the outcome of the match. The buses organised by regional supporter groups, or *peñas*, have a reputation for unruliness and attracting more volatile elements of the fanbase. Our bus was coming from San Martín, a working-class area outside the city's borders with a degree of notoriety.

'Going with these people is the riskiest thing I've done in the last five years,' Gonza had messaged me during the week. He had seen it all as a San Lorenzo fan, travelling home and away for every game in his younger days. But at 40, boisterous days at the football were becoming few and far between and his appetite for disorder had fully diminished. Gonza had barely been to a game since my last visit, but as always he was ready for action as soon as I said I would be in town for the Barracas game. Ever since we'd met a decade previously, he had assumed a kind of paternal role towards me with San Lorenzo and joined me for nearly every game I attended with an endearing sense of duty. Today would be no different.

Eduardo also brings generous *fútbol* guidance to our friendship. His extensive knowledge of the Argentinian lower leagues is invaluable when planning games to watch as a neutral, helping me navigate the always complicated and occasionally dangerous world of the *ascenso*. Thankfully, he had travelled with the San Martín group before and allayed Gonza's concerns about the bus journey. 'Maybe you'll find some *locos* at the back of the bus,' he said, 'but they're all good people.'

Two hours later, we were walking towards our pick-up spot on Avenida General Paz. The motorway acts as a border between Buenos Aires city and Buenos Aires province; or civilisation and danger, as more sheltered city dwellers tend to see the divide.

As we restocked beers for the bus journey, my unimaginative choice of Quilmes was once again mocked by the two Argentines. Like many 'national' lagers, Quilmes is at the cheap and insipid end of the spectrum, but to foreign eyes, the bold, elaborate type over the blue and white stripes of the Argentinian flag has a magnetic appeal. A cold can of pure Argentina. Still high on my return to the country, I was easy prey for simple branding tactics.

* * *

Bom, bom, bom-bom, tish. Bom, bom, bom-bom, tish. We heard the bus before we could see it; a beating drum and crashing symbols edging closer, with singing voices just audible within the cacophony. When the vehicle pulled over to our spot on the pavement, confirming itself as our transport to the game, Gonza would have turned around and walked home had Edu not already vouched for the trip.

The rickety red-and-blue bus looked as if it had just emerged from a war zone. The entire left panel of the windscreen had been shattered, cracks rippling outwards from where a missile had all but pierced the glass. A broken windscreen wiper dangled vertically over the other side of the front window. Below, a battered metal bumper revealed its own traumas, jutting inwards from the blow of a collision, while gaffer tape forlornly attempted to cover gaping holes under each headlight. On the rusty red flanks, drunken passengers leaned out of the windows and waved huge San Lorenzo flags, which billowed in the wind.

We hopped aboard and received an enthusiastic welcome. Jorge, with his neat black hair and sunglasses was the *Presidente* of the San Martín group and keen to add an air of professionalism to the operation. I thanked him for his help in planning my travel and tickets, but it was difficult to chat over the hammering drumbeat and raucous singing coming from the back of the bus.

'*La banda de Boedo zarpada de gira, quiere cocaína, no puede parar.*' – 'The gang from Boedo is on tour,' went the song, 'they want cocaine, they can't stop.' While illegal substances were not apparent on board, the booze was flowing and included some interesting concoctions. A large plastic bottle, cut in half and filled with a homemade cocktail, was thrust towards us through the mass of bodies.

Sipping from a sawn-off bottle is a familiar feature of the Argentinian pre-drinks, or *previa*, but the orangey mixture in this particular vessel was new to me.

I took a sip. *'Está buena!'* I said, wincing less than expected. 'What is that?'

'Red wine and grapefruit juice!' the mixologist responded proudly in his Lotto-made San Lorenzo shirt, which must have been 15 years old. Combining a carton of cheap wine with a fruity soda – typically from the brand Manaos – is a popular pre-match drink. As the cold, sweet liquid flowed through me and renewed my energy levels, I could understand why.

The cocktail washed away Gonza's inhibitions, while Eduardo had clearly forgotten his pledge to 'take it easy' after a heavy one the night before. Bouncing up and down, he belted out the words to an old-school San Lorenzo song, which felt particularly apt for the moment.

'If I were president, the presidential palace would be a nightclub,' they sang. 'And at the door a big poster would invite the drinker in. No waiter or counter, just everything filled with liquor' – a short pause – 'and the gang from Boedo soaked in alcohol!' they roared twice over. Beer sloshed from cans and the flag-bearers dangled out the windows, sweeping their poles from side to side as the bus roared down the motorway.

As a wild-eyed skinhead continued to orchestrate Edu and the singers from the back, I shouted through a conversation with Jorge, clinging on to the handrail so I didn't fall over every time the bus swung sideways to dodge traffic. There were now only 45 minutes until kick-off. The *previas* usually last hours and continue outside the stadium once the fans have arrived, so why were we cutting it so fine?

'*Día de la Madre*,' Jorge responded with a sage expression. Around 50 supporters were travelling from San Martín and he wanted to give everyone as much time as possible to see their mums before escaping to the match. It was this kind of lateral thinking which had surely earned him the presidency.

Our chat was suddenly interrupted by the skinhead, who was battling his way towards me at the front of the bus. He'd got wind of the foreign *cuervo* and the next thing I knew he was removing his top in front of me. To my relief, it was just to reveal his collection of San Lorenzo tattoos.

In the centre of his back, a row of lettered drums spelt out 'BOEDO', the neighbourhood where the club was born and made its name before being controversially removed by the military dictatorship in the 1970s – a traumatic episode which continues to define the club. Next to the drums was a huge crow and underneath, *'Este sentimiento es verdadero.'* 'This feeling is real.' Given the pain he must have gone through for the sprawling set of tattoos, I didn't doubt the claim.

I thanked him for his display and returned to my lukewarm Quilmes. But he wasn't done with me. *'Veni, veni!'* he urged, staring at me intently before dragging me to the back of the bus. After squeezing down the aisle, the skinhead seized the drummer's sticks and demanded silence. 'We have an English visitor!' He announced in hoarse Spanish. 'And he will choose the next song!' The bus fell quiet. Suddenly in the spotlight, I felt a little embarrassed so I launched into a chant as quickly as I could.

'Cuervo, sos mi alegriaaa ...' I offered. 'Crow, you are my joy ...' It may sound somewhat deranged in English, but my fellow passengers lapped up the terrace anthem. They were screaming the words and jumping around me before I could even make it to the second line.

When I broke away from the crowd to get some air, I witnessed the other side of *peña* travel. The bus made a final stop for the remaining fans to board, and a small red-haired boy, no older than four, apprehensively stepped on board, hand-in-hand with his dad. He looked shy and slightly perturbed by all the noise, but was ushered down the aisle like a VIP as we frantically swept the debris of cans and bottles aside.

The *Presidente* sprung into action, giving each seat a wobble to find the least-damaged option before frantically wiping down the surface with a tissue. The boy sat down, legs swinging below, as his dad laid an arm around his shoulder and sang censored versions of each chant in his ear. The bus to the game had its debaucherous streak, but the effort made to put the young family at ease was heartwarming.

I grabbed a window for the final stretch to the stadium, joining the line of bodies half-inside, half-outside the bus, flinging their arms out to the beat of each song. A man driving alongside our ramshackle mob rolled his eyes and veered away from us to another lane. A few drivers in San Lorenzo shirts beeped their horns in approval. As we entered the Bajo Flores neighbourhood and the Nuevo Gasómetro loomed ahead, the streets began to turn blue-and-red with murals and graffiti. One in particular caught my eye.

'San Lorenzo must be defended every day, all the time, everywhere you go,' it said. The quote belonged to Rubén Darío Insúa, a supporter, ex-player and former manager of San Lorenzo, who had left the club just six months previously. Today, in a twist of fate, he would be in the opposition dugout as manager of Barracas Central, plotting the downfall of his beloved club.

Our bus rolled to a stop. In the distance, the sun was dipping from view, sending a bright orange glow along the horizon. Buenos Aires is prone to a dramatic, fiery sunset. They seem to suit the personality of the so-called 'City of Fury' and its people. Bajo Flores is a poor, neglected area, but its lack of development means there are no modern high-risers to block your view of the skies overhead. Only the imposing silhouette of the Nuevo Gasómetro stood between us and the sinking sun.

On the streets, colourful swarms of San Lorenzo fans approached the ground on foot. When it comes to dressing for *la cancha* – the stadium – Argentines could not be more different from my British counterparts. At home, the 'casuals' style which once defined terrace trends still holds a subtle influence, with fashionable streetwear often favoured over club colours. Even those uninterested in fashion are usually wrapped in a dark jacket for most of the season anyway, keeping out the winds that whistle through our cold concrete stadiums. It leaves little opportunity for displaying club colours, barring the flash of a scarf or a shirt pulled over a hoodie. For some old-school fans, donning either item is something of a crime in itself, and may see you mocked as a 'scarfer' or a 'shirter'.

In stark contrast, the Argentines dress themselves in every piece of club merchandise they can lay their hands on, with colours proudly on display from head to toe. It is not uncommon to see an official shirt paired with club-branded tracksuit bottoms and a training jacket layered over the top. Colour coordinated bucket hats are also popular, while bracelets, necklaces and any other accessories with the team's badge or colours can be thrown into the mix. What the resulting outfits may lack in elegance, they compensate for in their contribution to the collective. The look of each individual is less important than what it lends to the overall image of the tribe; in this case, a sea of blue and red. Personal style sacrificed for allegiance to the cause.

The vibrant matchday scenes in Argentina always feel like the counterpoint to the dark silhouettes trudging towards the stadium in the paintings of L.S. Lowry, which depict the British football experience so aptly. Neither is better or worse (to my mind). There is beauty in Lowry's panoramas, and indeed that purposeful march towards a football ground on a winter's day, head slightly bowed, hands buried in pockets as you try to retain the heat you soaked up in the pub.

Likewise, stepping off our raucous bus into the warm evening air had its own sensory charm. The smell of barbecued chorizo filled the air as rows of ad hoc grills prepared the fans' favourite of *choripan* – a sausage sandwich – for incoming fans.

Over a nearby vendor's cries of *'chori, chori, choriii'*, one of the San Martín *cuervos* leaned in to ask why I, an Englishman, had come here, and why I liked San Lorenzo so much. I had plenty of reasons to throw at him, from the community and friendship it gave to an outsider like myself, to the unique history of the club and its faithful, ingenious fanbase. I was drunk and I was gushing.

Hearing a foreign voice speak so highly of his club visibly moved the young *cuervo*, and when I finished my explanation I received an unexpected hug. As he pulled away, he looked at me with a wistful smile, gently shaking his head. *'San Lorenzo y las mujeres,'* he said, before taking a pause and repeating the mantra. 'San Lorenzo and women.'

I couldn't help but laugh. His body language and the emotion etched on to his face had suggested a more poignant comment was coming my way. And yet, his slow, sincere delivery almost made it sound profound. This young man, no older than 18 or 19, already had it all figured out. There were only two things in life that mattered. Both gave him joy, both gave him pain, but he couldn't live without either.

With my new, simplified outlook on life, I followed Gonza and Eduardo through the open gates of Ciudad Deportiva – San Lorenzo's 'Sport City' complex – where the Nuevo Gasómetro awaited.

Chapter 2

We're going to kill a referee

Yo lo llevo a San Lorenzo	I carry San Lorenzo
Adentro del corazón	Inside my heart
A ver si los jugadores	Let's see if the players
Lo sienten igual que yo	Feel the same as me

MATCHDAY IN Argentina moves to the beat of a drum. Rolling percussion had soundtracked the journey to the ground and now it marked the destination too. Past the entrance of Ciudad Deportiva, beyond a cluster of training pitches, stood a semi-circle of tall concrete pillars. They supported the vast terrace behind the goal of the Nuevo Gasómetro and below them, dozens of drums banged the infectious rhythm of murga.

Argentina may not be famed for carnival, but the murga tradition endures. Throughout the year, but particularly in February for carnival season, marching murga bands bang their drums, crash their symbols and blow their brass instruments, while *murgueros* – elaborately dressed in satin, tassels and top hats – dance to the music with dramatic leaps and jumps. Murga has roots in southern Spain but, like many cultural traditions that made their way to the Río de la Plata, Argentines and Uruguayans transformed it into something quite different, as immigrant communities seasoned it with African and Latin American influences.

23

By accident or design, the clearing underneath San Lorenzo's all-standing home end – *la popular* – acts as a perfect concrete amphitheatre in the hours before kick-off. The thudding drumbeat of the murga has a visceral effect within it. The closer we got to the band, the more the rhythm morphed from being an exterior sound to an internal vibration moving through our bodies. By the time we'd got through the final line of security and the turnstiles, the deep *bombo* bass drums and clattering snares had completely enveloped us.

With just ten minutes to go before the start of the game, it was time for the hardcore of the support, the *hinchada* (pronounced een-chah-dah), to take their place on the terrace. Their theatrical entrance, led by the *barra*, is an important part of the matchday ritual and can draw as much attention as the arrival of the players on the pitch. For many teams, the moment even has its own song, 'Here comes the *hinchada*, they're out of their minds.'

Gonza, Edu and I latched on to the tail of the 200 or so fans following the *hinchada*'s procession. Giant flags on 15ft poles swept through the marijuana-filled air. Some flags were emblazoned with '*La Butteler*', the name of San Lorenzo's *barra brava*. Others featured a cartoon of a young boy sitting on his father's shoulders, with the words '*Desde chiquito te vengo a ver*' – 'Since I was little I've come to see you.' Right in front of us, a real-life father and son mirrored the image. The mini *cuervo* gripped his dad's head as the blue-and-red fabric of the flags fluttered around him.

As the decibels rose, the *hinchada* snaked out from behind the terrace and filtered towards the corner of the pitch, nearing the foot of the *popular* where they would eventually take their place. At the front, two or three tattooed *barras* with dark sunglasses coordinated the disorderly march, furiously waving their arms to beckon the drummers forward while maintaining the beat of the song. The 20 or so percussionists rattled on, flanked by red-faced trumpet players with their cheeks puffing furiously. Behind them, a delirious mosh pit of 50 or so fans jumped and shoved each other; bodies bouncing off the tall metal fence separating the terrace from the pitch.

Further behind in the pack, we arrived at the gap between the two imposing stands. Along the edge of the steep *popular* terrace to our left and the two-tiered *platea* to our right, hundreds of supporters gazed down on us, many filming our entrance on their phones. It was a surreal feeling, like entering the stage as the member of a giant band. Some 35,000 people had come to see San Lorenzo, but with scores turned away from the pitch to film our arrival, it briefly felt like we were the stars of the show.

And then, quite suddenly, the mood changed. Orchestrated by the *barra*, the joyful song that had soundtracked the fans' arrival was killed in favour of an angry, indignant chant. It was time to let the players know that another poor performance would not be tolerated today. According to the song, belted out with aggressive vigour, the players needed to show pride in the shirt, like two legendary San Lorenzo teams of previous decades: *Los Camboyanos* and *Los Matadores*.

'We want *Camboyanos*, we want *Matadores*, we want players that feel the colours.' The volume went up another notch. 'No more failed, mediocre players, San Lorenzo is a big club, we want to be champions.'

As the song spread through the stadium, I noticed that the protest had a visual ingredient too. Of the hundreds of banners placed around the stadium, every single one had been hung upside down in a show of discontent. I had only ever seen this among the famously demanding fans at Boca Juniors and was surprised that the comparatively patient San Lorenzo crowd had opted for the statement. But seven years of mismanagement on and off the pitch was taking its toll on the *cuervo* faithful. The lowly position in the league table was just the latest symptom of a chronic disease.

In Argentina, it is common to take your place in the stands more than an hour before kick-off. Leave your entry to the *popular* as late as we did, and working your way to a clear spot is like negotiating an assault course. Moving upwards, we sidestepped the brass band and the flying sticks of the drummers, ducked underneath the metal barriers and long banners draped overhead, and forced our way through a tangle of bodies on each step. Out of breath, we finally found a space halfway up the terrace. Down below, the players peeled away from their handshakes and the terrace released their fast, urgent cries of '*El Ciclón! El Ciclón! El Ciclón!*'.

With the floodlights twinkling under the early evening sky, I gazed out at the stadium with a hint of childlike wonder – just like every time I return to San Lorenzo after some time away. The pitch was so green, the terrace so packed, the chanting so relentless. But as the team made a nervous start to the match, those around me clearly weren't sharing the same moment of awe. Gonza was already shaking his head, palms together in a praying gesture which motioned back and forth. The Argentines are famous for evoking their Italian ancestry in gestures and even their Spanish accent.

San Lorenzo's young full-back Fabricio López was making his full debut in the kind of atmosphere that nobody would want on their first day at work. Clearly affected by the team's hostile reception, his first touch was to clumsily mis-control a simple pass which rolled out of play. Moments later, he gifted the ball straight to the Barracas winger in a dangerous area. It was painful to watch. Poor López was drowning.

Sensing the need to rebuild confidence, the *hinchada* began to cheer emphatically whenever López and his team-mates showed even basic levels of commitment. Blocks and tackles sent ripples of approval through the stands. A lack of quality could be forgiven if endeavour was on display and the players were 'feeling the colours', as the song demanded.

With some luck, they'd also 'sweat the shirt', to coin another local phrase. Argentinian football may be famous for producing supremely gifted, technical players like Messi, Maradona and Riquelme, but to the everyday fan, effort and commitment are still the attributes valued above all others.

Realistically, there was only one player on the pitch who could lift the game out of its scrappy, frantic state. Iker Muniain had recently joined San Lorenzo from Bilbao's Athletic Club in a move that made absolutely no sporting or financial sense. The classy attacking midfielder was wearing the captain's armband when Athletic won the Copa del Rey just six months previously, and now he was here in the chaos of the Argentinian Primera, being kicked to pieces by Barracas Central.

Muniain is a self-confessed football romantic and wanted to end his career amid the passion of Argentinian football. San Lorenzo was an unlikely destination, with mounting debts leading to a series of transfer embargoes from FIFA. But in Argentina, it's important not to let trivial matters like potential bankruptcy stand in the way of a dream. And so, the board sourced third-party sponsorship from an incoming kit manufacturer to pull off an historic signing for the club.

Before making his debut, Muniain was filmed in the dugout singing '*Cuervo, sos mi alegria ...*' along with the *hinchada*. 'He sings that song all day at home,' his girlfriend Ana Montoya told journalists after the game. Iker was catching the bug, but San Lorenzo needed a leader on the pitch, not just another fan.

Lower down the terrace, the *barra brava* was becoming increasingly animated as half-time approached. As always, the main protagonists stood above the rest, perched on top of the metal rails known as *paravalanchas* (literally, avalanche stoppers) and holding on to banners for balance. To highlight their role as de facto guardians of the *hinchada*, the *barra* stand with their backs to the game and observe fellow fans instead of the action on the pitch. If you're not joining in with a song, expect a telling-off and some forceful encouragement to raise your voice. It's not just the players who have a responsibility to show up and perform.

But with the fans in full voice and the players showing heart on the pitch, the *barra* needed an alternative scapegoat for San Lorenzo's inability to break the deadlock. Fortunately, the referee was happy to step into a time-honoured role. By waving away a penalty appeal when Muniain was tripped inside the box and refusing to punish some reckless Barracas challenges, the man in the middle, Luis Lobo Medina, quickly became the villain everyone needed.

In the UK, the chant for Medina would have been a simple 'The referee's a wanker', or perhaps the B-side, 'Who's the wanker in the black?' In Argentina, the lyrics are a little more threatening.

'*Tomala vos, dámela a mí, vamos a matar a un referí!*' the crowd chanted. 'Take it yourself, give it to me, we're going to kill a referee!'

You can see why police with riot shields so often accompany the officials to the dressing room on this side of the world. Unsurprisingly, when Medina blew the half-time whistle at the Nuevo Gasómetro, he did not head down the tunnel alone.

The *popular* seemed grateful for the break and dropped as one to sit on the concrete steps. I was quick to join them, my aching legs ready for some respite. Clearly I lacked the endurance of the hardcore, who had now clocked up hours of singing, jumping and flag-waving since the *previa* began. The physical exertion of supporting your team in the stands – as well as the bravery to defend their colours in the street – is such an important part of Argentinian fandom that it has its own name: *Aguante*.

Early in the second half, San Lorenzo's evergreen winger Ezequiel Cerutti suddenly rediscovered a burst of pace that I thought he'd left in his 20s. It changed the game. Skinning his man on the right flank, he stood up a teasing cross at the far end of the pitch. We tensed our bodies and strained our eyes. The ball looped towards the penalty spot in slow motion. Striker Alexis Cuello rose highest and nodded the ball goalwards. The advancing Barracas goalkeeper was in no man's land. The net bulged. '¡GOOOOOOOOOLLL!'

If the *popular* had a roof, it would have flown off. We exchanged frantic, ecstatic embraces on the terrace and roars of relief filled the air. Goal celebrations in Argentina are more primal and angrier compared to home. Shouting '¡GOL!' rather than 'YES!' creates a deeper, more guttural noise. Faces contort and eyes bulge as the cries of '¡GOL!' are repeated again and again and again.

The fear of relegation and dismay around the club had turned the Nuevo Gasómetro into a pressure cooker on this hot, humid Sunday – and Cuello's header released the valve. After the game, both players and journalists described the moment as a *desahogo*: a release, a letting go. Semantically, the word is the opposite of drowning or suffocating, which perfectly captured the fans' wild, open-mouthed celebrations. Oxygen rushed back into their lungs and hope returned to their eyes.

The *desahogo* seemed to settle everyone down. Instead of chastising players and referees, the chants turned joyful. 'We'll drink all the wine, we'll drink it all, and there'll be nothing left,' sang the *hinchada* in inebriated contentment. The words always make me smile. If British football chants reference beer and cocaine, in Argentina it's all cheap wine and weed.

But the San Lorenzo players weren't looking as relaxed as their fans. Barracas began to attack in numbers and the home side retreated nervously into their half. By the closing stages, the tension on the pitch was creeping up into the stands. The watching *cuervos* chose to sing through their nerves. The more the home defence creaked, the louder the volume rose. The *popular* seemed to hope that waves of sound could push the ball away from the goal that Barracas attacked below.

It worked. The visitors floated one final long ball into the San Lorenzo box but goalkeeper Gastón Gómez punched it clear and the referee blew the full-time whistle. '¡Vamos carajo!' Gonza shouted at me and we locked into a sweaty hug. An outpouring of delight from the stands was followed by sighs of relief. It hadn't been comfortable, nor particularly impressive, but three vital points had been secured. And isn't that all that ever matters? San Lorenzo had won a football match and life felt simple.

* * *

It was 11pm when I got back to the flat, and I was hungry. Being in Buenos Aires meant restaurants were open and people were still wandering the streets, even though we were technically just an hour away from the dreaded Monday morning. A dim light shone from a small, unassuming pizzeria on the other side of the road. As I looked through the red metal bars across the doorway, I noticed a small San Lorenzo flag hanging behind the counter. My choice of dinner had been decided for me.

If *choripan* – the chorizo sausage sandwich – is a pre-match staple in Argentina, pizza is a post-match classic. Many of Buenos Aires's traditional pizzerias are packed with football memorabilia and old shirts cover their walls. Old men in stained white aprons carve up the slices in steaming pans and deftly flip them on to metallic plates. More often than not, the TV in the corner will be showing highlights of the day's matches. It's a perfect venue for fans to reconvene and dissect their team's performance.

'A *cuervo* is here!' announced an elderly woman who sat waiting in the corner. She had spotted my shirt. The guy behind the counter asked if I had something to pick up and the elderly woman interjected with, 'A nice, pretty young girl!' *Porteños* can toe a fine line between cheeky and seedy in their sense of humour. The twinkle in the eye of this friendly grandmother put her in the former camp so I allowed myself a chuckle.

When I took the pizza up to the flat, I saw that two free slices had been added to the top of my large ham and pepper pizza. I had received special treatment from the fellow *cuervos*. One slice was fainá; a topping-free flatbread made from chickpea flour. Why Argentines feel the need to layer these triangles of stodge on to their deep-pan pizzas, I will never understand. But, hailing from Genova, fainá had been introduced to Argentina by Italian immigrants more than a century ago, and I wasn't about to argue with such a long-standing tradition – or indeed free food.

The other slice was a more enjoyable *pizza canchera*, which bucks the trend of excessively cheesy Argentinian pizza by not having any cheese at all. Just tomato sauce, garlic and oregano. Its name translates to 'stadium pizza' due to its origins in and around football grounds. The first-ever slices were apparently served at Club Atlético Atlanta in Villa Crespo, Buenos Aires. The servers in the pizzeria saw that I had been to the *cancha* and knew what I needed.

Underneath the bonus slices, the main event awaited. While a conventional Italian approach to topping the pizza would have seen a modest scattering of ham and pepper, that is not how things are done here. Instead, carpets of ham upholstered the surface from crust to crust, while thick slabs of red pepper oozed across every slice. With Argentinian pizza, *more* is more.

As I sat eating on the balcony in the warm night air, it occurred to me that more than a decade had passed since I attended my first San Lorenzo match. And here I was, still coming back. Something that began as a side hobby while learning Spanish in Buenos Aires had grown into an obsession. From flying visits to one-year stays, I had taken eight trips to Argentina in ten years, most of which were planned around San Lorenzo fixtures. I didn't want to see the damage it had done to my bank balance, but I didn't regret a single trip.

The day I had just experienced typified why. San Lorenzo were in the middle of a crisis on and off the pitch and the visit of Barracas Central was perhaps the least glamorous fixture of the season. The performance was underwhelming, and yet the entire day had been one of unbridled joy, set to the beat of carnival drums and bathed in sunshine. We shared drinks on a terrace, rode a party bus and bounced in the *popular*. When there is so much of the matchday to be enjoyed, the 90 minutes of football almost becomes a sideshow.

'Another game, another party for the Cuervos de San Martín,' the supporters club posted on social media the following day. 'We went to the stadium at full rhythm!'

The short description neatly summed up the outlook of San Lorenzo supporters and football fans across Argentina. Another game, another party. You cannot control what happens on the pitch but the rest of the day is in your hands, so make the most of it. Sing, celebrate, see old friends, make new ones and threaten to kill referees.

Chapter 3

Discovering San Lorenzo

Mirala que linda viene	Just look at them come
Mirala que linda va	Just look at them go
Es la banda de Boedo	It's the gang from Boedo
Que al Ciclón viene a alentar	That's come to support *El Ciclon*

BACK IN 2013, just months before my first visit to Buenos Aires and the Nuevo Gasómetro, I knew next to nothing about San Lorenzo. I was approaching my mid-20s and still living at home with my parents. My work as a technology journalist didn't pay especially well, but it was an improvement on my previous job at Sainsbury's Local. More importantly, with reduced outgoings at home, it was enough to save for a flight to South America.

I had visited parts of the continent the previous year, fulfilling the destiny of many a white middle-class graduate by backpacking across Peru and Bolivia. Although there were aspects of the trip I didn't enjoy, I was desperate for a return to the region. In fact, it was the unenjoyable parts that helped me shape the next trip, which eventually became a life-changing six-month stay in Argentina.

Firstly, I didn't want to move up and down the 'Gringo Trail': the South American route so well-trodden by foreigners that it ended up being named after them. The fast-moving nature of backpacking wasn't for me either. If you are in the extremely fortunate position of being able to travel to the other side of the world, it seems a shame to rush through it. The best times always came when I was in a place for longer than just a few days.

Settling somewhere for a period of time would also allow me to get acquainted with the local football scene. As this began to shape my planning, the more football-centric nations of Brazil, Argentina, Uruguay, Colombia and Chile emerged as potential destinations. My goal to learn Spanish meant Brazil quickly fell out of the running. Uruguay, Chile and Colombia were clearly beautiful countries but none of them had much chance against Argentina when it came to football.

Like most people, my reference points for the Argentinian game were mainly restricted to the Boca Juniors vs River Plate *Superclásico,* the country's World Cup triumphs, and the Argentine players who had moved to Europe. I also had a vague recollection of cockney actor Danny Dyer shouting, 'I think me head's gonna pop off!' during a lively Independiente match on the documentary series, *Real Football Factories.* It wasn't much to go off, but it was sufficient to build the image of a passionate football nation.

Adding to Argentina's credentials was its capital city. Buenos Aires attracted glowing praise from travel writers, with 'Parisien architecture', a 'café culture' and 'bustling nightlife' being the go-to observations, seemingly copy and pasted across articles and blogs. Research showed there were plenty of Spanish schools in town, as well as some international companies who, I hoped, might not be averse to employing a failed technology journalist who couldn't speak the native language. Enough boxes had been ticked and my choice was made. Buenos Aires was calling.

It was now time to better familiarise myself with the local football clubs. I had no intention of 'supporting' a new team, but liked the idea of following a side's results to add some interest. At this stage, becoming a fully fledged fan in Argentina felt beyond the realms of possibility. Supporting Charlton Athletic home and away from the age of five was, and is, utterly consuming. I assumed I would never have the emotional capacity to become properly invested in another club, but still wanted to keep my eye on a local team.

To assess the lay of the land, *Los Cinco Grandes* – the Big Five – were an obvious place to start. Boca and River had iconic stadiums and wonderful kits that I could waste a lot of money on, but almost felt *too* big as clubs. Their dominance and popularity were unappealing to my underdog sensibilities as a Charlton man. If a club wins a trophy every other year, how exciting can that really be? If they have followers all over the world, can they still be a community club? The answers are up for debate, but following the masses to the big two never felt like an option for me.

The remaining three *grandes* were Independiente, Racing Club and San Lorenzo de Almagro. The latter name felt the least familiar and the most exotic. I then remembered signing the striker Bernardo Romeo from them on *Championship Manager: Season 01/02*. Romeo was prolific in the computer-simulated sides I oversaw as an 11-year-old, and that alone seemed to warrant investigating the club a little further.

Immediately catching my eye were the supporters. As I scrolled down YouTube search results for 'San Lorenzo', videos of the packed stands seemed to outnumber those of the actual team. The jumping, flag-waving, flare-burning fans were the stars of the show and the scenes were mesmerising.

'*Oooooooh, San Lorenzooo, ooooooooh, San Lorenzooo,*' went the booming chorus in the most popular video. '*Dicen que estamos todos de la cabeza, pero a San Lorenzo no le interesa!*' I popped the lyrics through a translator. 'They say we are all crazy, but San Lorenzo isn't interested!'

San Lorenzo might not have been interested, but I was, and began to read more about the club. It's difficult to get the essence of a century-old institution from the utilitarian pages of Wikipedia, but there was one particular section that seized my attention. Financially stricken, San Lorenzo had been forced to leave its beloved stadium and the Boedo neighbourhood during the 1970s. The fans suffered the ignominy of watching their team play in the grounds of city rivals while mounting a struggle to return home that still continued to this day.

As a Charlton supporter, the story struck a chord. The defining episode of the club's modern history was a heartbreaking exile from our stadium, The Valley, in the 1980s, before a triumphant return home. The club was financially stricken and the disused Valley was about to be claimed by the council, until a unique fan-led movement created 'The Valley Party', which won nearly 15,000 votes in local elections against the political establishment. With newfound influence on the council and funding from supporters, Charlton finally returned home to a joyous, tearful Valley in 1992. The faithful supporters had transformed a tragedy into a fairytale.

San Lorenzo and Charlton had both suffered the pain of losing their home, the fear of extinction and the humiliation of becoming nomads in their own city. But in both cases, supporters had kept the clubs alive. The parallels were so striking that I was only slightly perturbed by San Lorenzo sharing the same blue-and-red-striped shirts as one of Charlton's landlords during the exile, Crystal Palace. Charlton never felt welcome at Selhurst Park and resented the long journey to a ground so disconnected from their actual home. As a proud London club, formed a stone's throw away from the River Thames in the Royal Borough of Greenwich, traipsing down to the suburbs of Croydon was a soul-sapping, identity-stripping experience. Crystal Palace have never been popular in Charlton circles.

* * *

As my trip drew closer, San Lorenzo were growing on me by the day. My plan to research all of the major clubs in Buenos

Aires had ground to a halt, while preparing for Argentina had been reduced to reading articles and watching videos on *El Ciclón*.

A handy byproduct of the San Lorenzo immersion was the new way it gave me to learn Spanish. Chris Hylland, author of the excellent *Tears at La Bombonera* and *Dame Bola*, explains in the former book that renowned Uruguayan writer Eduardo Galeano had taught him a lot of his Spanish. In many ways, my teacher was San Lorenzo's *hinchada*, known as *La Gloriosa*.

Hours were spent on the YouTube channel Musicuervo (essentially, 'Crow Music'). Sebastian Roldan and his late father knew better than anyone that the most interesting spectacle at the Nuevo Gasómetro was usually the *popular*, so angled their cameras away from the pitch and towards the *hinchada*. They uploaded the highlights to the channel, which was a revelation at a time when fan-focused content was scarce. Crucially for me, the video descriptions included the words to the songs, so my time watching Musicuervo led to an unorthodox study of the Spanish language.

Notebook out, pen in hand, I'd hit play.

'*Vamos San Lorenzo, Ciclón ponga huevo …*' I didn't need to look-up that first part, but the second? 'Cyclone lay eggs.' This was confusing. A quick google of Argentinian football colloquialisms revealed that 'laying eggs' was in fact a metaphor for showing heart and being strong. Interesting.

'*… quiero ser campeón, soy de Boedo.*' 'I want to be champion, I'm from Boedo.' Easy. I liked the fact that the chanting fan would also be 'a champion' if San Lorenzo were to win something. Glory wasn't just for the players.

'*Voy a todos lados, voy descontrolado, San Lorenzo yo a vos te amo.*' The fans follow the team everywhere, and they do it *descontrolado* – out of control. It seemed a fitting description for the supporters on the screen, tumbling around the terrace and climbing up the metal railings. The use of *vos* in the gushing 'San Lorenzo I love you' was also noted. The *tu* for 'you' as I'd learned in Spanish classes beforehand was nowhere to be seen. Just one of the endless examples that distinguished *castellano rioplatense* – the Spanish spoken by Argentines and Uruguayans local to the Río de la Plata basin – from what I'd seen in textbooks.

As I worked through the Musicuervo hits, my beginner-level Spanish was quickly evolving from comments on the weather, my age and the pets I had as a child, to aggressive demands for San Lorenzo players to put in more effort and claims that all Boca and Huracán fans were sex workers. It made for a bizarre mix of conversation that caught my Spanish teachers off guard when I eventually arrived in Buenos Aires. But for better or worse, *La Gloriosa* was adding much-needed colour to my experience of the language.

The closer I got to flying to Argentina, the more I started paying attention to San Lorenzo's results. Using the archaic Soccerway.com to find out what was going on, it became clear they were in a title race, as 2013 – and with it the Primera División season – drew to a close.

Boca had been beaten 1-0 at the Nuevo Gasómetro in November, which felt significant. Two weeks later, a 4-2 win against Belgrano put *El Ciclón* clear at the top with three games to go. Sure, I may have rejected supporting Boca or River in a performative stand against glory-hunting, but the idea of following a team that actually won things suddenly felt quite appealing. Hungry for vicarious glory, I started tracking games live on social media. And that's when the wins dried up.

Two disappointing draws put the title in the balance for a tantalising final day. San Lorenzo, Vélez Sarsfield, Newell's Old Boys and Lanús all had a chance of being crowned champions. To crank up the tension, a quirk of the fixture list meant they were paired off in head-to-head battles.

If San Lorenzo could win at Vélez, they would win the league. If they drew, they needed the same outcome between Newell's and Lanús in Rosario. A loss would not only mean squandering the title, but it would see local rivals Vélez lift the trophy in their faces. Somewhat removed from the final-day excitement in Argentina, I found myself in my childhood bedroom at my parents' house, laptop open, scouring for updates.

After a goalless first half in both fixtures, the score alerts sprung to life in the second period – but they all came from Rosario. Newell's led 2-1 against Lanús with time ticking down. With no news from Vélez, a Newell's side featuring Gabriel Heinze, Maxi Rodríguez and David Trezeguet was heading for the title. Spotting the trio was my first introduction to the sentimental side of Argentinian transfer policy. Before every season there is always a club pulling out the stops to bring a legend home.

But the drama wasn't over. Lanús fought back to make it 2-2 and the title seesawed back into San Lorenzo's hands. I was now struck by an urge to see more than the basic text updates I was reading on social media. I had no idea if it was possible to stream Argentinian football, but I had to check before the final whistle.

To my shock and good fortune, a high-quality video of Vélez vs San Lorenzo was streaming for free on YouTube. I had stumbled across Fútbol Para Todos, another online treasure trove that would serve me faithfully over the coming years. Football For Everyone was a free-to-air channel launched by Cristina Fernández de Kirchner's government, which argued that viewing the people's game should not be restricted to those able to afford cable TV. It may not have been designed for English football nerds living with their parents, but with five minutes remaining of an enthralling season, I was a grateful beneficiary.

So, in surreal circumstances, I found myself watching San Lorenzo live for the very first time – and they just happened to be playing out one of the most dramatic finales to a season in the club's history. *El Ciclón* had one hand on the trophy, but Vélez were attacking in waves and a vociferous home support could smell blood. Just one goal would snatch the title away from the tiring visitors.

I feared I was about to inflict my Charlton curse on this new team. I never back winners. I repel success and glory. I'd already stalled their title charge by taking a closer interest and now I could be responsible for them blowing it altogether; here, alone in my bedroom.

As the clock ticked past 89 minutes, a long diagonal ball entered San Lorenzo's box, sharpening the feeling of impending doom. It fell straight to Vélez midfielder Agustín Allione with a golden chance to win the match – and the title. His connection was clean and true, sending the ball flying towards the roof of the net. But before it bulged, the arm of San Lorenzo goalkeeper Sebastián Torrico shot up and his fingertips miraculously tipped the ball over the bar. What a save! A title-winning save.

Minutes later, the full-time whistle blew, and San Lorenzo were champions. It was a lot to take in on a small laptop screen. The frantic commentary was incomprehensible to my untrained ears, bar the repeated cries of '*San Lorenzo campeón! San Lorenzo campeón!*' As weeping players celebrated on the pitch, it felt like I'd gatecrashed a party. Little did I know that almost every year for the next decade, I would walk past a giant mural of the title-winning Torrico save I had just witnessed – underneath the *popular* of the Nuevo Gasómetro.

* * *

Two months after the drama at Vélez, I was able to see the champions of Argentina in the flesh. I arrived in Buenos Aires in January, during its summer inferno. Escaping the bleak midwinter of the UK, I had no issue with temperature reaching the mid-30s each day but the same could not be said for the locals.

Porteños complain about a lot of things, even if their animated, entertaining delivery means they rarely seem gloomy. The humid summer heat is high on their list of grievances and many vote with their feet in January, fleeing for the coast when the mercury rises.

As such, the Buenos Aires I first encountered was practically a ghost town. After my Spanish classes in the morning, I would wander down an unusually calm Avenida de Mayo, enjoying clear views of the stunning Palacio del Congreso at one end and the government's Casa Rosada at the other. Once I had exhausted this walk and the other routes connecting my flat with downtown, I was ready for some more extracurricular activity. Thankfully, as February arrived, so did the Argentinian football season.

San Lorenzo's first home game was a *clásico* against Racing Club. After *the* local derby with Huracán and the next biggest fixture vs Boca Juniors, most of my *cuervo* friends regard Racing as the third-most important match. At the time, I had no knowledge of the fixture's significance and simply wanted my first taste of San Lorenzo and live Argentinian football.

I needed to arrange tickets and travel for the game but had little faith in my Spanish to do the job. Indeed, when you're new to a city and only have a basic grasp of the language, every trip outdoors feels like a challenge. Early visits to the local Jumbo supermarket had been fraught with unexpected questions and confusion, forcing me to rehearse my checkout responses in the queue.

'*Puntos?*' No.

'*Bolsa?*' Si.

'*Factura?*' No.

No, I don't have loyalty points. Yes, I would like a bag. No, I'll go without a receipt. Thank you and goodbye. I wasn't bowling over Jumbo's checkout staff with my small talk, but I was beginning to understand a little more *castellano* beyond the words of San Lorenzo songs. Not enough, however, to confidently get myself to the Racing game, so I tracked down a football tour company to take care of the legwork.

When the bus collected the tourists for the game, I was the only one wearing a San Lorenzo top in a sea of Berghaus and Patagonia jackets. It was the first shirt of many I would buy, but I was still put off by Crystal Palace-esque blue-and-red stripes, so had opted for the navy blue third shirt with a more subtle red trim.

I quickly accosted the tour guide, Pablo, a Boca-supporting local, and grilled him on the Argentinian Primera and how to attend games. I was on a mission. Paying for the tour was a necessary evil to see San Lorenzo for the first time and obtain as much information as possible so I could go my own way after the Racing game.

We arrived an hour or so before kick-off so I had plenty of time to soak up the Nuevo Gasómetro for the first time. It was impressive. The stadium's austere, all-concrete simplicity was oddly alluring. Two steep, imposing terraces plonked behind each goal. Opposite, the neat, two-tiered Platea Norte, complete with a roof. And our stand, the Platea Sur, offering its long, uncovered stretch of backless seats. The large gaps between each stand exposed the sheer edges and striking angles of the stadium, and offered glimpses of life outside this blue-and-red fortress.

The teams came out and we were treated to a quintessential Argentinian football scene. Ticker tape burst from the stands and fluttered through the air. The *hinchada* raised the volume and bounced as one. This was it. My heart raced as I watched La Gloriosa move through the gears. I yearned to be in the thick of it, in the middle of the *popular* to my right.

On the pitch, a fellow debutant made it a perfect evening. After just seven minutes, the ball ricocheted skywards in the Racing box and Nicolás Blandi, a summer signing from Boca, met it with a flawless scissor-kick. The ball flew into the bottom corner in front of the *popular* and the stadium erupted; 1-0. The champions were in front.

There is little else I remember from the game itself, apart from the way in which San Lorenzo captain Néstor Ortigoza orchestrated everything from the middle of the pitch. He was the most overweight player I had ever seen, yet the midfielder pulled the strings with such ease it looked like he was jogging through a training exercise. Every loose ball was taken under his spell, every pass was delivered perfectly to feet and he never needed to break out of his gentle trot. Probably just as well, given his size.

After another fine piece of Ortigoza play in the second half, a chant rang out. '*Oleee, ole ole ole, Gordo, Gordo!*' I asked Pablo what they were saying. 'Fatty! They call him *Gordo*, which means fat,' guide Pablo said with a chuckle. It was the first time I'd heard the nickname, which despite its meaning, is a term of affection across the Spanish-speaking world.

When the referee blew the full-time whistle, I realised I'd spent as much time gazing at the fans' party in the stands as I had the match, which ended in a 1-0 win for San Lorenzo. It seemed like Pablo had been doing the same, albeit for different reasons.

'Did you know that the women of San Lorenzo are the most beautiful?' he told me with a twinkle in his eye. 'I am a Boca fan but I can tell you that San Lorenzo has the prettiest fans.' I shrugged it off as a typical, throwaway observation from an *argentino*, but it has been repeated to me by numerous people many times since. As it turns out, Argentines have been saying the same thing for nearly 100 years.

In a newspaper article from 1929, Roberto Arlt describes the matchday experience at San Lorenzo's Viejo Gasómetro stadium on La Plata Avenue, or Avenida La Plata in Spanish. 'All the gates on Avenida La Plata were decked out with magnificent young girls,' he writes. 'Boy, are there beautiful girls on this Avenida De La Plata!' I would soon learn a lot more about this fabled avenue and San Lorenzo's struggle to return there.

For many, the old wooden stands of the Viejo Gasómetro were as beautiful as anyone who gathered there. The stadium became a focal point for the area and an emblem of the Argentinian game – but it wouldn't last for ever.

Chapter 4

The Wembley of Buenos Aires

Señores, yo soy de un barrio   Gentlemen, I am from a *barrio*
Barrio, de corazón   A *barrio* of heart
Señores, yo soy de Boedo   Gentlemen, I am from Boedo
Y soy hincha del Ciclón   And I support *El Ciclón*

THE NUEVO Gasómetro is located in Bajo Flores, the lower part of the *barrio* known as Flores – literally 'Flowers'. It's a somewhat ironic name, given the distinct lack of greenery and nature near the stadium. There is also very little in the way of bars, restaurants and general places of interest, so apart from the occasional *previa* inside the Ciudad Deportiva complex that surrounds the ground, I have never been to Bajo Flores before a game. Very few *cuervos* do. As well as the insecurity of the area and lack of places to pitch up for a pre-match drink, you just don't feel like you are at the home of San Lorenzo.

Walk northwards for 30 minutes, along Avenida General Fernandez de la Cruz, then on to Avenida La Plata, and the feeling could not be more different. You are now in the *barrio* of Boedo, where San Lorenzo was born and where their famous old stadium, El Gasómetro, once stood.

Owing to its size, prestige and history, the stadium was nicknamed *El Wembley Porteño* – the 'Buenos Aires Wembley'. It hosted San Lorenzo from 1916 to 1979 and the streets of Boedo still echo its memory. Striking blue-and-red murals – most of them created by the talented Grupo Artístico de Boedo – mark the club's spiritual home. The works pay homage to *cuervo* players, myths and legends, as well the old wooden stadium itself. The *barrio* exudes *porteño* charm. Old-fashioned cafés and bars, their facades shadowed by overhanging trees, are full of San Lorenzo pictures and memorabilia. Smartly dressed waiters serve coffees by day and beers by night to the locals, who are usually debating something to do with the club or a recent match.

These are the places where I like to pass the hours leading up to a game at the Nuevo Gasómetro. As I look around, I hear the words my *cuervo* friend Martín said to me some years ago: 'Will, Boedo is San Lorenzo and San Lorenzo is Boedo.' While fans of every other club in Argentina celebrate winning trophies at the Obelisco monument in central Buenos Aires, San Lorenzo supporters gather in the middle of Boedo. It's a tidy illustration of the unique relationship between the club and its place in the world.

A couple of weeks after the Barracas game on my most recent visit to Buenos Aires, I made the most of a leisurely afternoon before a Tuesday night match by stopping by the historic Esquina Homero Manzi on Avenida Boedo. The bar is named after the writer of the tango song 'Sur', which references the street corner of its location in the opening line: Avenues San Juan and Boedo. Aside from a poster behind the bar showing the Copa Libertadores side of 2014, there isn't as much San Lorenzo on show compared to other bars in the area, but this is more than compensated for by the spectacular interior.

Long rows of polished wooden chairs and marble-topped tables line the black-and-white chequered floor, leading to a stage at the rear that's cloaked by a scarlet curtain. Waiters in white shirts, black aprons and red bow ties potter along the sprawling bar, elaborate chandeliers illuminating their unhurried work.

'Esquina Homero Manzi had its heyday in the 1950s, when the neighbours came to listen to the music from the two record players on the bar's stage,' the Buenos Aires city government states in a historical profile of the venue. 'Tango dancers, fans of San Lorenzo de Almagro, and the political world of the city gathered at its tables.'

Before a home game against Racing the following Sunday, I ventured to another Boedo institution. Roque is a *bodegon*: the term for a traditional, no-frills eatery serving large portions of typical Argentinian food like milanesas, pasta, grilled meat, and desserts that inevitably involve dulce de leche. As a rule of thumb, if a *bodegon* has a metal 'CINZANO' sign among its paraphernalia, it's probably going to be good. A leather-bound menu with laminated pages (that often stick together) is another reassuring sign of being in a 'proper' *bodegon*.

Alongside these features and its excellent food, Roque boasts 110 years of history and plenty of San Lorenzo memorabilia. There is a long-sleeved Uhlsport home shirt from the 1980s hung from the wall, which I always want to steal, and a Rosario Central pennant by the bar nodding to the clubs' friendship. Looking across the tightly packed tables during my pre-match meal before Racing, it was clear that I wasn't the only one heading to the *cancha* later that Sunday.

But to date, my favourite San Lorenzo-inspired Boedo experience has come in El Modelo Bar Cultural. Its white concrete exterior is decorated with perfect *fileteado porteño* – the distinctive lettering and pattern of Buenos Aires – with its dramatic strokes and intricate curls. Walking through the door of El Modelo is more like entering a museum than a bar. Every inch of shelving and wall space is occupied by a poster, photograph or historical artefact. San Lorenzo is the most common theme among them, but tango, leftist politics and pop culture feature almost as heavily. Above an antique jug and an ancient pair of scales is a poster of the

Beatles. A little lower, Che Guevara. To the right, Fabricio Coloccini alongside his San Lorenzo team-mates in 2001. It's an eclectic mix.

The bar has been passed down through generations and is now in the hands of Luciano, an affable *cuervo* in his late 30s. I messaged the bar on social media to see if I might strike lucky with their irregular opening hours before the Racing game. When the account replied by asking how many people wanted to come, I realised it would be opening solely for our visit. Sure enough, despite our modest party of three, Luciano was happily pouring beers, explaining the bar's history and even singing tangos for us with his guitar. It was like a private bar, museum tour and live gig rolled into one.

As we left, I noticed that the masters of the mural, Grupo Artistico de Boedo, were responsible for the beautiful paintwork on El Modelo's exterior. The signage included the year the bar institution first opened: 1908. Fittingly, a certain football club that played just two blocks away was born the very same year. Because Boedo is San Lorenzo and San Lorenzo is Boedo.

***

Football was introduced to Argentina by British immigrants who settled in the country during the mid-to-late 19th century. Businessmen, engineers and workers who were drawn to Argentina's rapid economic development and growing railway industry brought their cultural pastimes with them, including the nascent sport of football. British schools and railway-sponsored clubs were key to nurturing the game, and Buenos Aires Football Club – the first club in Argentina – was founded in 1867.

The Glaswegian Alexander Watson Hutton, who worked as a school headmaster in Argentina, is considered the father of Argentinian football. Watson founded the country's first football league in 1891, as well as Alumni

Athletic Club, which won 22 trophies in the game's early years before disbanding in 1913. The UK's legacy in Argentinian football remains visible in the names of many important clubs. I often wonder if the more nationalistic fans of River Plate, Boca Juniors and Newell's Old Boys are bothered by the very English names they graffiti on to walls and tattoo on to their bodies.

By 1908, football was quickly transitioning from a pastime of British immigrants and the upper classes to a game for the masses. Among those enchanted by the sport was a group of boys who played on the streets outside the San Antonio church in a part of Almagro, which later became Boedo. Father Lorenzo Massa had arrived at the church on a mission to get children away from the danger of the streets, and when he saw a tram nearly collide with a young player one day, he intervened. Massa offered the boys a safe area to play football in the grounds of the church, on the proviso that they came to mass each Sunday.

The deal worked. On 1 April 1908, the young group was ready to form an official club. They suggested a name they had already been using – Los Forzosos de Almagro, 'The Strongmen of Almagro' – but Massa wasn't keen. A bit rough-and-tumble for a priest, you'd assume. The boys then put forward San Lorenzo in his honour. Modestly, Massa didn't want the club to carry his name, but was willing to accept if it was instead dedicated to the Battle of San Lorenzo in 1813, which had helped to win independence for Argentina. To complete the name, the club's location was added. Boedo was not an official *barrio* at this point and the church fell within the boundaries of Almagro. And so, Club Atlético San Lorenzo de Almagro was born. Lorenzo Massa is a symbol of the club, and one of its many nicknames, *Los Cuervos*, is a reference to the long black cassocks worn by Catholic priests like Massa, which resemble a crow's plumage.

The San Antonio church remains open to this day, so I made a pilgrimage to the site during a trip to Buenos

Aires in 2023. The street was quiet, nondescript and largely residential. You could still quite easily have a kickaround on the same corner as the young Forzosos. It was surreal to think that an institution like San Lorenzo, with hundreds of thousands of followers around the world, had started in front of this small, unassuming church. As I got closer, I was pleased to see that the Grupo Artístico de Boedo had left their mark here too. Beside the entrance was a blue-and-red-bordered mural of Lorenzo Massa's foot trapping a football, standing in between tramlines on a cobbled street.

Not only did the site mark the beginning of a football club, it marked a turning point for the working-class boys of the Forzosos, and countless others like them through the years. Massa gave local youngsters a safe place to develop – as footballers and as people – away from the insecurity and violence that plagued the streets. From its very inception, San Lorenzo was an institution with a social purpose.

Across Argentina, the creation of football clubs heralded a transformation of the *barrios* and life within them. Football teams were, and still are (for now), part of member-owned social and leisure clubs where a variety of sports and recreational activities take place. The rapidly growing urban populations flocked to these local clubs, which, in the same way as social spaces like bars and cafés, became fundamental in establishing a sense of community, identity and even the idea of the *barrio* itself.

Matthew Hawkins, Professor of Anthropology at Carleton University (and a fellow foreign *cuervo*), described this social phenomenon in his excellent study on Boedo and San Lorenzo. Like Hawkins, I have generally used the specific term *barrio* rather than simply 'neighbourhood' in this book. As he explains, '*Barrio* translates as neighbourhood, but in the context of Buenos Aires, the word takes on a unique meaning that evokes an emotional connection to place and sites of social interaction: tango halls, the *barrio* café-bar, the community-based *murga*, and the football club. Beyond a category that is used to topographically organise the city, the *barrio* is a space of cultural activity, the refuge of familiarity in a chaotic city, and your football club.'

The historian and sociologist Julio Frydenberg – an expert in dissecting the relationship between Argentinian society and football – agrees that football clubs and going to the *cancha* played a key role in establishing the sense of *barrio* identity. 'One of the attractions of the football spectacle lies in building a sort of ritual,' he writes in *Society, City and Football in the Buenos Aires of 1920–1930*. 'In the case of Buenos Aires, football and the development of its ritual were part of the process of creating neighbourhood identifications.'

When you consider the mass immigration taking place in Argentina during this period, you can understand why creating this sense of identity and communal purpose was so significant. At the time San Lorenzo was founded, 46 per cent of Buenos Aires residents were foreign nationals. With so many immigrants – the majority from Italy and Spain – searching for belonging in a foreign land, you could argue that *barrios* and their football clubs took on an elevated role.

Of course, places and clubs provide communities with a sense of shared identity in countries all over the world, but the parallel timing of Argentina's development as a modern nation and the arrival of football created something distinct in cities like Buenos Aires. It was a perfect storm for people and clubs to become inextricably linked, producing the intensity of feeling that has helped to make Argentinian football so famous.

In the first half of the 20th century, San Lorenzo became the prime example of a football club which captured the imagination of its community. Opened in 1916, some ten blocks away from the Church of San Antonio, the Gasómetro stadium sat proudly in the middle of Boedo as the club's first formal home. By 1931, it could hold as many as 73,000 people, bigger than River's and Boca's grounds, which held 58,000 and 55,000, respectively. On the other side of the *barrio* and *clásico* divide, neighbours Huracán could host a sizeable 41,000 at their art deco-inspired Estadio Tomás Adolfo Ducó. Huge arenas were springing up across the densely populated *barrios* of Buenos Aires, packed into just a few square blocks of areas that were becoming increasingly defined by their clubs.

Aside from the bigger names, there were also Argentinos Juniors, Vélez Sarsfield, All Boys, Ferro Carril Oeste, Nueva Chicago and Atlanta (among others), all accessible within the 200 square kilometres of the capital. Just outside, the urbanised province had two more *grandes* in Racing and Independiente, not to mention the likes of Banfield, Lanús, Quilmes, Platense, Tigre, Gimnasia and Estudiantes. One of the world's great football hubs had been created. A century later, Buenos Aires remains a groundhopper's paradise.

* * *

With so many clubs competing for a finite number of supporters, I was curious to know how San Lorenzo and Boedo had risen to the top so quickly. It was one of many questions I had prepared for Adolfo Res, a club historian, the leader of the campaign to return the club to Boedo, and something of a San Lorenzo celebrity.

He invited me for a chat over some yerba mate (Argentina's omnipresent herbal tea drunk from a gourd with a metal straw) in the office he rents in downtown Buenos Aires. Like many office blocks in this part of town, the interior felt like something from the early 1980s. A windowless entrance and reception, dimly lit by a particularly artificial hue of overhead light, led me into a lift of 360-degree stainless steel.

I rattled up to the 18th floor and Adolfo ushered me into a roomy office where he teaches courses on the history of San Lorenzo. I say 'office'; it was more of a San Lorenzo shrine. Untold amounts of flags, pennants, posters and framed newspaper articles filled the space. There was so much to look at that 30 minutes had passed before we sat down to begin the interview.

A short man in his 60s with a fair complexion, Adolfo wears a stern expression. Even when he says something lighthearted, he does so with a frown. We were talking about San Lorenzo and that was a very serious thing. In case the wall-to-ceiling, blue-and-red mementos around the office didn't show Adolfo's allegiances clearly enough, he was sat in front of a large San Lorenzo flag, wearing a San Lorenzo shirt, pouring hot water from a San Lorenzo thermos into a San Lorenzo mate gourd.

Adolfo had been part of the candidacy that won the club election a year previously, adding much-needed credibility to the campaign of businessman Marcelo Morretti. But you don't see Adolfo in open-neck white shirts, shaking hands with suits in the modern offices at San Lorenzo's stadium. He prefers to be here, away from the business dealings and boardroom politics, with his students and his archives, in a place with no distraction from the only thing that matters: San Lorenzo.

'San Lorenzo made Boedo develop and grow,' he began in his husky voice and strong *porteño* accent. 'It was a *barrio* of extreme poverty when San Lorenzo was born. There were people in the area who didn't have hot water so they came to the club to wash. The club always had an important social aspect.' As the decades passed, the Gasómetro began to offer a lot more than just hot water for its neighbours – something that was fundamental to the growth of the club's support.

'In 1942 the club opened a library at the Gasómetro, which was majestic. It was of the quality of a university library. If you wanted to write something, San Lorenzo was like a public university. There was also a cultural centre underneath the terraces which had literary classes, language classes, folk dancing, photography courses …' The sport offering grew just as quickly. 'In 1945 we had one of the best presidents in the history of the club. Enrique Pinto. He built a complex that I used as a child and it brought even more members to the club. It had a pool, where I learned to swim, a shooting range, a bowling alley, mini football pitches, everything.'

The growth of the club off the pitch helped Boedo grow into a more prosperous *barrio*, and it didn't do the team any harm either. San Lorenzo picked up their third league title in 1946 and made their mark in Europe at the end of the year on a highly successful tour of Spain. The series of exhibition matches included a 6-1 against Spain's national team which left a lasting impression on the locals.

Speaking on the popular Spanish football show *El Chiringuito* in 2021, the commentator and ex-player Jose *Petón* Otín, said, 'Spanish football changed because in 1946, San Lorenzo de Almagro, with their star Ángel Zubieta [the Basque inside-right who joined San Lorenzo during the Spanish Civil War], changed everything. They gave Spanish football a thrashing. Every player linked up with one another, they played in a different way. Even the way they dressed – their boots were made of a finer leather. They changed everything.'

The tour also included a 4-1 humbling of Atlético Madrid, whose manager Emilio Vidal admitted, 'They are far superior to us. Their marking is extraordinary and this allows them to always have possession of the ball. They gave us a lesson in the game, which we must, without fail, assimilate to and instil in our own.'

After a leaner decade in the 1950s when just one further league title was added, the 1960s ushered in some legendary San Lorenzo sides and a golden era for the club. First came *Las Carasucias* – 'The Dirty Faces' – of 1964. The side was dominated by home-grown boys from Boedo, who played with a skilful, daring style, reminiscent of the talented street footballers of the *barrio* with their grubby faces. The baton was then passed to *Los Matadores* – 'The Killers' – who became the first unbeaten champions of Argentina's professional era in 1968, beginning a spell of four titles in six years for the club. The Buenos Aires Wembley was packed every Sunday. Boedo was the place to be.

A young Diego Maradona was often in the crowd – but only during the second half. In a TV interview, Diego explained how he went to games at the Viejo Gasómetro with his San Lorenzo-supporting friend, because the number 15 bus took them straight to the stadium from Villa Fiorito, the impoverished *barrio* in the province where Diego was raised. 'When they opened the gates of the Gasómetro five or six minutes into the second half, we would sneak in for free, climb up the railings and watch from there.'

The prestige of the Gasómetro was enhanced in 1973, when it played host to the first live gig by an overseas band in Argentina. The sounds of Santana echoed through the streets of Boedo, but despite the euphoric scenes inside the venue, clouds were beginning to gather above the Gasómetro.

Due to mismanagement in the boardroom, San Lorenzo were sliding towards financial trouble. The beloved Gasómetro was now the only major stadium still made of wood rather than cement and badly needed modernising. There were rumours of a move to a new, modern complex in Bajo Flores, which would make good money for the club's directors, even if no *cuervo* could imagine leaving Boedo.

At the time, Argentina was entering another period of tumult. Juan Domingo Perón had returned from exile in 1973 to lead the country for a third time, but his final term was plagued by violence as the left and right factions of his support effectively went to war with each other. I'd noticed an old pennant in Res's office which had the face of Perón over San Lorenzo's blue-and-red stripes, with the words '*El Ciclón y Perón, un solo corazón*' – '*El Ciclón* and Perón, one heart'. But if San Lorenzo were pinning their hopes on the president, they were in trouble.

Perón died from a heart attack in 1974. His third wife, Isabel Perón, stepped into power but failed to stabilise an increasingly violent and volatile country. Now, the military generals were circling. The club's fate, which already looked bleak, was about to become intertwined with the Argentinian nation and its Dirty War.

Chapter 5

Anatomy of a *cancha*

Y si tengo que morir	And if I have to die
Solo te pido un favor	I ask just one favour
Yo quiero que sea así	I want it to be like this
Con la banda del Ciclón	Here with the gang of *El Ciclón*

IN ARGENTINA, I tend to bore people with stories of my beloved Charlton Athletic and what it's like going to the football in the UK. Back home, I do the same with stories of my second love, San Lorenzo, and what football is like 'over there'. In these tedious tales, which can take place anywhere from Lincoln to La Plata, I often use *la cancha* interchangeably with 'stadium' or 'ground', which are the most direct translations.

But returning to San Lorenzo always reminds me that the two are not the same. *La cancha* looks different, smells different and feels different.

To me, the unique essence of the Argentinian *cancha* lies in the deep connection between the physical space and the fans who inhabit it. There is a one-ness between people and place that I have not seen elsewhere. Supporters in Argentina occupy every nook, cranny, step and railing in their *cancha*, taking an unusually active role in shaping and decorating the space.

In turn, the *cancha* transforms into a den for the tribe – one that begins to influence the behaviour of those inside it. The relationship is symbiotic, giving rise to the beautiful, if at times chaotic, images of Argentine supporters that now travel around the world.

The terraces may look like a chaotic mix of flares and flags, but there is a method to the madness. Hardcore supporters enter the stadium hours – sometimes days – before a game to prepare the stands. New inflatables and pyrotechnics enter the mix every season as fans look to outdo each other, but the basis of the traditional *cancha* adornments are the three Ts: *tirantes, telónes* and *trapos*.

Giving an Argentinian 'end' its distinctive look, *tirantes* are the long narrow banners resembling giant ribbons that run vertically down the stand. For big games, they will be placed across every stand, almost gift-wrapping the stadium for the occasion. River Plate's El Monumental offers a vivid example, becoming a giant red-and-white oval for the Superclásico with Boca or big nights in the Copa Libertadores. But the *tirantes* have a practical function too, offering vital support to the rabble-rousers on top of the *paravalancha* railings, who cling on with one hand while orchestrating fans with the other.

The second T of the *cancha* is the mighty *telón*. Translating literally as 'curtain', these giant flags can cover a whole stand or even an entire stadium, as supporters of Racing and Rosario Central have demonstrated with extravagant displays in the past. Every time I find myself under one of the Butteler's *telónes*, confronted with mild claustrophobia and unable to watch the game (they are sometimes unfurled while the match is going on), I am struck by how little the participant gets out of the experience. A *telón* is for show rather than to be enjoyed. The design, production and choreography is a significant undertaking for supporters, adding to their importance and mystique in Argentinian terrace culture.

These emotionally significant flags and banners are brought to the stadium by families, friends and supporter groups, and plaster every available surface around the stands.

They are often stacked in rows across the fencing behind the goal, forcing spectators to move further up the terrace just to be able to see the game. Most *trapos* proudly bear the name of the owner's origin, turning the stand into a patchwork homage to towns and cities across Argentina.

When supporters travel long distances to support their team, the display can be quite incongruous. As Boca Juniors fans flooded stadiums in the United States for the 2025 Club World Cup, *trapos* shouted names like 'BUDGE' – referring to Ingeniero Budge (pronounced 'Bood-he' with a guttural 'h') in the Buenos Aires province. The city was named after Swindon-born Oliver Budge, who was chief engineer of the influential East Argentine Railway. His name has now been immortalised in football stadiums around the world.

Such is the standing of the *trapo* in Argentinian terrace culture, there is a song dedicated to them by the cumbia band, Yerba Brava. 'La Cumbia de los Trapos' has nearly 200 million views on YouTube and includes the lines 'Jumping, singing, clinging to the *trapos*, we leave our souls on the terrace' and 'I'm crazy about my *trapo*, I'll follow my team until the end, no matter where you go'.

Depending on the size or clout of the group responsible, the flags can scale from handheld to the entire width of the pitch, opening up the possibility of slogans and messages. A *trapo* angled towards the TV cameras at San Lorenzo claims 'Silence is not my language'. Whisper it quietly, as Racing Club are not popular among *cuervos*, but I always enjoy one spotted behind the goal at their El Cilindro stadium. 'Racing and wine for every Argentine,' it preaches.

Unsurprisingly, the *barra brava* make sure their *trapos* are the largest and most prominently displayed in the *cancha*. Behind almost every goal in Argentina is a long banner bearing the name of the *barra* that currently controls the local *popular*. Higher up the terrace, they mark out their territory with further sprawling *trapos* which often deliver ominous messages to rival *hinchadas*.

Switch on any Argentinian match and you'll spot all of these eye-catching elements. Get close in person, and you notice the unusually galvanising impact they have on people inside the *cancha*. Fans grab on to fistfuls of their team's precious colours, screaming, weeping or praying into the material when tensions rise. *Barras* gather behind *trapos* on the terrace like demonstrators at a protest, parading a message to their team, to their club's directors, to the world. *Tirantes* swing from side to side as the *hinchada* tries to generate an energy that may somehow transmit to the players.

* * *

From my days as a regular at the Nuevo Gasómetro to streaming San Lorenzo matches from the UK, I've had a constant window into the ways that *cuervos* decorate their *cancha* and express themselves within it. But each ground is different and every trip to Argentina offers the chance to visit another team's lair. In late 2024, I made a long-awaited trip to Nueva Chicago to watch their B Nacional (second tier) play-off tie with Racing de Córdoba. I was keen to see some of the most notorious supporters in Buenos Aires in their habitat.

Nueva Chicago are located in the *barrio* of Mataderos, meaning 'slaughterhouses', owing to the area's history of meat production. The industry also inspired the *barrio*'s nickname and the football club itself. 'New Chicago' is a nod to its namesake in the USA, once famous for its slaughterhouses and meat packing plants.

As a bonus for the day-tripper, the Estadio Nueva Chicago is just a few blocks away from a gaucho-themed fair held every Sunday. My visit landed on such a day, so before the match I tucked into a juicy *bondiola* sandwich (barbecued pork in a bap) while watching some live *folclore* music. I could have browsed the market's popular trinkets and leather souvenirs, but the green and black plumes of smoke in the distance – Nueva Chicago's distinctive colours – soon coaxed me towards the *cancha*.

The Chicago fans created a rousing pre-match build-up on the streets of Mataderos, and the fireworks, flares and smoke grenades continued inside the stadium. On my way in, I walked past a large *trapo* with the image of Diego Maradona and the words '*Siempre tengo a mi lado a mi D10S*' – 'I always have my God at my side' – with Diego's number ten embedded in the word 'God'. Maradona does not need a direct connection to your club to feature on a *trapo*. He is a god for all.

Completing the design was the emblem of the Justicialist Party, synonymous with Peronism – the omnipresence movement started by three-time President Juan Perón. Depicting one hand lifting another, the symbol popped up on *trapos* throughout the ground. It's a particularly common sight in Mataderos, given the area's historic ties to the movement, but the same badge can be spotted in *canchas* across the country. Peronism's popularity among the working class – or at least its symbolism – still endures more than 80 years after Perón first came to power. While Peronism may mean different things to different people, its blue-collar, nationalist bent has long resonated with football fans.

The *popular local* at Chicago runs across the side of the pitch and was as densely packed as I have ever seen a terrace in Argentina. The seething mass of bodies seemed to sway as one, before intermittently breaking out in frantic pogo jumps. I was grateful to have paid the extra few pesos to sit in the comfort of the *platea*, where I had a prime view of the *barra*'s main *trapos* unfurling opposite me.

'YOU KNOW WHO WE ARE', the top one read. Below it, 'THE NIGHTMARE OF EVERY HINCHADA'.

With only rare exceptions, away fans had been banned in Argentina for more than a decade due to security reasons, but I'm not sure how many Racing de Córdoba fans would have fancied making the 700km journey to Mataderos anyway, given the reception that would have awaited them.

The early afternoon sun beat down fiercely but energy pulsed from the stands. A draw or a win for Nueva Chicago would get them to the quarter-finals of the B Nacional's protracted promotion play-offs, but Racing de Córdoba hadn't travelled all this way to lie down. After just seven minutes, a spectacular 20-yard strike gave the visitors the lead. The now customary hush of an away goal descended on The Slaughterhouse. Only the celebratory shouts of the players and dugout could be heard, before the locals kicked back into their chants.

Fifteen minutes from time, the sun-soaked sardines in the *popular* were rewarded with an equalising goal. The celebrations around me were full-blooded and emotional, but the scenes on the terraces were quickly upstaged by events on the touchline.

Racing de Córdoba's goalkeeper had been time-wasting since his side took an early lead. And not subtly. His antics had wound up the locals and, with the teams now level, he became a prime target for abuse. As angry as anyone was Chicago's official mascot, Tito El Torito – the bull dressed in full green and black stripes.

Soon after the equaliser, when the offending goalkeeper went to retrieve the ball, Tito smelled revenge in his giant furry nostrils. First, he tried to obstruct the ball from being returned. When it finally made its way back to the pitch, the mascot launched a tirade of abuse at the goalkeeper. The Racing players turned around in disbelief, but the bull continued to shout insults, lifting up his oversized head by a few centimetres so the expletives could escape through the costume's neck. With no hint of irony, the referee brandished the red card at the raging bull. Tito El Torito had been sent off.

The mascot threw his arms up and stormed along the touchline. The incident had taken place behind the goal, a considerable distance from the tunnel, making his walk of shame gloriously long. Tito continued to point angrily at the referee throughout his protracted exit, then ripped off his head in one final undignified flourish before disappearing down the tunnel. It remains one of the greatest incidents I have ever witnessed at a football match.

'The lower leagues in its purest state!' celebrated the football newspaper *Olé* on social media, alongside photos of an angry Tito. The football public revelled in an episode that felt both unprecedented yet somehow familiar, and perfectly befitting of Argentina's chaotic *ascenso*.

* * *

The characterful *cancha* and eventful match in Mataderos stoked my curiosity to see how other *hinchadas* operate in Argentina's second tier. Within days, I was back in the B Nacional, this time with Chacarita Juniors. Just like Nueva Chicago, Argentines will tell you not to visit Chaca, due to the infamy of the supporters and the local area. But just like Chicago, it's the perfect destination for enjoying the colour and ferocity of the *ascenso*. Applying the usual rules of caution and common sense is more than enough to keep you feeling safe – especially in the post-away fans era.

Overall, Chacarita is better known for its violent supporters than footballing achievements. A Chacarita fan once referred to his club as 'the Millwall of Argentina' as we chatted about the game in our respective countries. On another occasion, I asked a Rosario Central-supporting taxi driver which game he most feared in the days of travelling as an away fan in Argentina. Chacarita Juniors was his immediate response.

Somewhat ominously, the club is known as *El Funebrero* – the undertaker – although that's due to its original location near the famous Chacarita Cemetery rather than the antics of the fans. The Buenos Aires *barrio* of Chacarita has become a trendy, up-and-coming area, capturing the overspill of modern cafés and small plate restaurants from neighbouring Palermo – a tourist hotspot. But since the 1940s, the club has played in the working-class area of San Martín, the home of my travel companions for the Barracas game.

With no away fans to fight anymore, the Chaca fans have turned on themselves. It is the only ground in Argentina I have visited with two local *hinchadas* positioned on opposite sides of the stadium, singing different songs at the same time. In-fighting between *barras* has created opposing factions – a common occurrence at Chacarita and, sadly, right across the country. One of the most notorious conflicts at Chaca involved two sisters, Angélica and Ana Molina. The Molinas not only fought for the rare distinction of being female leaders of a *barra brava*, but they waged war on each other for the privilege, following an acrimonious split during their rise on the terraces.

Walking through the streets of San Martín on a matchday, you are blissfully unaware of this nonsense. That was my experience at least, when I and my friend Gavin – who has married into a Rosario Central-supporting family – stumbled into a group of friendly *funebreros* for beers and fernet – the dark spirit that Argentines mix with coke to create their iconic, frothy drink. They were delighted to know that people from abroad had taken an interest in their club and were soon taking photos with their new foreign friends.

In stark contrast to the party in and around the ground, Chacarita versus Gimnasia de Jujuy was a truly appalling event. A gaping chasm between the matchday atmosphere and the quality of football is a familiar theme in Argentina, and the gap only seems to widen. But the show provided by the Chaca faithful more than made up for their team's laboured performance, in a match that oozed 0-0 from every orifice.

The bigger of the two *popular* stands was a spectacle in itself. Just before kick-off, a gargantuan *telón* swallowed up the entire stand behind the goal. 'There is only one *hinchada*' it pointedly proclaimed. Below were three huge badges. One of the club, one of the *barra*, and one, naturally, of Peronism. President Javier Milei was once on Chacarita's books during his teenage years as an aspiring goalkeeper. You wonder how the hotheaded libertarian coped with Chaca's very public Peronist affiliations.

Taking in the *cancha* from our warm patch of concrete at the back of the *platea*, we could sense the Chaca fans were keen to wrestle back some form of control on the day. The *previa* was a carnival, their pre-match display was impressive, but the match – the part they could not control – had been a resounding disappointment. As the game stuttered past the 70-minute mark, the *hinchada* took matters into their own hands and launched an act of both protest and celebration.

Suddenly, swarms of *barra brava* at the top of the *popular* began to coordinate a second, impromptu release of the prize *telón*. With play ongoing, the swathes of red-white-and-black material swept back down to completely obstruct the *hinchada*'s view of the game. The fans had effectively drawn the curtains on the pitiful performance. They didn't want to watch these players anymore.

But Argentinian *hinchadas* like to be the heroes and this was also a tribute to themselves. Screaming out their message, 'There is only one *hinchada*', the *telón* was shaken with vigour for what felt like five minutes or more. It was a celebration of their loyal support during an end-of-season dead rubber, but also a message to their enemies at the other end of the *cancha* and the underperforming players on the pitch. 'We are the only ones who matter here.'

The Chacarita fans are an odd bunch. Their commitment to the cause is admirable and, given the dire game, their *fiesta* had rescued the day for Gavin and I. But it was a bit like watching an abusive relationship unfold. The team and the *hinchada* seemed to need each other, without either enjoying the other's company. The players ran out in front of the league's biggest and most passionate support, clapping, waving and thanking them, but then looked scared of their presence within minutes and wilted under their noise. For their part, the *hinchada* gave its all in the stands, but was it to support the team or just prove to themselves – and rival groups – that they were the best?

It was a complex dynamic, but this is the theatre of the *cancha*. When turf wars, political allegiances, choreographed shows and angry mascots collide, the match can feel like the least important thing happening.

Chapter 6

An *hincha* is born

Nos dicen enfermos   They say that we're crazy
¿Qué le voy a hacer?   What am I going to do?
Mi único remedio   My only cure
Es volverte a ver   Is coming back to see you

IN THE early 20th century, Prudencio Miguel Reyes worked as a saddler in Montevideo, Uruguay, maintaining leather saddles and reins for riding horses. Club Nacional de Football, which became one of the country's 'big two' alongside Club Atlético Peñarol, would send their punctured footballs to Reyes to be repaired.

'With hands like mallets and fingers that looked like sausages, the guy had a masterful skill for stitching the ball shut,' wrote the Nacional player-turned-author, Luis A. Sciutto, as relayed by *Marca*. 'From the outside it might not seem like much, but that's an art like any other.' After skilfully repairing the ball, Reyes would breathe life back into it using nothing but the oxygen in his lungs. The modern-day football pump was not yet a part of the kit man's arsenal.

Reyes began to attend Nacional games and support the team, but he did so in a more vocal and animated way than anyone had ever seen before. '*¡Arriba Nacional!*' he bellowed from the touchline, using his considerable, ball-inflating lung capacity. The middle-class spectators in their top hats usually offered no more than polite applause for the players. Who was this loud man? '*El hincha*' was the response – the man who inflates (*hinchar*) the balls.

To this day, football fans across Latin America are called *hinchas* (pronounced een-chahs). *Hinchada* is the collective noun, but as noted, this term is usually reserved for the more vocal supporters. Reyes the saddler had given birth to one of the most commonly used terms in *fútbol*, and more importantly, the very concept of passionately supporting your team.

By way of contrast, the term *aficionado* is still more common in Spain. If you look around a Spanish stadium, any spectator who is not in the small band of ultras does indeed have the air of an aficionado. They sit down and observe the action, engaged but passive, chomping through their packs of sunflower seeds. In Uruguay, Argentina and now the whole of Latin America, even those positioned far away from the *hinchada* prefer to be on their feet, singing, shouting, jumping and flinging their arms in the air to lift their team.

'*Alentemos todos juntos, pa' que pongan huevos nuestros jugadores*,' they sing at the Nuevo Gasómetro. 'Let's lift the team together so the players show some balls.'

'*Que los partidos se ganan dentro de la cancha y aca en los tablones*.' – 'Because games are won on the pitch and here on the terraces.'

The idea of the '12th man' is more than a football cliche in Argentina. The fans have an active role to play throughout the season. They are praised for wins, blamed for defeats and, just like the players and managers, regarded as protagonists in the overall fortunes of their club.

Taking this sense of responsibility into each game, the *hinchas* – particularly those in the *popular* – do their best to influence proceedings from the stands. It all starts when the players emerge from the tunnel before kick-off. At this moment, all the elements of the terraces, from the instruments, to the flags, to the fervent chanting, are shaken up in a bottle and the cap is flipped off. What explodes into the air is known as the *recibimiento*, literally the 'reception', as fans roar their team on to the battlefield in a cloud of ticker tape and smoke.

The songs then continue throughout the 90 minutes. When I'm at Charlton, I often think that 'song' is a generous term for what leaves our mouths. Like nearly all fanbases in the UK, we support our team through short bursts of shouting and chanting rather than actual singing. A penchant for speed – fuelled by pints of lager and sometimes more powdery substances – means even longer club anthems like 'Valley Floyd Road' are belted out in fast-forward, effectively killing any sense of rhythm or tune.

In Argentina, the chants are surprisingly melodic. They tend to include at least one full verse as well as the chorus. The band complements the *hinchada* by holding a steady rhythm and building to crescendos for key moments of the song. Fans write full sets of lyrics to honour their club and put them to tracks from cumbia, rock and even reggaeton.

When it comes to celebrating goals, the Argentinian *hincha* tends to respond with less physical movement than in other football cultures, relying heavily on those lung-busting roars of '*GOL*'. But there is one notable exception, 'the avalanche'. When I first arrived in Argentina in 2014, it was one of the first things I noticed when watching highlights of the Primera.

Peering at an old box TV in my flat near downtown Buenos Aires, I have vivid memories of a Racing player scoring a bicycle kick, which prompted an almighty surge forward from the fans behind the goal. (A retrospective check shows it was Valentín Viola against Club Atlético Colón). My initial thought was that someone may have been crushed to death in the celebrations, but I soon learned that this was just an *avalancha* – a well-established feature of watching your team from the *popular*. The terrace seems to tip fans forward when a goal goes in, creating a dramatic rush of human dominoes.

For an avalanche to happen, you need a terrace packed with hardcore support – making its occurrence a source of pride for fans. Mocking the sparse, low-key home support of their bitter rival Huracán (nicknamed *El Globo*), San Lorenzo once unleashed a giant *trapo* in their away end for a derby match. '*Globo*,' it asked, 'will you ever see an avalanche?'

* * *

Of course, the antics of a noisy Uruguayan saddler alone cannot explain the world-famous passion of the Argentinian *cancha*. To create such a phenomenon, you need a society and culture that is completely drenched in football from top to bottom.

Walking through Buenos Aires on any given day provides reminders of the country's football obsession. Every second person seems to be wearing an item of clothing dedicated to their team. Stadiums pop up every 20 blocks and the streets that separate them are smattered with football graffiti. If there is a big game in the evening, you will hear screams of joy or anguish escaping apartment windows.

The media coverage is relentless. Newspapers, social media and TV stations scrutinise every game to the nth degree. Journalists stay planted at training grounds throughout the week. You wonder if they ever are allowed to go home. Every conversation and tactical consideration that could be taking place behind them is relayed to the camera. Their Chinese whispers are broadcast live in cafés, bars, restaurants, barber shops and shopping centres. When Argentina won the 2022 World Cup, it didn't celebrate like other countries. The population lost its mind. Four million people gathered around the Obelisco in Buenos Aires – and that was just one part of one city.

Where does this all come from? It's something I tried to extract from nearly everyone I met in the creation of this book, but few could bring as many perspectives from inside the game as Mariano de la Fuente.

Mariano is a rare breed. Over the course of his career, he has been a professional player, manager and a pundit, without ever breaking his routine of supporting his beloved team from the *popular* every other week.

'Even when I was a player, San Lorenzo always had the priority,' he says firmly. I sensed this was never negotiable with his employers. We are both in Buenos Aires for the conversation, but we've had to settle for a video call on WhatsApp. Mariano is a busy man, working full time as a hotel chauffeur from Monday to Friday and spending the weekend analysing San Lorenzo and the Argentinian Primera for his 35,000 subscribers on YouTube.

It's a warm Sunday night and he's 'gone skins' for the call. I've never before interviewed a topless man (or woman), but Mariano's appearance reflected his persona. His stylish glasses and neatly trimmed grey beard were a nod to his talking-head punditry, while his hairy chest, thick medallion and upper-arm tattoos embodied the everyday fan at the *cancha*.

Mariano had a successful career in the second tier of Argentinian football during the 1990s, including nearly 200 appearances for Defensa y Justicia. But every weekend involved meticulous planning to ensure he could also go to watch San Lorenzo. Even if he was playing on the same day, transport would be arranged in advance so he could get to the game. Fortunately, his matches in *la B* were usually in the Buenos Aires city or province, and played earlier than San Lorenzo fixtures in the Primera. 'Sometimes I'd still be carrying my dirty kit when I entered the Nuevo Gasómetro,' he recalls.

One particularly delicate moment came when he was playing for Quilmes in 1995. At the time, Mariano was taking painkilling injections to get through training and matches. Meanwhile, San Lorenzo were fighting for the league title and their first trophy in 21 long years. It all came down to the last game of the season, in which San Lorenzo could clinch the *campeonato* with a win at Rosario Central. Devastatingly for Mariano, Quilmes were playing on the same day. There would be no time to make the trip to Rosario. Unless …

'On Tuesday I decided not to take the injection. At the weekend I went to Rosario to watch San Lorenzo. That was it. Bye. See you later.' Mariano was one of 35,000 *cuervos* who watched San Lorenzo seal an historic title with a 1-0 win. His gamble had paid off, even if he was terrified of being captured by 'the 7,000 TV cameras they had in the stadium which were filming everything!'

Mariano's intense relationship with the game surfaced in a more public manner during his managerial career. In 2017, his JJ Urquiza side were struggling near the foot of the third tier when a particularly limp performance against San Martín de Burzaco tipped him over the edge. With Urquiza 1-0 down at half-time, his exasperated rant in the dressing room was secretly recorded. It went viral online, and became the stuff of lower-league legend.

'We're not marking anyone! Fuck all of you!' Mariano shouts hoarsely. 'You can't play football like that! Kick them! Grab their shirts! Just do something! You're going to kill me. I don't want to die in a dressing room … You're going to kill me! Mark up! Then start to play. But mark up!'

Listening back, it's impossible not to smile. Just like his life as a player, it seems Mariano could not let go of the *hincha* within. But there isn't just anger in his voice; there is desperation too – which points to something deeper in the Argentine psyche. The popularity of the video suggests many fans could hear themselves in that half-time tirade. Football is a passion that pushes Argentines to breaking point. Yet the emotion seen within the game is just the symptom of a wider cause.

'In football, you release the frustration of everything you're living in your daily life. And the daily life of an

Argentine is complex and difficult. My mum is 80 years old and she still has to work ten hours per day because her pension isn't enough to pay the rent. What's happening to her will happen to me and will happen to my kids. For 20 years I've been battling on. I have to work 12 hours a day, six days a week as a driver for a hotel. And if someone speaks badly to me I have to keep my mouth shut, because if I react badly, I'm in the shit.'

The more I heard, the more I sympathised with the man on the edge of a breakdown in JJ Urquiza's dressing room.

'Our society is a little unhinged and on the edge because the day-to-day frustration in the country is enormous. Football helps you forget, but the anger of everything you encounter stays with you. You're so pissed off with everything that you have to release that somewhere.'

Our conversation had touched a nerve. But it also reinforced what a priceless outlet football is for so many people. 'It generates what nothing else in the country can generate,' Mariano said. 'Not politics, not F1, not tennis, nothing. Celebrating a goal in the stands is one of the best feelings a human being can feel, only topped by celebrating a goal on the pitch.'

It's not often you meet someone who has scored in a professional match in front of thousands of people. I wanted to know what it felt like. 'Will, you know that I am not vulgar, but let me tell you this so you understand. Scoring a goal is better than shagging Pampita [as Argentinian model Ana Carolina Ardohaín Dos Santos is commonly known]. And the feeling doesn't just come and go, the feeling stays with you for years. I scored eight goals in my career and I remember celebrating every single one of those eight goals. That's the feeling football has. Nothing can equal it. And it's born from the moment we all receive that first present as a baby: a football.'

Mariano was keen to emphasise just how early Argentines are indoctrinated into football. I didn't doubt him. But in case I did, a telling example appeared on my social media feed just days after our conversation. A friend of a friend posted a picture of a San Lorenzo membership card featuring the photo of a new-born baby. The post read, 'The day I was born, my grandfather arrived at the hospital with a San Lorenzo membership card. That card, in many ways, defined my life. Today my son arrived. And he's already received his membership card. It bears my grandfather's name. Because love is cyclical. And because San Lorenzo is always present.'

The sentiment was touching, but the fact that somebody had gone through the lengthy administrative process to sign his baby up to the club on the very same day of his birth took me back. The baby was a paid-up San Lorenzo member before he could even open his eyes.

I didn't want my conversation with Mariano to end. His love for football radiated through the screen. His observations were astute and full of humour. I also liked that he never spoke from the perspective of a player, manager or pundit, apart from when I asked him to. Everything came from the perspective of Mariano the *hincha*.

'Football unites people,' he said. 'Argentina is a very unequal country; there are very rich people and there are people that go through a really hard time. But in the stadium we are all equal. Maybe social stratification still exists in the *platea*, but in the *popular* we are all equal.'

By not earning millions in football and now working in a 'normal' job, perhaps it is easier for Mariano to maintain the perspective of an everyday fan. But his mentality reminded me of the many Argentine players who, like him, never stopped being an *hincha*.

Just months after leaving Boca Juniors in 2024, ex-Argentina striker Darío Benedetto was pictured on top of the *paravalancha* railings during a match at the Bombonera, right among the *barra brava*. He was wearing a yellow Boca vest and singing along with the fans. His tattooed arm was aloft as he willed on his former team-mates in their battle against Independiente. Looking at the photo, he is indistinguishable from the fans and *barras* around him.

Former River Plate striker Daniel Villalva was photographed in similar circumstances in 2023. The *Millionario* fan was bouncing on the *paravalanchas* wearing a replica shirt with 'Lanzini' – Manuel, the ex-River and West Ham midfielder – printed on the back. Carlos Alcaraz left Racing for the Premier League in 2022 and later played for Juventus, but he has also been spotted behind the goal at his former club – dressed head to toe in Racing clothes and passionately chanting with the *hinchada*. Most famously of all, Diego Maradona was a regular at La Bombonera and visibly felt the highs and lows like any fan, albeit in his hospitality box rather than the *popular*.

It is common to see ex-players return to their clubs in other countries, but they tend to do so in a very different manner. They wear smart clothes and are seated high in the VIP areas of the stadium. They shake hands with dignitaries. They smile and applaud the goals, much like the well-heeled Uruguayan fans before Reyes the *hincha* came along. It is all very different from the rough and tumble of the *popular*, going shoulder to shoulder with everyday fans and breathing in the sweat, marihuana and smoke bombs.

Reyes planted the seed for a different way of experiencing the game. But he was merely reflecting something that was already inside his people. As the British influence on South American football receded, this exuberant way of supporting a team took hold. Now, it has become second nature to match-goers. The ex-players returning to the *popular* of their boyhood clubs shows that the *hincha* inside never leaves, even if your journey in football takes you away from the terraces.

The *hinchas* have created an entire subculture that Argentina and indeed much of the continent can hang its hat on. And given the declining standard on the pitch, this subculture is more important than ever. Feeding off the Latin American economies which they exploited for centuries, wealthy European clubs have been able to buy up the region's most-talented players at an increasingly young age, and reduce the quality of the leagues that raised them. But there are some things they can't buy, like the spirit of the *hincha*. As long as that survives, there will always be Europeans like me flocking to the *canchas* of Argentina and beyond, just to see, hear and feel something that you cannot find at home.

Chapter 7

Las barras bravas

En el barrio de Boedo hay una banda In the *barrio* of Boedo there is a gang
El aguante es lo primero que aprendí *Aguante* is the first thing that I learned
En el barrio te vas haciendo picante In the *barrio* you start to toughen up
Es el barrio mas hermoso para mi It's the most beautiful *barrio* to me

WHEN YOU tell someone you're going to a football match in Argentina, be it a local or a foreigner, you often get the same question in response, 'Is that safe?'

Argentines are all too aware of the violence that has plagued their game. Although people continue to fill the stadiums, trips to the match are often planned with a degree of caution. In the eyes of the locals, an unsuspecting Englishman will surely sleepwalk into danger. Those who have never even set foot in the country draw similar conclusions, such is the reputation of Argentinian football.

The infamous *barras bravas* play a central role in creating this image. Their name literally means 'fierce group' and is frequently translated to 'hooligans' in English, but that is a touch misleading. When they weren't fighting, British hooligans blended in with everyday fans on the terraces and, crucially, held no power within the organisation of their clubs. Conversely, the *barra brava* is deliberately conspicuous in the ground, with *trapos* and *tirantes* marking their patch and reflecting their elevated status. Over recent decades, the *barras* have branched out from fighting and fully infiltrated almost every aspect of club operations.

Although the *barra* phenomenon didn't fully cement itself until the latter half of the 20th century, violence in Argentinian football has existed from the beginning. A full stadium riot took place as early as 1916, when a match between Argentina and Uruguay in the South American Championship (which later became the Copa América) had to be abandoned after just five minutes.

Football hadn't been around long, but it seems that the Uruguayans were already embracing the 'away day' concept. Nearly 2,000 supporters travelled from Montevideo to Buenos Aires via steamboats for the match. The Argentines were just as eager, with tens of thousands arriving from all over the country to see the continent's two footballing heavyweights go head to head, in a game marking the centenary of Argentina's independence.

Unfortunately, it was this very eagerness which became the problem. As many as 40,000 people forced their way into a stadium which could only accommodate half the number. Fans spilled on to the pitch and made play impossible, not least for the Uruguayan players who had fired-up locals literally breathing down their necks while taking throw-ins. When the match was abandoned early on, violence broke out throughout the stadium.

Incensed fans stole one goal as a trophy and set the other one alight. The flames caught a wooden terrace and three stands were burned down in the blaze. Somehow, there were no fatalities, although a heroic act of comradeship nearly cost an Argentina fan his life. When Juan Pallas saw that the fire was about to catch a Uruguayan flag hanging from the stand, he climbed through the flames to rescue it and received an ovation from onlookers. Unable to breathe in the smoke, he fell to the pitch and was rushed to hospital, where he survived.

Football violence at the time was neither isolated, nor limited to supporters. Just two years previously, the secretary of Racing Club invaded the pitch with a revolver during a friendly with Exeter City. He was furious with the 'rough play' of the English and threatened to shoot the referee for not taking action. 'Thankfully, tempers were calmed and the game resumed after the interlude,' reports Exeter club historian Martin Weiler, in a glorious downplaying of the incident.

By 1922, Argentina had its first death related to football violence. During Tiro Federal Argentino versus Newell's Old Boys, Enrique Battcock, a railway worker and supporter of the home team, punched Newell's treasurer Francisco Campá during an argument. Campá left the stadium and returned with a gun. He shot Battcock dead.

With football-related disorder continuing to surface, the term *barra brava* started to be coined during the 1920s. Historian and sociologist Julio Frydenberg highlights the first examples in the Argentinian press, including an article from the newspaper *Crítica* which described *barras* as 'madmen who only go to matches with the aim of showing their base instincts'. In 1928, the magazine *La Cancha* proposed the banning of the 'aggressive, brutal, fanatic and unsportsmanlike *barras*'.

Among the first recognised *barras* was San Lorenzo's Barra de la Goma. 'The Rubber Barra' got its name from the weapons cobbled together by its members. The young rebels would slice open rubber tyres and fill them with sand and stones. Sewn back up, they formed a lethal truncheon.

Those of a *cuervo* persuasion claim the Barra de la Goma were founded to protect San Lorenzo players and fans, and not to fight rival supporters for the sake of it. This, admittedly, has been a defence used by most *barras bravas* throughout their history. It is said that in 1927, when San Lorenzo were riding high in the league, fans from city rivals Huracán and Boca Juniors would go to the Gasómetro to support whoever San Lorenzo were playing. During their visit, they would hurl missiles at the San Lorenzo players from the away end.

The aggrieved *cuervos* saw that their players needed protecting and formed the Barra de la Goma. Each time they saw a missile fly towards their players from the away end, the perpetrator would feel the force of the rubber truncheon.

In his book on the aforementioned magazine *La Cancha*, Rodrigo Daskal uncovered a note penned by the Barra de la Goma which was published at the time. It supports the view that the group was founded to protect the players, though its ominous tone suggests its members weren't completely averse to idea of a good scrap either: 'Each and every one of you is warned, whether we are home or away, we will demand respect, and we would rather a match was abandoned than to see our players mistreated and our chances in the league diminished by the criminal action of certain beasts with brightly coloured shirts [Boca and Huracán fans]. If our opponents want good football, we will provide it to them, as we have some great players in the squad. If you prefer a fight, we will deliver it at your discretion, even at your home. Take your pick, there will be something for everyone.'

By the midway point of the century, a win-at-all-costs mentality in Argentinian football had long since replaced the values of sportsmanship taught by the game's forefathers. And with that mentality, the ugly incidents became evermore common.

In 1946, Newell's Old Boys and San Lorenzo played out a cracker in Rosario, as Newell's clawed back San Lorenzo's 2-0 half-time lead to make it 2-2 in the second half. With just five minutes remaining, Newell's were denied a dramatic winner by referee Osvaldo Cossio, who blew for a marginal offside which his linesman had not flagged. To further incense the Newell's contingent, San Lorenzo went down the other end and made it 3-2 with a controversial goal.

An angry pitch invasion from Newell's fans forced Cossio to abandon the match on 88 minutes and 50 seconds, according to the referee's official report. Fearing for his safety, Cossio bolted through a gap in the stadium's perimeter fence and fled through the surrounding Parque Independencia. He spotted a slow-moving car and jumped on to its roof to quicken his getaway, but lost balance and toppled to the ground.

A group of Newell's fans who had given chase set upon Cossio, beating him violently and dragged him to a tree. 'Let's hang him!' was the chilling cry as the mob held him down and removed his belt. A crisis was averted when three patrolling soldiers spotted the mob and dispersed them, allowing Cossio to be taken to safety.

Tales like this add a more sinister edge to the 'we're going to kill a referee' chants I have heard at San Lorenzo, or the *trapo* once hung at Huracán which claimed, 'When we kill a referee, you will stop robbing us.' Yet Argentina's steadfast commitment to chaos means that even the dark side of the game can throw up some amusing quirks. Following the abandonment, Newell's and San Lorenzo were reunited in a candidate for the shortest match ever played in the professional game.

Instead of writing off the 70 seconds that had remained before the pitch invasion, the Argentine Football Association insisted that the sides complete the 90 minutes on a rearranged date in Buenos Aires – the day after Newell's were already in town for a match at Vélez Sarsfield. Following orders, the sides convened at the neutral venue of Ferro Carril Oeste. Not only did they obediently play out the remaining 70 seconds, but they did so by playing two halves of 35 seconds.

San Lorenzo kicked off, began an attack, and the referee blew for half-time. The same thing happened in the second half, with a brief Newell's foray interrupted by the final whistle. A 3-2 win for San Lorenzo was confirmed.

It could be assumed that the farcical one minute and ten seconds of football would at least give the stand-in referee, Valentín Rey, an easy afternoon. But according to *La Capital*, Rey had angered Ferro with his refereeing of their defeat to Racing the previous afternoon, and when Ferro fans heard that he was officiating at their ground again the next day, a group went down to hurl abuse and criticise his performance throughout the 70-second contest.

A defining moment in the history of *barras bravas* came just over a decade later. Eighteen-year-old Alberto Mario Linker, a Boca Juniors fan, was invited by a neighbour to go to watch Vélez Sarsfield versus River Plate on a Sunday afternoon in October 1958. Crowd trouble led to the police throwing grenades of tear gas into the stand where young Linker was located. One struck him on the head and killed him. The police attempted to cover up the incident by claiming the missile had come from supporters – a story the press ran with until it was debunked.

In the wake of the incident, newspapers began to tackle the question of football violence in greater detail, describing the inner workings of these *barras fuertes* ('strong groups') or *barras bravas*. Thirty years after they were first mentioned in print, the *barras* had finally gone mainstream. The phenomenon had anchored itself in both local football culture and the wider public's imagination, where it has remained ever since.

After the tragic death of Linker, football fans became increasingly aware that their enemy was not just on the other side of the stadium, but in the ranks of those paid to protect them. Many felt threatened by the police and looked to the *barras* to organise and protect them, especially when travelling to away matches.

Over the second half of the 20th century and up to the present day, the *barras* have grown in strength. Perhaps not in a literal sense – since fist fights have given way to knife attacks and shoot-outs – but certainly in the power they wield. By building relationships with club directors, government authorities, drug gangs and even the old enemy of the police, many *barras* have become untouchable. And with far greater sums of money flowing into football since the 1990s, their business opportunities have grown exponentially.

Initially, club directors would simply pay for *barras* to travel to games. This made sure that the players were well supported and that injustices on the pitch were discouraged, thanks to the presence of strongmen on the terraces. In return, *barra* members would mobilise fan support for directors running for club president, helping to consolidate their political base.

As many club presidents moved into regional and national politics (Mauricio Macri led Boca Juniors in the 1990s and eventually became president of Argentina in 2015), politicians began to tap into the power of the *barras*. In particular, they transported them across the country to bolster rallies and marches. With this political cover, the *barras* had an 'access all areas' pass and could convince the relevant authorities to turn a blind eye to their violence and nefarious business. Inevitably, many of these alliances fractured and ended up with *barras* behind bars. But the damage was done. The *barras* had become an insidious presence throughout football and society at large.

The dynamics explained here are deliberately over-simplified, but broadly outline how many *barra* groups have established themselves both inside and outside of the *cancha*. On a matchday, whether you know it or not, the *barra* may be selling you anything from tickets and merchandise to a parking space and a gram of cocaine. La 12, Boca Juniors' main b*arra brava*, has expanded operations to such an extent that in 2024 it opened a restaurant bearing its name in Puerto Madero, one of the most upmarket parts of Buenos Aires.

* * *

There is a great deal of discussion about the *barras* among supporters and the press in Argentina, but I was curious to know if those inside the game felt the weight of their presence. During my conversation with Mariano de la Fuente, I asked whether his career had ever been affected by the *capos* on the terraces.

'It's ugly, really ugly, but you know it will happen to you at some point in your career. It's not normal, but it's become normalised. The directors of clubs often know that the *barra* are planning to intimidate the players at the training ground and are happy for it to happen, because it gives the players a telling off without them having to get involved.'

When I pushed Mariano on whether he'd ever feared what *barra* members may do, he revealed a troubling episode during his time as manager of JJ Urquiza in 2015. His team were in a closely fought relegation battle with arch-rivals Club Atlético General Lamadrid, and the two sides were set to face off in one of the final games of the Primera C season.

'I've lived my whole life in Villa Devoto, which is the *barrio* of Lamadrid,' said Mariano, 'and a few days before the game I received a threat from their *barra* via an unknown number on my phone. It said, "Watch what you do. Because if you win, you won't get out of the stadium. We know where you live."

'On the day of the game there were police absolutely everywhere. I was well protected but I also knew that I was being watched by their *barra* wherever I went, so my behaviour didn't have to be a ten out of ten, it needed to be a 15 out of ten. I managed to contain myself for our goals but at the end of the game I entered the dressing room and burst out crying. It was a release of all the tension that had built up. We won 3-1, I made it out alive, and on the final day of the season we overtook them in the league to send them down. It was the perfect ending.'

Mariano said his main fear was the safety of his children. 'They went to school in the local area and knew a lot of Lamadrid people. They were walking to and from school every day and I was really worried, constantly checking whether they had arrived home safely. It was extremely stressful.'

Two years before Mariano's run-in with the dark side of the game, away fans were banned across Argentina. The final straw was the death of a Lanús supporter in 2013, after violence broke out during their game at Estudiantes.

Ironically, like the Mario Linker death, it was the police with blood on their hands once again. Daniel Jerez found himself in a melee of Lanús supporters outside the stadium when the police began to fire rubber bullets into the crowd. According to Daniel's friend, Adrián, he was trying to shield younger fans from bullets amid the chaos. 'Daniel's message was always to stay out of trouble,' Adrián told national newspaper *La Nación*.

One of the rubber bullets was fired into Daniel's chest from just a metre away. 'Stop shooting!' were his final words as he pleaded with the police. But it was too late and he died in hospital.

According to the organisation Salvemos Al Futbol – 'Let's Save Football' – Daniel Jerez was the 274th person to die in football-related violence in Argentina since 1922. But as fans and *barras* continue to clash away from the stadium, stopping away supporters from attending matches has not solved the problems with violence. Salvemos Al Futbol's records show that a further 78 people have died since the away ban was imposed, supporting the view that the issue belongs to society at large, not just football.

The ban's relative ineffectiveness makes the absence of away supporters in the Argentinian leagues (there are exceptions in the cups) all the more sad. Wherever you are in the world, the back-and-forth between two sets of supporters is one of the key elements of the matchday experience. In a football culture like Argentina's, where terrace expression is so vibrant and rich, being denied the famous 'battle of the *hinchadas*' is a particular blow.

Although pilot schemes for their return began in 2025, away fans have been mostly absent since I began watching Argentinian football. Those brief, tense silences when the visiting side bear down on goal still take some getting used to. When the chance is missed, deafening whistles follow from the home crowd. When the chance is scored, the silence intensifies for a few more eerie seconds. The scorer wheels away and those in the technical area celebrate manically, but the mute button is on. It's a surreal spectacle.

When the silent goal is not against your team, there is a strange beauty to that moment of quiet – like nothing I had experienced in a football ground before visiting Argentina. But it will never get close to compensating for the loss of one of live football's great protagonists: the away fan. As the banners hung at Argentinian canchas often say, '*Que vuelvan los visitantes*' – 'Bring back the away fans.'

Chapter 8

Coffee with the *capo*

Vengo del barrio de Boedo	I come from the *barrio* of Boedo
Barrio de murga y carnaval	*Barrio* of murga and carnival
Te juro que en los malos momentos	I swear that even in the bad times
Siempre te voy a acompañar	I will always follow you

'YOU MUST never, ever, *ever*, mention *barras bravas* in that conversation.'

The advice came in a WhatsApp voice note from a San Lorenzo-supporting friend as I set off for my next interview. It wasn't really the advice I wanted. The interview was going to be with an ex-*barra brava* leader and the point of the interview was to talk about the *barras bravas*. This was a spanner in the works.

Christian Evangelista, formerly nicknamed *Sandokán* (after a fictional pirate created by Italian writer Emilio Salgari), was the head of San Lorenzo's famed *barra brava*, La Butteler, from 2011 to 2017. He has since made the controversial journey from the battlefield to the boardroom and is now a 'vocal' within the San Lorenzo hierarchy, giving him a voice and a vote on club operations, if no day-to-day responsibility.

In light of his newfound professionalism, I suspected Christian may not have wanted to reveal too much detail about his *barra* life, but my friend's stark warning made me even more wary. Implicating him directly with La Butteler and the criminal underworld of the *barras* could make the conversation go south very quickly, the voice note said. This was a man trying to build a very different reputation. With just 30 minutes until the interview, I began to hastily edit the questions I had noted.

I'd never met anyone from La Butteler so I was keen to get an impression of the group – and *barras* in general – from the inside. The prevailing opinion in Argentinian society is that any member of a *barra brava* is a violent criminal who should be avoided at all costs. Football fans may not view them in such a black-and-white manner, but trepidation still looms large on the terraces. Even within the intimacy of a friendship group, I have seen *cuervos* get shifty and uncomfortable when La Butteler come up in conversation, as if any critical comments could escape the room and land them in trouble.

With 'Don't mention the *barra*!' ringing in my ears like Basil Fawlty's 'Don't mention the war!' I arrived early for the meeting. Getting Christian to agree to the interview had been fairly straightforward, but I'd been left hanging for our initial arrangement the previous week. So, as per many social arrangements in Argentina, I couldn't be certain it was happening until it was *happening*. The restaurant where we'd agreed to meet was closed when I arrived, which didn't fill me with confidence. 'Find someone and tell them you're meeting me,' Christian reassured me in a text. Sure enough, when I tracked down a waitress setting up for the evening and passed on the message, I was quickly offered a seat and brought coffee.

Christian arrived shortly after and greeted me with a surprising amount of warmth, as if we already knew each other. His impossibly deep, growly voice, dark, shadowy eyes and imposing stature could have made him intimidating company, but his relaxed demeanour made conversation easy. His phone pinged incessantly for the hour or so in which we spoke, but with impeccable manners he did not look at it once.

I decided to focus the start of the conversation on Christian's life as a fan and his new role within the club. If I could ease the chat towards his past, I would use the word *hinchada* instead of *barra* to reference the hardcore of the support without inferring criminality. Any other details of his time in La Butteler could reveal themselves.

'I can tell a thousand stories about my relationship with San Lorenzo,' he began. 'From sleeping at the club as a child to travelling for days and days to see away games. San Lorenzo is like a member of my family. I'm from the *barrio* [Boedo] and I've spent my whole life going to the *cancha*. At eight years old I escaped from my house to attend games because my parents wouldn't let me go. The older fans from the *barrio* adopted me. They saw I was young and that I was often hungry, so they began taking me to games. That's how it all started.'

Christian's journey to becoming *capo* of La Butteler highlights the close relationship between the murga and the *cancha*. He is passionate about Argentina's carnival culture and in 1998 created his own group, Los Chiflados de Boedo ('The Boedo Nutters' or 'Headcases'). He was part of a group that successfully lobbied the Cristina Fernández de Kirchner government to restore Argentina's carnival as a national holiday, decades after the military dictatorship took it away as an attempt to shut down public gatherings. Running the murga, combined with his work for trade unions and constant presence on the San Lorenzo terraces, gave Christian the platform and contacts to rise to the highest level of the *barra*.

'I come from a humble, working-class family. We couldn't afford to go on a holiday so our summer activities were going to a municipal swimming pool during the week and going to carnival at the weekend. All of my neighbours and family would go. It's what we did to have fun, but it was also an opportunity to leave behind a lot of the problems we had at home. It was an escape.'

I was already aware of murga's influence on football terrace culture in Argentina, but was unaware of its wider social impact. In addition to their performances, Los Chiflados de Boedo run social projects such as an annual Children of the Barrio day, where food parcels are given out to families in need. The group, which Christian continues to run with his wife, also opened a centre for the elderly which organises social events, psychological support and excursions.

'It's a sociocultural murga, not just a cultural murga,' he explained. 'We wanted to create something with a social purpose rather than just an artistic one, so we could help people in the area. In a murga you often have kids from families which don't have the resources to buy them the shoes they need, so if a kid like that joins us, we always have a whip-round and buy them the right shoes. Murga is a great activity for kids and teenagers as it helps people express themselves. In the middle of a carnival, shy people relax and come out of themselves through the music and movement.'

It was hard not to be impressed with Los Chiflados' social dimension and its dedication to supporting the community. Under Javier Milei, Argentina is now embracing a doctrine that promotes a small state and free markets as the solutions to all societal problems. Welfare cuts have left pensioners and other vulnerable groups without vital support, making the values Christian grew up with feel more important than ever.

'Older people are going through a really tough time in this country. Pensions don't last them until the end of the month, they can't buy their medication. Our message is always that one person alone can't save themselves, it's about the community coming together.'

Given the division and tribalism sewn by the *barras bravas* in Argentina, I wondered if the murga's social work was Christian's way to correct the wrongs that may have come with his *barra* life. There were moments in the conversation when he seemed determined to distance himself from stereotypes associated with his past. 'The murga is very different from football,' he said. 'We have fans of all different clubs in our group and there is never any lack of respect towards one another. No one is ever criticised for turning up with a Boca or River badge on their clothes.'

Perhaps recognising the contradiction between this and the actions of the *barras*, he launched into a defence of his time with La Butteler. It caught me off guard and my note-taking hand froze. Had I implicated him with the *barra* in my questioning? Even worse, had I inadvertently criticised him for leading La Butteler?

'People point the finger and want to tarnish you all with the same brush!' I tensed up. 'They try to connect the *barras* with anything bad that happens.' The way he said 'they' reassured me that I was not among the finger-pointers. I exhaled and relaxed back into my chair. 'Sometimes the criticism is fair but sometimes it's not. There are people in the *barra* who live for the club and want what is best for everyone.'

Christian continued his defence. 'When I was in charge, we tried to build something positive for the future. We organised activities for kids like martial arts and boxing. We encouraged people to be polite and respectful, to not rob others in the stands. At San Lorenzo you're always taught to respect the families who go to games. Eventually you get tired [of managing the *barra*] because it is viewed so negatively by the public and everyone calls you a delinquent.'

Now the topic had been broached, I began to probe a little more around his time in the *barra* – particularly the pre-2013 era when away fans were allowed to attend.

'Every weekend was an adventure and you never knew where you'd end up. It was a dangerous adventure with lots of fights. Things kicked off on the way to games, things kicked off on the way back – it was constant fighting. There were some beautiful adventures and there were some horrific adventures. You could travel to a game for 24 hours and the bus would break down in the middle of nowhere. People see you're from another part of the country and trouble begins. You don't even know if you'll make it to the game. The problems that kick off with fans now are now very minor in comparison with those days.'

But Christian insisted that going to matches was also about looking after the everyday fan who wanted to travel safely. 'After every away game, the *hinchada* was the last to leave the ground so we could check that everybody was OK and that nobody was left behind, then all the buses could leave together.'

The former *capo* is now middle-aged and a grandfather. His appetite for those hairy 'adventures' with the *barra* has gone and he is proud of earning a role within the club he loves. Given his past, 'it is very difficult to get to where I am now,' he says. The day before our meeting, he had attended a conference run by the Argentine Football Association. For our chat, he wore a smart, grey, collared shirt and sipped an espresso. He is now embracing a very different kind of networking to that of the terraces, but admits he struggles to shake the mindset of a fan in his work.

He constantly referenced the 'mercenary players' at San Lorenzo who weren't showing love for the shirt. He bemoaned the 'coldness' of club politics which 'run against your emotions'. It reminded me of a story I read about his time in charge of La Butteler, when he broke into the training ground and punched underperforming defender Jonathan Bottinelli in an altercation.

You can take the boy out of the *barra*, but can you take the *barra* out of the boy? I was curious to see whether Christian still cared about old scores with rival fans, but preferably without insulting his leadership credentials. Stealing and parading a flag from another team is a big deal in *barra brava* folklore, and during his time in La Butteler, fans of arch-rivals Huracán famously robbed a large San

Lorenzo *trapo*. The Parque Patricios gang proudly showed off their prize in the home end of their stadium and still sing about the triumphant episode to this day. La Butteler claim their enemies 'cheated' by sneaking over a wall and grabbing the *trapo* without throwing a punch.

I nervously prodded the old wound. 'Look, in the laws of the terraces, we always say the same thing: flags are robbed in a fight,' Christian fired back, bristling in his seat. 'You don't do it by jumping over a wall and taking them when San Lorenzo fans weren't there. The flag is won in combat. If you want my answer, that's it. For those small-timers [at Huracán], because they are small-timers: you rob in a fight.'

'I'll pass that on,' I thought.

* * *

Conflicting thoughts about *barras bravas* and La Butteler have swirled around my head ever since I met Christian. Capturing flags and the occasional fist fight seem like relatively harmless ways for young men to burn energy and testosterone. Their behaviour didn't make them criminals or monsters. Christian was a likeable and thoughtful man. He knew what it was like to grow up in difficult circumstances and spoke passionately about helping the most vulnerable people in society. By all accounts, he backed up his words with action too.

A few days after the interview with Christian, I was able to meet another ex-member of La Butteler. 'Gallego' cemented my view that you cannot dismiss people simply for having history in a *barra*. He was as warm and friendly as they come. He dropped everything in the middle of a busy day to come and chat to me over a coffee. He was a family man who adored his football club. Like almost every young male in his working-class neighbourhood, there was a time when he used to get into scraps. Football matches just became a vehicle for some of those conflicts.

Then I wondered if I was being naive. Had I taken a small sample size of *barras* at face value and began to view a dark world too sympathetically? The *barras bravas* may be a refuge for some disaffected young men, but they have also inflicted untold damage on other lives. You can be sure they would have played a role in many of those 350 football-related deaths in the country. Two of them even occurred at the hands of La Butteler when the *barras* I met were active members. Twice in the 2000s, a Huracán fan was killed in clashes before a *clásico* with San Lorenzo. Christian called the incidents an 'unspeakable tragedy' and acknowledged the 'terrible suffering' of the victims' families.

Perhaps I needed to encounter other *barras* at work to fully realise the impact they can have on the everyday fan. During my time as a *cuervo*, the terraces of San Lorenzo have been relatively free of trouble. Christian's gang quashed an uprising from a young group known as the Banda del Mástil who tried to seize control of the *popular* some 15 years ago, and order had been maintained ever since. The same couldn't be said for the volatile terraces of Rosario Central, as I was about to find out.

Chapter 9

Sun and shade in Rosario

Mire mire qué locura	Look, look what madness
Mire mire qué emoción	Look, look what emotion
Son las dos hinchadas juntas	Both *hinchadas* together
La de los Canallas y la del Ciclón	The *Canallas* and the *Ciclón*

AFTER BUENOS Aires and Córdoba, Rosario is the nation's third-largest city. It lies 300km north of the capital; a mere stone's throw away in a country as vast as Argentina. A bus from Retiro station in Buenos Aires can take you there in three to four hours, which seems to pass quickly. Secure a reclining seat on the upper deck and you're treated to sweeping views of the Pampas. The endless plains roll past hypnotically, usually sending me into a long, peaceful nap. Maybe that's why the journey always feels so short.

On my four visits to the city, the sun has never stopped shining. Rosario has a more relaxed atmosphere than Buenos Aires, with the long path along the Paraná River offering the perfect route for a leisurely afternoon stroll. For added bliss, you can stop for some freshwater fish in one of the riverside restaurants or sip yerba mate in the shade of a palm tree.

But what you experience as a tourist could not be further from the harsh reality lived by many *Rosarinos*. According to figures from Homicide Monitor, the city's murder rate was 22.3 people per 100,000 in 2022, higher than Rio de Janeiro, Medellín and Quito – three South American neighbours sadly renowned for their bloodshed. Crime and violence is a chronic issue, fuelled by the drug shipments flowing in and out of the city via the Paraná.

However, when you enter Rosario, you are reminded that it has another story to tell. Huge painted letters on the side of a bridge greet you with the message 'ROSARIO, THE FOOTBALL CAPITAL OF THE WORLD'. World Cup winners Leo Messi and Ángel Di María hail from the city and came through the academies of Newell's Old Boys and Rosario Central, respectively. The two teams play out arguably the most passionate *clásico* in Argentina.

My last visit came just weeks after San Lorenzo's 1-0 win against Barracas. San Lorenzo were on the road, looking for three much-needed points at Rosario Central. Having persuaded a few friends to join me, I managed to buy some tickets in the home end a week before the game. Central's Estadio Gigante de Arroyito is one of Argentina's famous football cauldrons. It also hosted Argentina's controversial 6-0 win against Peru in the 1978 World Cup, when the Peruvian players were allegedly threatened and bribed to throw the match by Argentina's military dictatorship. I had wanted to see Central at El Gigante for years. A visit would be all the sweeter with San Lorenzo as the opposition.

With no away fans allowed, the Cuervos de Rosario supporter group was determined to celebrate *El Ciclón*'s visit however they could. The day before the game, they discovered that the squad was staying in the city's Holiday Inn (which felt like a telling indication of the club's budget), so the hotel entrance became the site for an impromptu pre-match party – or *banderazo*, as it is known.

When I arrived, hundreds of *cuervos* had taken over the street and blue-and-red smoke was hanging in the air. Songs rang out, flares were lit and fireworks exploded above us. We were only standing outside a Holiday Inn, but the atmosphere rivalled that of many full-blown matches I've attended back home. I spoke to a few fans but none had planned to attend the match as an *infiltrado* – 'an infiltrator' – the term used for undercover away fans. Most simply didn't trust themselves to keep quiet if San Lorenzo scored.

Experience had taught me how tricky that can be. Some years before, I was infiltrating Independiente with my friend Richard when San Lorenzo went ahead after just 30 seconds. Adrenaline surged through my body as the net rippled. Unable to celebrate, I ended up biting Richard's shoulder to suppress a cheer. It was an unfortunate reaction but at least I hadn't revealed *cuervo* sympathies, which would have guaranteed our ejection and probably led to a beating.

Infiltrators being discovered has produced ugly scenes in Argentinian *canchas*. In 2017, a Belgrano fan was wrongly accused of being a Talleres supporter during the *Clásico Cordobés* at the Estadio Mario Kempes. He was brutally attacked and tossed over a gangway on to the concrete floor, before being taken to hospital where he tragically died.

* * *

Rosario is the most football-obsessed place I have ever visited. It feels as if every street is painted either red and black or yellow and blue to mark the territory of Newell's or Central. The next day, after following a street of yellow-and-blue-striped lamp-posts near the Gigante de Arroyito, we arrived at Parque Alem. It was the perfect *previa* spot for a hot afternoon. We sat in the shade of the towering trees to glug cold cans of Santa Fe lager, surrounded by packs of 'scoundrels' – the rough translation of *Los Canallas*, Central's nickname. The name dates back to the 1920s and their alleged refusal to play a charity match for a leprosy clinic. Newell's had agreed to play, earning them the nickname *La Lepra* – 'the lepers'.

The *cancha*, just a five-minute walk away from our idyllic park *previa*, was a visual treat inside and out. The imposing two-tiered stands almost backed on to the rows of houses behind them. The vast blue terraces were decorated with bright yellow *tirantes* which fanned out behind each goal. Central are famed for their vociferous support but the atmosphere on this sunny Saturday evening was joyful rather than hostile, with an unusual amount of goodwill in the air. We were told that La Butteler had been treated to an *asado* from Central's *barra brava* before the game, as the two groups marked their historic friendship – a common practice between certain *barras*.

With the game still goalless midway through the second half, a betting man would have put his pesos on a 0-0 draw. Then, quite out of the blue, San Lorenzo's mercurial Nahuel Bustos collected the ball 25 yards from Central's goal and unleashed a right-footed rocket which flew into the corner of the goal we stood closest to. Silence among the scoundrels. The ultimate test for the *infiltrado* had arrived and I fought to suppress the adrenaline surging through my body. If someone sensed my *cuervo* sympathies, we could have been in trouble. I grabbed my friend Gavin and frantically whispered '*¡golazo!*' in his ear with some swear words. San Lorenzo held on for a 1-0 win.

The Bustos strike will live long in the memory, but it was overshadowed by events that unfolded just one hour later. Having replenished ourselves with post-match pizza and beers just 200 metres or so from the stadium, we hopped into a cab and drove past a street corner that, unbeknownst to us, had just become the scene of a homicide. 'Central's top barra shot dead,' read a WhatsApp message from my friend Eduardo. 'Leave the city before that escalates.'

Rumours spreading on Twitter not only suggested Eduardo was right – but that the shooting had happened just two blocks from where we'd been eating. Supporters leaving the stadium had fled the area in panic, bolting in the opposite direction to where we were stationed. An ambulance had been and gone but a police presence was mysteriously absent. Talk in the city was of a *zona liberada* –

a 'liberated zone' – meaning the police had collaborated with the murderers and vacated the area for the killing. It was a depressing detail. Families and children were everywhere, yet right among them the authorities had seemingly allowed bullets to spray with impunity.

In the following days, neighbours reported that the streetlights on Calle Avellaneda, where the shooting had taken place, had mysteriously gone out that evening, while all the nearby CCTV cameras had blacked out due to 'a technical failure', reported C5N. The victims were Andrés *Pillín* Bracamonte, the long-standing leader of Central's *barra brava*, Los Guerreros, and his right-hand man, Daniel Raúl *Rana* Attardo. According to national news station Canal 5 Noticias, *Pillín* had seen it coming. 'If something happens to me, this city will burn,' he'd said.

Despite the warnings from Eduardo and *Pillín* himself, our bus to Buenos Aires wasn't until the following evening, so we had to spend another 24 hours in a city on edge before leaving. Burials are arranged swiftly in Catholic countries, but no funeral services would accept *Pillín* for fear of reprisals. Central fans were just as wary. *Pillín* was a known criminal but had brought a degree of stability to the terraces by acting as a buffer between the fans and the feared narco-trafficking gang that had been running riot in Rosario for more than 20 years – Los Monos.

Like many criminal gangs in Argentina, Los Monos have viewed the *popular* as an important sphere of influence. Since 2010, their men have been planted within the leadership of both Los Guerreros at Central and La Banda de la Lepra, the *barra* at Newell's. Their insidious presence at each club has helped the gangsters sink their claws deep into the game. A telling example is the network of youth players signed up to agents connected with the gang. According to Argentinian news website Infobae, around 120 players have effectively been under the management of Los Monos, including Argentina internationals Éver Banega and Ángel Correa –

the latter once of San Lorenzo. It was not yet known whether Los Monos, an enemy within Los Guerreros, or an outsider was responsible for the killing of *Pillin*.

On our way to the bus terminal the following day, I noticed a Central tattoo on the arm of our taxi driver. As we talked about the killing, the driver said he'd seen the close connection between the *barra* and Los Monos first hand. The previous year, he'd wanted to brighten up his street with a lick of paint. He lived in a Central-supporting area, so the idea was to proudly slap some yellow and blue stripes on the walls and lamp-posts. He was told to collect supplies from a member of Los Guerreros, but when the door was left ajar, he could see there was a lot more than just paint being looked after at the property.

'There was a table with a huge mountain of cocaine like this,' he raised his hand high above the steering wheel, 'and guns everywhere. I was so scared. I wasn't meant to see that and I thought if they knew what I'd seen, they would kill me. I just got the paint and ran.' I asked if he thought the *barras* were more dangerous in his city than in Buenos Aires. 'Without doubt,' he said. 'In Buenos Aires there is a lot more money around, so when there is a problem you pay people off. You offer them pesos, then you offer dollars, and everything is negotiated. If there is a problem with someone in Rosario you just shoot them.'

In the aftermath of *Pillin*'s death, the fearful driver said he would not bring his children to watch Central for the foreseeable future. The Gigante Arroyito stadium would be too dangerous until a hierarchy was restored in the *popular*. We rolled past a large mural of Messi and Di María as we chatted. Both players had publicly stated a desire to return to their boyhood clubs but, at the time, neither had been able to fulfil their dream because of threats from gangs and *barras* against their families.

Di María was close to a move back to Central in 2024, until the severed head of a pig with a bullet lodged inside was sent to his sister. An accompanying note promised that the head of Ángel's daughter Pia would follow if he returned. 'How can I come back when these things happen?' he said. In 2025, enough security was put in place for Di María to finally complete the move to Central, though it's unlikely to be the carefree homecoming he may have once imagined.

Supporters afraid to go to the game, heroes of the city afraid to come home. It was a sad state of affairs. Rosario may be a mini football paradise for the groundhopping tourist, but its people must live in the shadow of Argentina's criminal underworld.

Chapter 10

School of the terraces

Es la banda del Ciclón   It's the fans of *El Ciclón*
La que suena diferente   The ones that sound different
La que copian los demás   The ones that everyone copies
Es la envidia de la gente   The envy of the people

WHILE A spectre of violence may linger in the background of Argentinian football, it does not come close to defining your experience of going to the *cancha*. Despite the inevitable hostility from the police and opposition fans – when they are present – I have never felt in danger at any of the 50-odd matches I have been to, spanning 11 years and 18 different grounds. The matchday atmosphere is one of camaraderie and joy, orchestrated by the country's vibrant *hinchadas*.

At every World Cup, the cameras fixate on the Argentine fans. Regardless of the tournament's location or the fortunes of La Selección, the support is always numerous, boisterous and relentless. For each competition, they produce at least one song that's more elaborate and infectious than anything else, such as 'Muchachos', the soundtrack to the team's victory in 2022. But these anthems are not conjured from thin air every four years. They grow out of the brilliance that is heard in *canchas* across the country each week.

Which fanbase has the biggest influence on this culture of creativity? Look no further than San Lorenzo. I suppose I would say that, so don't just take my word for it.

'Listen up, San Lorenzo fans make almost all the songs,' Sergio Agüero, the former Independiente player and lifelong fan, explained on his ESPN streaming channel in 2023. 'All the songs that you hear from other *hinchadas* – be it River, Boca, Independiente – San Lorenzo always sing it first.'

Agüero's ex-father-in-law was in agreement. In a section about San Lorenzo in his book, *Yo Soy Diego de la Gente*, Maradona said, 'For me, they have the most vibrant *hinchada* in Argentina: they make the most ingenious songs, they entertain you. I love them very much, I would have liked to have played in that shirt.' His praise has been immortalised on a mural near the Nuevo Gasómetro. 'Diego said it', it reads. 'The most ingenious *hinchada*.'

The songs of La Gloriosa – the name associated with San Lorenzo's *hinchada* – have even reached European shores. 'In Italy, many players ask me about the San Lorenzo fans and I tell them that they are unique,' said Papu Gómez, formerly of San Lorenzo, Atalanta and Argentina, in an interview with YouTube channel La Cuerveria. 'The songs they make are unique, they're super authentic. I show them to the Europeans over here and they go crazy.'

Italy legend Gennaro Gattuso is one of those Europeans, according to Lucas Biglia, who played under him at AC Milan. 'Gattuso watches a lot of videos of Argentine support in his office,' the Argentina international told ESPN in 2018. 'He is in love with San Lorenzo's *hinchada*. They are the ones that impress him the most with their chants and how they enter the *cancha*.' The reputation of the supporters proved to be a factor in the unlikely signing of Iker Muniain from Athletic Bilbao. 'I loved everything I saw of the *hinchada* and it excited me,' he said after joining the club. 'When you're a player and you see a *hinchada* as great as San Lorenzo's – with the creativity they have, how they support the team – it moves you inside.'

In general, Argentines struggle to say anything positive about clubs they don't support, but the creativity of La Gloriosa has almost become part of the country's football folklore. When my conversations with taxi drivers, barbers, waiters, shopkeepers and new acquaintances take the inevitable turn towards football, the influence of San Lorenzo supporters is nearly always recognised by other fans.

It's a consensus that seems to span multiple generations, too. While younger fans pick up the modern-day chants that go viral online, older supporters recount the songs started by La Gloriosa nearly half a century ago. A prime example is '*Cuervo, mi buen amigo*'. Nowadays, virtually every fanbase in the Spanish speaking world sings an adapted, '[Team name], *mi buen amigo*,' from General Lamadrid in Argentina to Real Madrid in Spain, but it all began at San Lorenzo.

Bizarrely, the original song came from a state-sponsored advert in 1981, discouraging people from bringing their pets to the beach over the summer holidays. It opened with the line '*Boby, mi buen amigo*' as a girl explained to her dog that he would be staying at home this year. The catchy jingle was adopted by San Lorenzo fans who wanted to express their support for the team after a crushing relegation to the B Nacional. San Lorenzo were the first *grande* to ever be relegated – a source of great humiliation – but throughout the B Nacional season, the supporters pledged their loyalty to the team through the song:

Cuervo mi buen amigo
Esta campaña volveremo' a estar contigo
Te alentaremos de corazón
Esta es tu hinchada que te quiere ver campeón
No me importa lo que digan
Los de Boca y Huracán
Yo te sigo a todas partes
Cada vez te quiero más

Cuervo, my good friend
This season we'll be with you again
We'll cheer you on with our hearts
This *hinchada* wants to see you become champions
I don't care what they say
Those from Boca and Huracán
I follow you everywhere
Every day I love you more

A similarly ubiquitous chant is '*Ole ole ola, cada día te quiero más*' – 'Each day I love you more'. Having become a staple throughout the Argentinian leagues and at *La Selección* matches, it can now be heard across South America. But, as confirmed by the sports newspaper *Olé*, it was first sung by San Lorenzo supporters in September 1987. As part of a promotion for the club's new shirt made by Uhlsport, branded handkerchiefs were handed out to fans. The *cuervos* swung these in the air while singing their new chant, starting a tradition that still accompanies the song.

The global decline of handkerchiefs now means that any available item of clothing is swung above the head, often rendering the singer topless. At San Lorenzo, the chant usually kicks in for the very final minutes of a game when the team is in the lead. The extended '*Oooh, un sentimiento …*' ('Oooh, it's a feeling …') and thousands of shirts circling in the air seems to send out waves of energy that pushes tiring legs over the line.

Inspired by their forefathers in the *popular*, younger fan groups like Escuela de Tablones ('School of the Terraces') now convert modern pop hits into chants that spread rapidly across the world via social media. When 'Despacito' by Luis Fonsi became a global smash at the beginning of 2017, Escuela de Tablones created their own version for the terraces, including the line, 'This is the glorious band from Boedo, the one that the whole world listens to.'

Sure enough, the world was listening. Escuela's song was adopted by fans in Spain, Portugal, Italy, Brazil, South Korea and more, reported sports magazine *El Gráfico*. Even Luis Fonsi himself felt compelled to acknowledge their ingenuity, recording a thank-you message for San Lorenzo fans. He described the song's reincarnation as 'beautiful', adding, 'I want to go to one of your games!' He's not alone. Glance across the comments section of San Lorenzo fan videos on YouTube and people from all over the world dream of visiting the Nuevo Gasómetro to sing with La Gloriosa.

* * *

The history of creativity among *cuervos* has always intrigued me. The songs are worthy of playing through a speaker at home. The lyrics are tattooed across the bodies of fans. The inventiveness forms a significant part of the San Lorenzo identity and experience, and to my mind, requires some sort of sociological explanation.

Martín Cutino is an actor, playwright, San Lorenzo fanatic and lovely bloke. I can tell he's thought a lot about this tradition of creativity too, and as someone who's entrenched in the culture of Buenos Aires, he is well placed to offer some theories. Our relationship is almost exclusively restricted to emails, texts and voice notes, but he approaches every conversation with the warmth of a close confidant. Messages are signed off with *un abrazo azulgrana* – a blue-and-red hug.

For Martín, the *barrio* of Boedo, San Lorenzo's home, was fundamental in fostering the expressiveness of the fanbase. 'We need to get back to the beginning of the 20th century to understand all this,' he says. 'Boedo is a neighbourhood of artists, criminals, *murgueros* and dreamers. It's the cradle of tango, a home to writers, painters, actors, visual artists, dancers and sculptors, all living together. Art is a source of beauty and it permeates the club, because Boedo is San Lorenzo and San Lorenzo is Boedo.'

Boedo's cultural heritage in Buenos Aires has long been recognised. Take the famous tango song 'Boedo' by Julio De Caro and Dante A. Linyera, first recorded in 1928. 'You are the cradle of the scoundrel and the poet,' De Caro sings, describing the place in similar terms to Martín. Even more famously, Boedo was home to the literary and art collective Grupo de Boedo, known for its leftist ideals and a connection with the labour movement, which put it in opposition to its less political, avant-garde rivals, Grupo de Florida, which included Jorge Luis Borges.

The prominence of art in working-class areas characterises much of Buenos Aires and remains apparent in Boedo. Tango halls, cultural centres, street art and sculptures intersperse the more mundane and run-down parts of the *barrio*, giving it a bohemian but grounded feel. Importantly, none of these features are restricted to the artsy upper classes or designed for tourists. With tango singers popping up in everyday bars and intricate murals covering the doors of garages and workshops, you don't need money or status to taste the culture of Boedo.

'All of these elements of the *barrio* made the San Lorenzo fan a creative exponent by nature,' Martín says. 'There's a poetry in our songs that is different; I don't know of another *hinchada* that uses such an extensive vocabulary and terms like "utopia" in the middle of a chant. It's like we are born with the DNA to invent songs for the club. We have all gone through that creative exercise – some with more talent than others – but we have all done it. Being creative like this has been passed on from generation to generation.'

Guido Gallo, a *cuervo* friend I met through Martín, embodies this spirit. Guido is a writer, a member of the Escuela de Tablones group, and a fountain of knowledge when it comes to Argentinian football culture. Like Martín, his passion is matched by a generosity in sharing it. I popped to his flat near Vélez Sarsfield's stadium a few weeks before *El Fortín* won their surprise league title in late 2024, to catch up and discuss what he thought made San Lorenzo's *hinchada* so unique.

I only planned to stay for an hour, but as Guido talked (and talked) with a manic enthusiasm befitting his wild hair and intense gaze – darting between his book shelf, rolling joints and gushing about Dennis Bergkamp – one hour quickly became four. 'In five-a-side I play just like him!' he said, grinning. It was hard to imagine this gangly, six-foot-four writer spinning away from Nikos Dabizas like the great Dutchman, but I took his word for it.

Guido's football song epiphany came from an unlikely rendition of 'Bad Moon Rising' by Creedence Clearwater Revival. 'One day when I was still a teenager, I travelled on my own to a game and the bus was packed with San Lorenzo fans,' he recalled. 'They began to sing a song I had never heard before. They sang it for the entire journey without stopping and I started to recognise the tune. I kept thinking, "Is this Creedence? It can't be Creedence. Hang on, this is Creedence!" They'd grabbed a song from the 1960s and made it into a terrace chant. I couldn't believe it. Most of the songs were coming from radio jingles or cumbia tracks at the time. I'd never heard anything like this before.'

The song's lyrics are simple but emotive. Drawing on the culture of the *barrio* and San Lorenzo's macabre joy of suffering, it translates to:

I come from the *barrio* of Boedo
Barrio of murga and carnival
I swear that even in the bad times
I will always be with you

The song's writer, Juan Manuel, had taken a song from far across the Americas and converted it to a hit for the *cancha*. Within a few years, it was travelling back around the world. Argentina fans created an extended version which became their anthem for the 2014 World Cup in Brazil, before versions spread to fanbases in Europe and beyond. *'Brasil, decime qué se siente, tener en casa tu papá'*, as the Argentines sang on the beaches of Copacabana. 'Brazil, tell me how it feels, to have papá in your home.' In Argentinian football, *papá* ('dad') is used to describe the superior, dominant team. The inferior rival is known as the *hijo* (son).

'Vengo del barrio de Boedo' is just one of a staggering 2,000 San Lorenzo songs and chants that Guido compiled in his book, *La Hinchada que Hace Cantar al Mundo* – 'The *Hinchada* That Makes the World Sing'. In the painstaking process of building the archive, Guido could proudly add a few he had penned himself, so I asked him how a song makes its way from his head to the stands.

'For me, it starts when I hear a song I like and send it to our Escuela de Tablones WhatsApp group. To see if it could work in the *cancha*, we check the tempo by putting in some generic words that rhyme and hearing how it sounds. If it sounds good, we sing it under the *popular* before matches and if people like it, they join in.' There was a time when the likes of Guido would have to print off the lyrics and hand them out on squares of paper, but the internet has sped up the circulation of terrace hits.

'In the case of my Maluma song [the reggaeton track, 'Me Llamas'], I was at a friend's birthday in a nightclub. The song came on and I thought, "Yeah, this could sound good at a game." It's a simple melody. I passed it on to the lads and it ended up getting all the way to the *cancha*. I never listen to Maluma at home but I knew it would sound good on the terraces.'

But the creative process doesn't always take place in such carefree surroundings like the dance floor. Another of Guido's creations was the product of raw anger as he sat at home. 'It was after a match we lost against Tigre when we were robbed [by the referee]. It was such a scandalous robbery that I couldn't even sleep after the game. Because I couldn't sleep, I made the song.'

Guido's chant gives an excellent insight into the mindset of an Argentine fan reeling from a harsh defeat. Hell hath no fury like an *hincha* scorned. Rather than simply attacking referees or the Argentine Football Association, the song attributes the loss to an entire journalistic conspiracy. Using the catchy melody of Rodrigo's 'Amor Clasificado', the beginning of the song translates to:

> We want to tell the press
> Don't act like idiots
> They want to destroy San Lorenzo
> They're supporting Boca and River

If San Lorenzo are in a title race with Boca and River, there is usually paranoia among supporters that the big two will collude with the media, the AFA and referees to clip the wings of *El Cuervo*. This sometimes extends to the notion of a wider operation to prevent San Lorenzo from returning to its home of Boedo, as indicated in the second half of Guido's song:

> Even if they steal another title from us
> We're telling you to make it very clear
> That San Lorenzo will return to Boedo
> To build the stadium in their *barrio*

Another song, another mention of Boedo. The omnipresent reference; the *barrio* that created a distinct type of fan. How did the club lose its famous home? Why are they so hell-bent on getting it back? The dark story of rebellion, betrayal and repression continues to unravel to this day.

Chapter 11

A Dirty War in Boedo

Hay una mancha en la historia	There is a stain on history
Un gobierno de facto que nos desterró	A de facto government that evicted us
Para todos los militares	To all the military generals
San Lorenzo les grita	San Lorenzo shouts
Ni olvido ni perdón	We don't forgive, we don't forget

'APARICIÓN CON VIDA DE NUESTROS HIJOS'

'Bring our children back alive.' It was a demand and also a plea from the Mothers of Plaza de Mayo, the activists searching for their children who had been 'disappeared' by Argentina's military dictatorship. The slogan became synonymous with the Mothers' marches that continue to this day – and it was first seen on a banner at the Viejo Gasómetro in Boedo.

During my visit to the office-cum-San Lorenzo shrine of historian Adolfo Res in downtown Buenos Aires, I was keen to hear more about the significance of the banner. His ever-present frown deepened as he poured me a yerba mate. In sombre tones, he explained how this, one of Las Madres' earliest protests, had come to pass. In June 1977, the recently formed group discovered that members of the military dictatorship were set to attend a San Lorenzo match at the Gasómetro. They bravely chose this day to make their statement, in the faces of the generals, with tens of thousands of people in attendance.

Had they unfurled it during the match, 'they would have been disappeared there and then,' Adolfo said. So the mothers scaled the wooden terraces before the game and hung the flag on the outside of the stand. They did so 'with great fear' but it was an effective move. Hordes of people travelling down the busy Avenida La Plata and entering the stadium could see their message. Life under the military junta had been characterised by a paralysing fear of speaking out, as any form of dissent could lead to arrest, torture and death. But with the Gasómetro as their stage, the mothers made an historic stand.

It is difficult to imagine the feeling on the streets of Argentina at the time. Even before the generals seized power in 1976, guerrilla warfare and political murders were causing daily havoc and claiming dozens of lives. Isabel Perón had failed to rein in the People's Revolutionary Army and the Montoneros on the left, and the Argentine Anti-Communist Alliance on the right. Amid the bloodshed and chaos, a *coup d'état* was planned to remove her from government in the Casa Rosada.

The US Secretary of State Henry Kissinger met the Argentinian military generals multiple times before and after the coup. Part of his briefing was for the junta to destroy their opponents as swiftly as possible. 'If there are things that have to be done, you should do them quickly,' he advised.

On 24 March 1976, Perón was detained in the middle of the night. The generals interrupted TV and radio broadcasts with a blare of military trumpets and delivered their first official communication to the country in ominous fashion.

'People are advised that as of today, the country is under the operational control of the General Commanders Junta of the Armed Forces. We recommend to all inhabitants strict compliance with the provisions and directives emanating from the military, security or police authorities, and to be extremely careful to avoid individual or group actions and attitudes that may require drastic intervention from the operating personnel.'

From the beginning of the regime, congress was suspended and political parties were banned. Hundreds of unionists, students and political activists were abducted from their homes or the streets, as anyone believed to have an association with left-wing Peronism, communism or the Montoneros was hunted down by security forces and death squads.

Imprisonment, torture or death – sometimes all three – awaited the victims. Many were drugged and taken on 'death flights' from which they were dropped into the Atlantic Ocean. Human rights groups in Argentina estimate that the Dirty War campaign of state terrorism saw as many as 30,000 people disappeared between 1976 and 1983.

Among the disappeared were leaders of the Mothers. From their early protest at the Gasómetro through to their weekly marches at Plaza de Mayo in downtown Buenos Aires, they were a thorn in the side of the dictatorship and those who wanted to hide the truth. The fate of a football club pales into insignificance against the loss of human life, but ever since the Dirty War, San Lorenzo fans have questioned whether enabling the Mothers' demonstration contributed to the club's eviction in 1979.

The late journalist and human rights activist Osvaldo Bayer suspected it did. 'On March 24, 1976, a sinister period began in Argentina. And also in Boedo,' he wrote for ANRed, the alternative Argentinian news platform. 'The Gasómetro on Avenida La Plata and its headquarters, a symbol that sums up the institution, disappeared along with 30 thousand Argentines.'

When the junta took power in 1976, Brigadier General Osvaldo Cacciatore was installed as the mayor of Buenos Aires. He became the scourge of San Lorenzo, leading a regime which, according to some, had a score to settle with the club. Matthew Hawkins points to the work of anthropologist Silvio Aragón, who claimed that the leader of San Lorenzo's *barra brava* during the dictatorship – a man nicknamed *Milanesa* – was known to have links to the Peronist party and the far-left Montoneros. According to Aragón, San Lorenzo's *hinchada* experienced heavy repression and was regularly targeted by the police before and after matches, leading to violent clashes.

Hawkins also cites philosopher José Sebreli, who said the Boedo *hinchada* was the only fanbase in Argentinian football to successfully reject efforts by undercover police to infiltrate its leadership as they tried to gather intelligence on left-wing activism within the *cancha*. Other *cuervos* have told Hawkins that San Lorenzo riled the generals by being the first to sing the Peronist anthem at a game in 1976, and by unveiling a banner in support of the Montoneros. There may have been more overtly Peronist *hinchadas* at the time, but it is fair to assume that the San Lorenzo community was in the bad books of the junta.

Back in 1972, under another unconstitutional military government, the Buenos Aires urban planning committee had approved the controversial building of a highway that would run through Boedo and cut the Gasómetro in half. The plans had stalled but were revived under Cacciatore and the junta, who wanted to modernise cities and stadiums ahead of hosting the World Cup in 1978. The tournament was the regime's prize propaganda tool. Their big bet to show the world that Argentina was safe, free and functioning, despite the stories of brutal repression that were escaping the country.

In a chillingly literal example of the junta's hush-up, the cheers of Argentina fans in the Monumental Stadium almost drowned out the screams of torture victims at the secret detention unit known as ESMA (Escuela Superior de Mecánica de la Armada), located just a few blocks away in Núñez. Once a naval facility, the regime's most infamous murder centre was also discovered to have stolen babies born to imprisoned mothers, hidden their identities and allowed military families to illegally adopt them.

At the end of the 1970s, Cacciatore was unhappy that San Lorenzo still lingered in their old wooden *cancha* – unfit for modern football and obstructing his lucrative development plans for Boedo. According to Osvaldo Bayer, 'Efforts were under way to seize San Lorenzo's stadium.' Conveniently for the generals, 1978 saw a new board installed at San Lorenzo which had little intention of serving the interests of supporters. The president Moisés Annan caved under Cacciatore's pressure and began to sell off club infrastructure – including parts of the Gasómetro complex on Avenida La Plata. San Lorenzo's grand old home was being auctioned off.

According to Bayer, Cacciatore threatened that 1979 would be the last year for San Lorenzo in Boedo. The brigadier got his wish. Claiming the terraces were unsafe, the Buenos Aires city inspectors ordered the stadium to be closed indefinitely on safety grounds that year. The end was nigh. One final game was played at the Gasómetro against old rivals Boca Juniors on 2 December 1979. The sadness of the stadium's closure seemed to envelope the players and the game itself, which ended in a 0-0 draw.

'It was a surprise for all of us,' recalls the legendary San Lorenzo defender Sergio Villar. 'But who dared to say anything at that moment?' The Uruguayan played the final match in Boedo and remembers the fear that gripped the country. 'We couldn't speak out about what was happening – we didn't dare, for fear of reprisals. The San Lorenzo directors had to accept it, no matter what.'

Villar's own pain no doubt reflected how every San Lorenzo supporter felt at the time. 'I felt sadness because they took away my second home. There was a deep sorrow and sense of helplessness,' he told Infobae.

A week before leaving his presidency in 1980, Annan agreed to grant the City of Buenos Aires a portion of the land at Avenida La Plata in exchange for written recognition of the club's ownership of a plot in Bajo Flores, which they feared would be repatriated due to the growing debts. Cacciatore's office was keen to uphold the narrative that the land obtained in Boedo would be used for the benefit of the city. They informed Annan that a new elementary school and housing complex would be opened on the site.

Neither were built. Nor was the transformative highway that had been proposed nearly a decade earlier. And so, with the disused Gasómetro still standing in 1981, San Lorenzo's next president Vicente Bonina attempted to reopen the stadium and end the club's humiliating groundshare at *clásico* rivals Huracán. Cacciatore was having none of it. His requests for Bonina to sell the remaining land in Boedo soon became threats. Bayer reports that according to sources close to Bonina, Cacciatore asked him if he had children at school. Bonina's response was affirmative. 'Then I recommend that you do what I ask of you,' Cacciatore replied.

In 1983, San Lorenzo sold the plot of Gasómetro to a newly opened company called Banco Mariva for a reported US$900,000. The plot was subsequently sold to the supermarket multinational Carrefour for US$8m. It is rumoured that members of the Buenos Aires city government had interests in Banco Mariva, but these have not been proven. Whoever was involved profited from a 1,025 per cent increase on their investment.

Boedo, on the other hand, received nothing but a supermarket in return. The *barrio* had lost its social club, the centre of its community, its economic motor and an irreplaceable part of its history. San Lorenzo too, had lost nearly everything. Homeless and in financial ruin, *El Ciclón* were staring into the abyss. Many *cuervos* feared their beloved club would soon cease to exist.

Chapter 12

We will return

Nos fuimos al descenso	We got relegated
Nos vendieron la cancha	They sold our stadium
Lo que nunca pudieron	What they could never do
Fue parar esta hinchada	Was stop this *hinchada*

AT ANY other time in Argentinian football history, it's difficult to imagine the plot to evict San Lorenzo succeeding. Supporters across the country have long shown their willingness to confront injustice or betrayal in order to protect their club, and from the Barra de la Goma in the 1920s to the modern-day struggle to return to Boedo, San Lorenzo fans have been among the most assertive. But even as it became clear that their home was being taken away, the dark shadow of the military dictatorship ended any form of resistance before it could even begin.

Taking to the streets to vent your anger meant putting your life at risk, so the schemers in the city government and the traitors in the San Lorenzo boardroom could commit their crime without reprisal. After the junta was toppled in 1983, democracy returned to Argentina, but San Lorenzo did not return home to Boedo.

In 1981, the homeless club was relegated from the Primera División for the first – and so far and only – time, deepening its state of peril. A 1-0 defeat against Argentinos Juniors at the home of Ferro Carril Oeste condemned a *grande* to the second tier for the first time in the history of Argentinian football, bringing great shame to the club. However, in an emotional display of unity, the fans applauded the players off the pitch and stayed in the ground to sing songs of support. In 2011, River Plate supporters responded to their only relegation by setting fire to their stadium and vandalising their *barrio*. It may have happened in a different era, but San Lorenzo fans like to point out the contrast.

'I always remember that when the match ended, there were no insults,' said striker Walter Perazzo, who played in the fateful defeat in Caballito. 'What happened was incredible, it was a sea of tears, but for an hour no one left the stands. Today, 40 years later, I can say that the relegation ended up being good for San Lorenzo. The club came together and following 1982 it had a couple of really great years,' he told Argentinian football history website Abrí la Cancha.

The fans at Ferro sang through their tears, '*Ciclón, Ciclón*, it's only one year, we'll keep following you, wherever you want to go.' And they were right; it was only one year. San Lorenzo stormed to the second division title while their fans broke attendance records in the stands. Perhaps as a result of being unable to demonstrate in the streets over losing El Gasómetro, the *cuervos* decided to double down their support in the *cancha* – whichever it may be.

The mass mobilisation of *cuervos* in *La B* became something of a phenomenon as demand outstripped the capacity of stadium after stadium. Ferro's ground was quickly upgraded to Vélez Sarsfield, then again to River for a match against Tigre, where the club recorded a staggering attendance of 73,948. A week before, just 45,000 fans had watched River play Boca in a Copa Libertadores *Superclásico* in the same stadium. The news channel TN, among others, claims that until the Estadio Monumental's recent expansion, only the 1978 World Cup Final and the 1986

Copa Libertadores Final saw more people in the stadium than San Lorenzo's humble B Nacional league fixture.

Argentinian football had never seen anything like it. 'San Lorenzo's participation in the 1982 Primera B tournament was a true revolution for the division,' reported newspaper *Clarín*. 'According to the AFA, 884,473 general tickets were sold the year before the arrival of San Lorenzo. In 1982, the numbers doubled to 1,637,714.'

It is said that Vélez Sarsfield's president Ricardo Petracca wanted San Lorenzo out of his stadium as soon as possible, because Vélez fans were becoming so enamoured with the *cuervo* parties in Liniers that some were defecting to support their new guests. Posters were displayed around the club facilities imploring that only Vélez shirts should be worn on the property.

'Mr Petracca, it's too late ...' sang the San Lorenzo supporters at the time, '... the Vélez boys now support *El Ciclón*.'

* * *

San Lorenzo returned to the Primera, but their nomadic existence was unsustainable for a *grande*. An essential part of Argentinian terrace folklore is the *cargada* – basically taking the piss out of other teams – and from the 1980s to the present day, San Lorenzo's home being replaced by a supermarket has been a source of *cargadas* galore for rival fans. Among the more creative efforts was this song from River, sung to the tune of 'Cuervo, mi buen amigo':

> *Cuervo*, you're an idiot
> I went to your stadium but I only found a supermarket
> With a red and blue flag, and a little trolley that said Carrefour
> I stole some bread, wine, milanesas, and even a fish
> River has a stadium, San Lorenzo has a shop

Thankfully for the *cuervos* getting constant grief from other fans in bars, cafés and *canchas*, there was light at the end of the tunnel. It flickered 3km away from Avenida La Plata in Bajo Flores, where the club retained some land. Money was tight, but momentum grew behind the idea of building a new stadium outside Boedo.

The supporters had dragged San Lorenzo through its darkest hour in the B and now they were dipping into their wallets so the club could have a home once again. As work on the stadium began in 1987, fans paid an additional eight peso donation on top of their ten peso match ticket for every 'home' game, almost doubling their spend to raise funds for the construction.

By 1992, the Nuevo Gasómetro was edging towards completion. The large Platea Norte was the first stand ready and was tested in the only way a stadium in Argentina can truly be tested. A group of fans was invited to jump up and down on the new structure to check its suitability for supporting thousands of bouncing *cuervos* on a matchday. Fortunately, it didn't collapse, and a year later the stadium was finally ready to hold its first match.

The Nuevo Gasómetro, officially titled the Estadio Pedro Bidegaín, was inaugurated on 16 December 1993 in a friendly against Universidad Católica from Chile. San Lorenzo won 2-1 but the match was secondary to the feelings of joy and relief in the stands. It may not have been in Boedo, but San Lorenzo had a place they could call home once again. Wounds were beginning to heal.

'When I first arrived at the Nuevo Gasómetro, I kissed the rail in the stands and started crying,' actor Martín Cutino tells me. 'I was 19 years old. I had never known the Viejo Gasómetro, so I waited 19 years to have a home. I used to ask, "How can it be that all these people have a stadium and we don't?" When the team came out the tunnel we sang, "Here is the glorious *banda* of San Lorenzo, the one that had no ground, that stood firm through relegation. Despite all the years and the moments we've had, I'll always be by your side my dear San Lorenzo."'

Having a stadium breathed life back into the club. Just 18 months after moving into the Nuevo Gasómetro, San Lorenzo won their first Primera title since 1974. The *campeonato* was clinched in Rosario, where an astonishing 35,000 *cuervos* crammed into Central's Gigante Arroyito stadium to watch the vital 1-0 win. The 'injured' Mariano de la Fuente was of course among them.

* * *

Just five years after the move to Bajo Flores, unrest had set in among certain sections of the fanbase. Yes, the club now had a ground, but the unsuitability of its location was becoming apparent. In its heyday, San Lorenzo was on par with the biggest clubs in Argentina thanks to the enormously popular social and sports club in Boedo. Locals of all ages flocked to the Gasómetro, which saw membership numbers explode and helped the team grow on the pitch. The community nurtured San Lorenzo and San Lorenzo nurtured the community. This has never seemed likely to happen in Bajo Flores.

According to Adolfo Res, the insecurity of the area, fuelled by problems in the sprawling Villa 1-11-14 shanty town next to the *cancha*, has placed a ceiling over San Lorenzo as a club. His verdict is born out by the conversations I've had with *cuervos* over the years. People don't want to spend time in the area before and after games. Parents are reluctant to send their children to train at the club. *Socios* – members – rarely venture to Ciudad Deportiva to use the facilities they are entitled to. Match-goers worry whether their cars will still be intact when they return from the ground. Some choose not to attend altogether.

'If this office was one block away from the stadium in Bajo Flores and I said, "Let's meet here at 9pm," I don't think you'd come,' Adolfo said, leaning towards me across the desk. 'If you did decide to come, the Queen of Great Britain would probably send a security convoy to look after you.'

By 1998, Adolfo and his brother Diego had begun to float the idea of a return to Boedo. As well as the impracticalities of Bajo Flores, the draw of the *tierra santa* – 'holy ground' – was too strong to ignore. 'Why do I want the return to Boedo? For memory, for the sense of belonging and to honour the founders of the club,' Adolfo was looking at me with a sense of urgency. 'They didn't want to play in Bajo Flores. They wanted to play on Avenida La Plata. It's also for the memory of my dad. He was a San Lorenzo supporter and first took me to the Viejo Gasómetro.'

The campaign titled La Vuelta a Boedo – 'The Return to Boedo' – didn't begin with a ready-made army of activists. 'In 1998, there were two people on the streets of Boedo preaching about the return to Avenida La Plata,' Adolfo said. 'They were me and my brother. We gave speeches in the cafés and the bars and people said we were crazy. How were we going to remove a multinational like Carrefour? Especially when the supermarket in Boedo was one of their most successful, highest-selling branches. But we took them on.'

Little by little, the Res brothers rallied support through their speeches and impassioned broadcasts on local radio. In 2005, they founded a supporters' committee dedicated to the cause, which included close confidant Daniel Peso and ex-*barra brava* leader Claudio De Simone. A year later, the committee made its first big move, presenting the Historical Reparation Bill to the Buenos Aires legislature.

They claimed that a portion of the Viejo Gasómetro's site in Boedo should be returned to San Lorenzo, as the military government failed to build the school and houses it had promised for the plot of land. The legislature approved the bill and La Vuelta had its maiden triumph; 500 supporters celebrated outside the chambers in downtown Buenos Aires in the knowledge that their efforts – not those of the club directors – had allowed San Lorenzo to plant a flag back in Boedo. A grassroots movement was gathering pace.

While the committee plotted the downfall of Carrefour, it continued to raise funds to acquire as much property as possible in and around Avenida La Plata 1700. Boosting their piggy bank and their publicity was the Hollywood actor Viggo Mortensen. Born to an American mother and Danish father, Mortensen spent a large part of his childhood living in Buenos Aires, where he became an avid *cuervo*.

During his career, he has become an ambassador for the club, brandishing San Lorenzo flags on the red carpet and having the badge stitched on to his designer suits on full display for the paparazzi. He eulogises about San Lorenzo in interviews and even sneaks blue-and-red props on to the film set, hoping they creep into shot.

'I would rather see San Lorenzo win the *campeonato* than get an Oscar, definitely,' Viggo told *Gente* magazine. In another interview with La Nación, he said, 'I'm spreading the *cuervo* gospel all over the world. That's not only my mission, but my career, that's my job. Cinema, poetry and all the rest are hobbies. Spreading the *cuervo* gospel, that's what I'm dedicated to.'

Mortensen made a significant financial donation to the Vuelta committee, helping to secure new headquarters in Boedo directly beside Carrefour. If the French supermarket hadn't yet been concerned about these meddling football fans, it now had little choice but to take notice.

Riding the momentum, the siblings played their next hand in 2010. It was their most ambitious move to date. A new proposal known as the Historical Restitution Bill was presented to the Buenos Aires legislature, this time demanding the entire property at Avenida La Plata 1700 be declared a public utility, thus returning it to San Lorenzo. Two years of lobbying in the legislature was accompanied by a series of mass supporter demonstrations to apply maximum pressure on the city's lawmakers.

Ten thousand *cuervos* gathered outside the French embassy and handed a petition over to Carrefour's compatriots, demanding the supermarket leave Boedo. Twenty thousand marched outside the legislature offices to pressurise the city authorities into passing the motion. Forty thousand returned to celebrate the Tourism and Sports Commission's official backing of the bill, and then, on 8 March 2012, the mounting waves of support broke the floodgates altogether.

An estimated 110,000 San Lorenzo fans and supporters of La Vuelta took over the iconic Plaza de Mayo in the centre of Buenos Aires, directly outside the government's Casa Rosada. The sea of blue-and-red protestors was splashed over the front and back pages of the newspapers as La Vuelta became a topic of national conversation.

Who wanted to tell tens of thousands of fanatical *cuervos* that they couldn't return home? Not the Buenos Aires government. On 15 November 2012, the Buenos Aires legislators voted unanimously in favour of the Historical Restitution Bill. Thirty-three years after the military dictatorship had seized the club's home, San Lorenzo's right to Avenida La Plata in Boedo was written into law.

Hundreds of fans had squeezed into the chamber and burst into song when the announcement was made. Bewildered legislators turned in their seats to see supporters crying, hugging and singing an ode to the campaign at the top of their lungs:

And bring joy, joy to my heart
The return to Boedo is my obsession
To have a stadium like the days of old
And to be champions on Avenida La Plata
We will return
To the neighbourhood where San Lorenzo was born

Thanks to the Res brothers and the supporters committee, San Lorenzo had changed the city's laws. Now the club needed the money to pay off Carrefour. The committee's next initiative, officially taking off in 2014, took the form of a fundraiser which allowed fans to buy a symbolic square metre of the plot at Avenida La Plata. The movement would stay true to its popular roots.

At this stage of La Vuelta, I had just spent my first six months in Buenos Aires and was desperate to play my own small part in the story. I wanted a square metre. After filling out the required forms and paying around £130, I was the 'owner' of a tiny patch of land underneath a supermarket in Argentina. When I eventually bought my symbolic square metre to support La Vuelta a Boedo, I was curious to see if fellow Charlton Athletic fans were as moved by the campaign as I was, given the parallels with our own club's plight in the 1980s. I posted a long message on the Charlton Life forum explaining the history of La Vuelta and asked for donations to help fund some extra square metres I was buying with Eduardo. The response did not disappoint. Addicks supporters need no lesson in what 'home' means to a football club and the vital role supporters play in preserving it. The donations flew in.

By now, Mortensen wasn't the only famous figure pledging his allegiance to the cause. Pope Francis, the most famous San Lorenzo fan of all, had been installed at the Vatican. Argentina is a Catholic country, so for many *cuervos* there was nobody on planet Earth capable of influencing the fate of their club quite like Jorge Mario Bergoglio.

Born and raised in the *barrio* of Flores, around 4km west of Boedo, Pope Francis was a lifelong San Lorenzo fan. His father played for the club's basketball team and the Pontiff still held a *socio* membership card from 2008 until his death. Fellow *cuervos* would regularly bring him azulgrana gifts at the Vatican, which he received with a broad smile – and sometimes – the remark, '*¡Que gane San Lorenzo!*' – 'May San Lorenzo win!'

His death in 2025 saw a tremendous outpouring of emotion at the club. In a *recibimiento* dedicated to his memory, yellow and blue *tirantes* replaced the normal blue-and-red to honour the colours of the Vatican flag. The players held a banner reading 'San Lorenzo and Francis, together for eternity', while the Pope's face adorned a vast *telón* in the *popular* alongside his immortal words, '*¡Que gane San Lorenzo*'.

During his papacy, Daniel Peso from the supporters' committee saw an opportunity for La Vuelta to get the ultimate blessing. During an encounter with the Pope in Rome, he handed him a 'Vuelta a Boedo' T-shirt and three San Lorenzo books authored by Adolfo Res.

'How is La Vuelta going?' the Pope asked, gifts in hand. Peso explained that a financial agreement with Carrefour was getting close, thanks to the 20,000 square metres that had now been bought by supporters. 'And what about mine?!' the Pope responded. Whether or not a donation from the Vatican ever arrived – or if the world's most prominent religious leader had time to work his way through Adolfo's hefty books – San Lorenzo and La Vuelta had secured some priceless publicity.

* * *

Back in Buenos Aires, San Lorenzo supporters were running out of patience with Carrefour. As the French conglomerate continued to stall on the club's offer for its land, campaigners organised a human blockade of the entrances to the Carrefour on Avenida La Plata and 15 other branches across the country. It did the trick. Just four days later, Carrefour accepted the offer.

Competitive sport returned to Boedo in 2016, as the club finished the Roberto Pando indoor arena on the periphery of the Viejo Gasómetro's site. La Vuelta will never be complete without the football stadium, but it was significant to see the club's basketball, volleyball and futsal teams have a home in the *barrio*. Indeed, the opportunity to support a San Lorenzo team in Boedo captured the imagination of fans, who continue to fill out *El Pando* to watch those sports.

In 2019, at long last, the supermarket closed its doors for good. Carrefour had been defeated by a hardy group of football fans and their beloved club. Twenty years previously, the Res brothers were called crazy for trying to turf out such a formidable presence. And yet, on 1 July 2019, the supermarket was shut and San Lorenzo celebrated on the land that was rightfully theirs.

The gutted site was given a blue-and-red exterior, a stage was mounted and 130,000 *cuervos* flooded the area where the car park had been. As bands played and fireworks exploded in the sky, thousands of fans could not even reach the hallowed plot, instead packing out the surrounding streets to create the biggest party Boedo had seen since the military dictatorship. The brothers were invited on to the stage and given a deserved ovation.

The celebrations crowned a remarkable feat, but sitting opposite me more than five years later, Adolfo is not happy. In the intervening period, development of the stadium has still not begun at Avenida La Plata. The Covid pandemic and financial ruin for both the club and the country are legitimate factors that have delayed La Vuelta, but Adolfo blames people, not circumstances, for the lack of progress. He says that club directors – particularly under the presidency of TV host Marcelo Tinelli – wrestled control away from the fans and made a mess of the project.

'This has been a popular movement; it belongs to the people,' Adolfo said, struggling to keep his anger at bay. 'When we managed it, we got the law we needed in two years. Since the directors have managed it, 12 years have passed and we haven't seen a brick laid.' Passing me his refilled mate cup, he added a phrase that stayed with me,

'Abajo se progresa, arriba se frena.' Below, at grassroots level, society progresses, while above, those in power put the brakes on. Nothing in English captures the sentiment so succinctly as Adolfo's crisp rhyming motto.

'People get mixed up in modern-day society. They believe the millionaire will save you, and that's when you begin to lose,' he added. 'The people believed in Marcelo Tinelli and not Adolfo Res.'

Perhaps this explains Adolfo's decision to support the presidency of Marcelo Moretti, the successor to Tinelli. Res says he rejected the chance to be vice-president alongside Moretti, but agreed to take a role dedicated solely to La Vuelta. He may have renewed licence to drive the campaign, but he is far from content with the status quo.

'When will I be happy? When I see those first steps built for the stadium. It's time to start building. Avenida La Plata may be nostalgia for me, but for younger generations it's the future of the club. I'll be pushing for this until I die.'

As I left Adolfo's office after more than two hours of conversation, I tried to make sense of his extraordinary, unwavering commitment to the cause. Despite everything he'd said about the past, present and future of San Lorenzo, it was the personal reference to his late dad which stuck in my mind. I thought about my own dad, and how returning to The Valley to watch Charlton had been such an influential part of our relationship for 30 years. From the age of five to 35, we had walked the same streets and sat in the same stands, side by side. I now see him at The Valley more than I see him in either of our own houses. The Valley is a home for Charlton, but it is also a home for our relationship.

It reminded me of a cartoon by the Argentine artist known as *Chulengol*. His simple, Microsoft Paint-style drawings are usually designed to make people laugh, but there is one that's capable of making any *cuervo* cry.

In the first of four frames, a father and son wearing San Lorenzo shirts are standing side by side outside the Viejo

Gasómetro at Avenida La Plata. In the second frame, the stadium has been closed, and the figure of the elderly father is fading away next to his son.

Below, the son stands all alone by the empty site on Avenida La Plata. Then, in the final frame, the stadium is being rebuilt. The grown-up son is in tears and the hand of his late father enters the frame to rest on his shoulder.

Chapter 13

The invisible neighbours

A los 'anti-vuelta'   To the 'anti-returners'
Le decimos que no lloren   We say stop whining
Falta poco   There's not long left
Y el Ciclón se va del Bajo Flores   Until *El Ciclón* leaves Bajo Flores

AT SAN Lorenzo, the scars of 1979 run deep. Being evicted from Boedo by the military dictatorship may have given rise to one of the game's most impressive fan movements, but it has also created an underlying resentment of the club's current home. Because to many, it will simply never *be* home.

The Nuevo Gasómetro itself is enjoyed by fans, who have coalesced with the sweeping blue-and-red terraces after three decades of supporting their team in Bajo Flores. But their connection with the wider area is almost non-existent. At the heart of this disassociation is the presence of Villa 1-11-14; the biggest shanty town or slum in Buenos Aires, located directly opposite the *cancha*.

San Lorenzo has taught me a lot about Argentina. From its immigrant communities who founded the club, to the deep significance of *barrio* identity, to the cruelty of the military dictatorship and the resilience of Argentine people. Sadly, the precarious stack of ramshackle, crumbling flats within metres of the Nuevo Gasómetro shines a light on another inescapable part of modern Argentina – its endemic poverty.

According to the country's INDEC statistics agency, 53 per cent of Argentines were living in poverty in 2024. That's nearly 24 million people in a situation where 'household income is insufficient to cover basic expenses'.

UNICEF reports that some five million people live in *villas* like the 1-11-14. In these *villas*, 97 per cent of residents are not connected to any sewage system, 92 per cent have no drinking water and 66 per cent do not have access to a formal supply of electric power. Findings also show that 87 per cent of the women living in *villas* head their households, but only 31 per cent have paid jobs.

In Brazil, backpackers and holidaymakers can go on organised tours of *favelas* – the equivalent to a *villa*. The same is available for *comunas* in Colombian cities like Medellín. These tours, often dubbed 'poverty safaris', have not reached the Argentinian *villas*. The areas are very much off limits. As a foreigner, simply mentioning a trip to the Nuevo Gasómetro triggers a barrage of warnings because of the *villa's* proximity. Don't go alone. Don't leave alone. Don't travel there by bus. Don't bring valuables. Don't speak English in front of people.

As I have experienced no trouble in 40-odd visits to the ground, the general perceptions of the area can seem slightly hysterical, but they are not baseless. Stoked by the drug trade, robberies, murders and shoot-outs are commonplace in Bajo Flores and there is a reason the club generally requests not to play home matches after dark.

Despite the legitimate concerns of being in the area, I have often found the stigmatisation of the 1-11-14 uncomfortable. The everyday fan views the *villa* as a threat more than a neighbour. On matchdays, you are supposed to give it a wide berth and just look the other way. The idea that everyday people – fellow *porteños* – live there is seemingly forgotten. The *villa* feels so distant from the world inhabited by most match-going San Lorenzo fans, even though it stares them in the face every other week as they enjoy their favourite ritual. It's a strange paradox.

I was curious to meet those you rarely hear from regarding Villa 1-11-14: the people who actually live there. Is life in the *villa* how the outside world perceives it? What did they make of the neighbours and their obsession with upping sticks for Boedo? I went to ask these questions on a spring afternoon, without security organised by the Queen – and not just because she's dead. I didn't have the heart to correct Adolfo on that detail.

* * *

On the day of my visit, Buenos Aires was in its comfort zone. There was a strike on. President Milei was set to remove long-standing transport subsidies and increase travel fares for the public, prompting bus, train and metro operators across the country to suspend their services by way of protest.

Standing at an out-of-service bus stop a full 6km away from my destination, I was stumped. I looked down at my phone. Walking the full distance would take an hour and 20 minutes. I looked up at the sky. It was clear. Ahead, bright purple dashes of jacaranda trees – the calling card of Buenos Aires's beautiful springtime – lined the street leading out of Caballito and towards Bajo Flores. It was a day for walking, so I set off on foot.

My journey south neatly marked the different social strata of the city. While not boasting the luxury of Recoleta and Belgrano, nor the trendy hangouts of Palermo and Villa Crespo, Caballito – meaning 'little horse' – still offers a middle-class blend of cafés, restaurants and tree-lined streets. The *barrio* is pretty but reassuringly unfancy and lies just beyond the haunts of tourists and 'digital nomads'. I like staying in Caballito because I like to avoid people who remind me of me.

I crossed the bridge running over the train track and turned on to the fabled Avenida La Plata – though I was still some 20 blocks away from the site of the Viejo Gasómetro. Boedo is slightly rougher around the edges than Caballito, marking the transition into a lower middle-class *barrio*. Children poured out of schools wearing their uniform of white smocks, filling the pavement like swarms of miniature scientists. Cafés were busy with families on the afternoon school run or lackadaisical workers enjoying a bonus break between the more orthodox pauses of lunchtime and *merienda* at around 5pm – similar to teatime in the UK.

I arrived at Avenida La Plata 1700 and took a moment to appreciate the building site where the Carrefour supermarket had stood on each of my previous visits to Buenos Aires. Its disappearance gave a triumphant air to giant blue-and-red lettering along the wall outside.

'*ESTO ES TIERRA SANTA*', it read. 'THIS IS HOLY LAND'.

Directly opposite was Café Bar San Lorenzo, with its eye-catching walls (painted by Grupo Artístico de Boedo, of course) depicting the wooden terraces of the Viejo Gasómetro, Padre Lorenzo Massa, flying crows and elegant San Lorenzo badges with a flourish of *fileteado porteño*.

My final steps within the borders of Boedo took me past the Plaza Butteler, a small square hidden between a cluster of houses. This is where San Lorenzo's *barra brava* used to meet on matchdays and how they got their name. When I asked Gallego from La Butteler why they no longer met here, he said its layout was a dream for the police and a nightmare for the *barra*. With a chuckle, he recalled how *la yuta* – 'the cops' – would launch a coordinated ambush from each of the four cobbled streets leading into the plaza, locking the Butteler boys in for a heavy beating. It sounded horrific, but the memories tickled Gallego.

As I moved from Boedo into the working-class *barrio* of Nueva Pompeya, the tall apartment blocks and cafés disappeared. Cars and buses roared past, but I was almost alone on the pavement, marching past shuttered garages and modest low-rise flats towards Bajo Flores and the Nuevo Gasómetro.

Arriving at the fringes of Villa 1-11-14 marked the final stage on my journey across the social spectrum. If you are not from the *villa*, you do not enter alone, so I'd arranged company in advance. Further highlighting the disconnect between the 1-11-14 and the San Lorenzo community, not one person in my varied network of *cuervo* contacts knew somebody in the *villa* who could help me.

Searching for an 'in', I remembered hearing of a social organisation that worked in the *villa* called Club Atlético Madre del Pueblo (CAMP), so I sent them a message. 'Sure, come down. There'll be someone here to show you around and chat over some [yerba] mates,' was the response. That person was Jennifer Frost – a *porteña* despite what her name suggests – and one of the lead organisers of CAMP.

Jennifer insisted on meeting me some five blocks away from the *villa* to ensure I was safe for the final leg of my journey. After questioning whether the staged arrival was overkill, I was soon grateful for the company. Two worse-for-wear men in tatty clothes began to square up to each other beside me. They swayed and staggered across the pavement, confronting the handful of other bystanders as well as each other. When one cracked a clean blow on to the skull of the other, sending him toppling into the busy road, I decided to step away from the action.

On cue, my phone started buzzing and Jennifer was waving from the other side of the road. Jenny, or *Shenny* in the local accent, said her name came from 'a mix of Polish and Yankee' heritage. With her small but sturdy frame, sandy, sun-bleached hair and white CAMP polo shirt, she had the look of a PE teacher back home.

After breaking the unfortunate news that she was a fanatical River supporter, Jenny talked me through CAMP's operation. Founded in 2012 by the local Church of Santa María Madre del Pueblo, the organisation ran programmes dedicated to education, sport, culture and social welfare. While local residents of all ages got involved, the programmes were focused on young people. The average age in the *villas* of Buenos Aires is just 24 years old compared to 40 in the rest of the city, reported *La Nación*.

The *barrio* borders I crossed on my walk to Bajo Flores were invisible without a map, but there was a clear threshold dividing Villa 1-11-14 from the world outside. The sequence of two-storey houses stopped quite suddenly at the entrance to the *villa*. On the other side, the street narrowed and curved up a slope, breaking free of the grid layout across the rest of the city. Walking inside, much of the *villa* resembled a construction site. Incomplete-looking stacks of three- and four-storey buildings lined uneven, potholed streets, amid a tangle of electric wires criss-crossing overhead.

We soon reached a concrete pitch, which acted as a focal point for CAMP activities and also the 1-11-14 community in general. The area was tightly boxed in by colourful flats on each side of the *canchita*, creating a compact rectangle arena which reminded me of a mini Loftus Road. Murals ran along one side of the pitch, including the head of Maradona and a giant waving Pope Francis popping out of the Nuevo Gasómetro. We were, of course, in the Pope's home *barrio* of Flores. In the early days of his priesthood he had given sermons in the *villa*.

A painted Pope may have been watching from the side, but the holy presence did not stop brutal tackles flying in when *fútbol de potrero* was played here. Born in the *villas* and working-class *barrios* of Argentina, this version of the game sees amateur teams go head to head on dusty pitches and concrete courts, often with money at stake. The football is technical but highly physical and can spiral into violence, often encouraged by the boisterous crowds which gather to cheer on friends and neighbours.

Fútbol de potrero is credited with giving many Argentine players the distinctive mix of technique and tenacity. The best *potrero* players will tease opponents with step-overs, nutmegs and mazy dribbles, but be equally adept at poaching the ball in a 50-50, protecting it from incoming tackles and bouncing off heavy challenges.

Maradona, with his spellbinding footwork and low centre of gravity, would be the classic example, but the *potrero* style can also be seen in the harrying and hustle that Carlos Tevez combined with his skill, or the way Juan Román Riquelme would hand off opponents and ride tackles before elegantly dribbling away and releasing a pass. These little pitches produce their own brand of 'total football'.

In 2024, Sergio Agüero brought the game to mainstream attention by founding the Copa Potrero – a cup competition where amateur teams link up with ex-pros to compete in televised *potrero* matches. Agüero himself is a graduate of the game, having grown up in a *villa* in Quilmes in the Buenos Aires province. Of course, not everyone had the talent of *El Kun* to lift themselves out of the *villa*'s instability. A year after making his debut for Independiente at just 15 years old, Agüero returned to visit his former neighbours.

'When I asked about the boys I hung out with, one was dead, another was in prison, another was wanted by the police,' he revealed in an interview with *El País*. 'These are boys aged 15.'

* * *

Jenny continued our tour of the club. Cheery men enjoying a smoke on top of a roof waved at us as we climbed the steps to a music room where murga practice was taking place. A teenage boy in a Liverpool shirt handed me some tereré – a cold version of mate often mixed with fruit juice, which is popular in Paraguay. The cool liquid leaving the metal straw was a pleasant slaker, the bitterness of the yerba offsetting the sweetness of the orange juice.

Outside the CAMP offices, the salty scent of stew wafted by. Jenny pointed to the queue of people snaking on to the main street opposite the Nuevo Gasómetro, as neighbours waited for their serving from the *olla popular* – 'communal pot'. It smelled good, but I had to settle for mates poured by Jenny as we sat down at her desk. It was nearly 30 degrees, but soaring temperatures never stop the flow of mate in Argentina.

What the heat does stop, however, is electricity in the *villa*. Jenny explained how power cuts routinely plunged homes and streets into total darkness, which in turn increased the already prevalent crime and violence. Was assistance on hand when trouble occurred? 'There are parts of the villa where police and ambulances don't even go,' Jenny said. 'In the last few years we've had a bit of help from the fire brigade nearby, but before that it was just a case of "sort yourself out".'

With drug gangs running certain zones of the *villa*, it was clear the police had limited authority. But given their history of corruption and collaboration with criminal operations in the city, 'More police doesn't mean more safety,' said Jenny. The famous *zonas liberadas,* which had enabled the murder of the *barra* leader Pillin in Rosario, were a feature across Bajo Flores too.

One particularly egregious example came to light in 2015 when social activist Gustavo Vera publicly denounced a *zona liberada* of ten cocaine kitchens in the *villa*. The police may not have been present, but former combatants of the Peruvian armed forces were – recruited to guard the kitchens with AK47 rifles and an anti-tank bazooka.

Vera was a friend of Pope Francis after the pair worked together supporting victims of human trafficking in Buenos Aires. He claimed that while residents of the *villa* lived in terror from the armed group and the trouble they attracted, the police protected their operation with a cordon. Neighbours complained but the Ministry of Security did nothing. It doesn't take long to work out what may have persuaded the authorities to turn a blind eye. 'A kilo of high-purity cocaine sells for US$12,000 on the market and each kitchen can produce up to ten kilos per day,' Vera told Radio El Mundo. 'We must fight drug trafficking ... You can't fund a political campaign with narco money.'

Jenny lives in the wider *barrio* of Flores and is not from the *villa* itself. 'My parents were worried when I started this job ten years ago but have no problem now. I love it here. People speak about this place without knowing anything about it, or they just pretend it doesn't even exist. There's so much ignorance.'

Her younger colleague Andrea, who pottered around us as she prepared to teach a dance class, has lived in the *villa* nearly all her life. Jenny hauled her into the mate rotation so she could share her own experiences of growing up in the area.

'Seven or eight years ago you couldn't walk down these streets,' she said. 'In front of my house there was a war between Paraguayans and Argentines to take control of the area [for drug trafficking]. It was almost impossible to leave the house. Now things are a little better.'

Like Jenny, Andrea was open and engaging. Having to share the office with a pale, overheated Englishman asking lots of questions must have been distracting during a busy day of work, but they humoured me enthusiastically. I thought how tiring it must be to live in a place which is exclusively portrayed in negative terms, and wanted to know what Andrea liked most about living in the neighbourhood.

'This club,' she responded without hesitation. 'It's given me an opportunity to grow personally and move forward with my life. I've developed physically and mentally here. It's helped me as a person and a teacher.' She broke into a smile. 'It's also easier for me now because I know the people that might want to rob you, and they know me. I teach their families so I'm less likely to be targeted.'

As we compared the merits of Argentinian mate versus Paraguayan tereré, Andrea revealed that she, like so many residents of the *villa*, was born elsewhere in South America. 'I love Argentina, but I am Paraguayan. I like my country and its culture and that's where my roots are, so I always say I'm Paraguayan even though I've lived here nearly all my life.'

She wore her dual identity with an easy-going pride, but the same cannot always be said of the *villa* itself. 'The whole area is split up by countries,' she said, adding that the national divides contributed to playful rivalries but also serious conflict. 'You've got the Paraguayans, the Bolivians, the Peruvians, and in recent years the Venezuelans. Obviously the Argentines too, but they are more spread out.'

The door of the office swung open again. This time it was a priest in his late 30s or early 40s called Federico. Although CAMP was founded by the local Catholic church and relied heavily on its funding, Jenny and her colleagues admitted they weren't especially religious. Federico probably saw his opportunity to explain the valuable work the church does in the *villa*, but before we got to that, I quizzed him about the football club next door.

'San Lorenzo are very good with us,' he said. 'It's a deep relationship that's existed for many years now. They lend the facilities in Ciudad Deportiva, which are really valuable to us, like the swimming pool, the handball and volleyball courts, and the open grassy spaces, which you don't get in the *villa*. They also subsidise sports memberships for families that are from the *villa*, so people here get to use their facilities at a reduced cost.'

Federico wasn't a *cuervo*, but recognised that the club's off-the-pitch work was in keeping with its history. 'San Lorenzo has a really big social dimension. That dynamic has existed since its foundation, when a priest saved the kids who were playing in the street. From the very beginning the club has had a strong social consciousness.'

As Jenny and I stepped out of the office, we finally stumbled across something that had been strangely absent up to that point: San Lorenzo fans. The most outgoing of three young *cuervos* was *Chochy*, a smiley, dark-skinned, dark-haired teenager at least six feet tall. San Lorenzo were already in Bajo Flores when *Chochy* was born, and being part of the *villa* and CAMP gave him unrivalled access to his beloved club. Surely, therefore, he wanted them to stay in the *barrio*. 'Nooo, no. San Lorenzo is from Boedo. We have to return, that's it!'

As we chatted about the club, *Chochy* mentioned that he had met Hector *Tito* Villalba. *Tito* was raised in Villa 1-11-14, grew up as a fanatical *cuervo*, and played more than 100 games for the club, winning three major trophies. Like Andrea, his family's roots are in Paraguay and he has represented the country at international level. The winger's fairytale story includes one of my favourite-ever San Lorenzo goals – his first for the club. Frustratingly for me, it came the year before I started attending matches but it is now etched into my memory, having watched it back 100 times on YouTube.

It came in a *clásico* at home to Racing in 2013. There were just six minutes on the clock when 18-year-old *Tito* collected the ball beside his own penalty area. With the exuberance of youth, he embarked on a lung-busting 90-metre run through the middle of the Racing side, eyes wide, arms pumping. After skipping past three challenges, he blasted the ball into the roof of the net and fell to his knees, overwhelmed with euphoria. Within touching distance of the *villa* that raised him, he had announced his arrival in the Primera División with a *golazo* for the ages.

After his successful San Lorenzo career, *Tito* moved to Major League Soccer. His cult status at San Lorenzo was cemented when he turned down a move to Boca Juniors from Atlanta United, owing to his *cuervo* allegiances. 'Those who know me knew I was never going to play for Boca,' he said in an interview with Infobae. *El Xeneize* pay big money and would have been the biggest club on *Tito's* CV. 'I don't regret it; I took the decision as an *hincha*.'

Away from football, his family have shown similar loyalty to their roots despite *Tito*'s wealth. 'I always go back to the *villa* to visit. My mum and sisters live there and they don't want to leave,' he said. 'Sometimes we talk about the possibility of them moving, but it's no use, they are comfortable and happy.'

* * *

Jenny was approaching the end of her shift as we made our way out of the *villa*. The hours after clocking off was when the worry set in, she said. Whether it was *Chochy* in a game of *fútbol de potrero* which turned violent, or one of the children going without dinner that evening, there was always a lingering fear about what happened after the club closed its doors. 'One more kid in the club is one less kid in the street,' was one of their mottos.

I caught a glimpse of the Nuevo Gasómetro's imposing blue-and-red pillars through a gap in the buildings and thought of the dream it holds for young footballers in the *villa*. Were there more *Tito* Villalbas on the way?

Ultimately, though, professional football is just that; a dream, for all but a very select few. San Lorenzo offers a chance to the most gifted and plays its part in helping the community, but it's organisations like Club Atletico Madre del Pueblo which truly make the difference. Day after day, year after year, it gives young people a safe place to learn, develop and enjoy themselves. It's a priceless operation, run by smart, kind-hearted people who were devoted to helping others.

As if to underline everything I had seen that day, one of the girls from the club, no older than five or six years old, gave Jenny an almighty hug as we passed. Jenny smiled but it was tinged with melancholy as we walked away. 'Some children don't have an adult to give them hugs at home,' she said. 'Those are the ones that hug you tighter.'

Chapter 14

South America's obsession

Y dale alegría, alegría a mi corazón	And bring joy, joy to my heart
La Copa Libertadores es mi obsesión	The Copa Libertadores is my obsession
Tenes que dejarlo todo por El Ciclón	You have to give everything for El Ciclón
Tenes que poner mas huevo	You have to show more balls
Pa' ser campeón	To be champions

FITO PÁEZ is one of the legends of *rock nacional* – Argentina's homegrown rock movement which swept through the country and much of South America during the second half of the 20th century. Despite his early success in the genre's post-dictatorship boom, Fito's record label EMI refused to publish his more experimental work at the end of the 1980s and he fell into debt.

Warner came to the rescue by publishing his sixth album, *Tercer Mundo* (Third World) in 1990, which shocked even Fito by becoming a chart-topper in Argentina. The Rosario native, who disappointed his Newell's-supporting dad by becoming a Central fan, said *Tercer Mundo* held a mirror up to the continent: 'The album reflects what I saw on my travels through Latin America: pagan festivals, priests mixing with terrorists, prostitutes trying to take money from Americans.

'I said to myself: there is a very intense world down here. I wanted to reflect that – it's a kind of film about the American continent and its countries.'

It is fitting, therefore, that one of the album's hits, 'Y Dale Alegría a Mi Corazón', became the soundtrack to arguably the continent's biggest pagan festival of all: the Copa Libertadores.

'*Y dale alegría, alegría a mi corazón, la Copa Libertadores es mi obsesión ...*' sing supporters across South America. 'And bring joy, joy to my heart, the Copa Libertadores is my obsession ...'

The song was first popularised by fans of Uruguayan giants Peñarol and is now sung by nearly every *hinchada* when their team plays in the tournament. During my first game at the Nuevo Gasómetro, La Gloriosa had been singing their version with gusto and it stayed in my head for days. When performing the original at his piano, Fito throws his head back and sings with a deep, aching desire. The San Lorenzo fans around me, who had never seen their team lift the famous trophy, sung with the same sense of yearning.

I studied the words so I could rehearse them on my walk to Spanish school in Buenos Aires each morning. I told myself it would help me find my speaking rhythm before the real thing in the classroom, like a perfectly judged pre-match warm-up before the 90 minutes. In class, students would often mention their matchday tours to the Bombonera and the Monumental and wear the shirts of Argentina's big two. It made me sing one particular line of San Lorenzo's Libertadores chant with added relish.

'*Ya van a ver, nosotros no somos Boca ni River Plate!*' – 'And now you'll see, we are not Boca or River Plate!'

Whenever I talk to South Americans about the Copa Libertadores, it seems to mean more to them than the Champions League does to Europeans. The hunger to win *La Copa* transcends football. It is the hope of humbling giants in your *barrio* and overcoming the odds in faraway lands. The ambition not just to lift a trophy, but to conquer a continent. The vastness of South America, the extreme and unpredictable conditions, and the unparalleled hostility of away trips impart a unique kind of glory on winning the Libertadores.

During the San Lorenzo trip, the Boca-supporting tour guide scoffed when I brought up the Champions League in our conversation about the Libertadores. 'Anyone can play on those pitches in Europe! Home and away games have the same conditions,' he said. 'The Copa Libertadores is another thing altogether. It's the Tour de France of football. You travel for days, you play in 40-degree heat, you play in the mountains, you play at altitude … To win you have to overcome everything.'

Of those famously variable conditions, altitude is the most feared. Two years after playing in the Champions League with Manchester United, the Brazilian midfielder Anderson travelled to the Bolivian capital of La Paz, 3,650 metres above sea level, to play Internacional's Libertadores away tie at The Strongest. Suffocated by the altitude, the star signing was substituted just 36 minutes into the game. He slumped on to the bench, gasping for air, and was handed an oxygen mask.

Bolivian fans have come to celebrate the role of their energy-sapping atmosphere – particularly since the national side's historic 6-1 thrashing of Diego Maradona's Argentina in La Paz during World Cup 2010 qualification. It is not uncommon to see supporters of the city's big two – The Strongest and Club Bolívar – taunt Argentines by dressing up as the 'ghost of altitude' in the stands. Grown adults draped in bed sheets with 'ALTURA' painted on the front remains one of my favourite images of the Libertadores.

But it's not just Mother Nature who's responsible for the testing conditions. Fans, players, club officials and local residents all conspire to make life as difficult as possible for visiting teams, particularly if a continental heavyweight comes to town. My friend Eduardo, who has been on his fair share of San Lorenzo trips, once said *Copa* away games were like 'going to war'. In recent years, nearly every fixture for an

Argentinian side in Brazil has backed up his claim. Locals attack away fans in the street with alarming regularity, and the Argentines don't exactly roll out the red carpet when the fixtures are reversed.

Of course, not all Libertadores passion is expressed through violence. Eduardo also told me about an acquaintance who had named his newborn son 'Ivael' as a tribute to River's Libertadores triumph against Boca in the 2018 final. I didn't grasp the connection, so Eduardo sent me a video of the last-minute goal which sealed the 3-1 win for River.

'*Y va el tercero, y va el tercero!*' goes Mariano Closs's now-famous commentary. 'Here comes the third, here comes the third!' '*Y va el*' had been converted to 'Ivael' for the young boy's name. Naturally.

* * *

I was keen to find out if the Copa Libertadores had always come with such a large side order of mania, so I arranged to go for coffee with an expert on the tournament. Luciano Wernicke has written more than 20 books on sport, including *Historias Insolitas De La Copa Libertadores*, re-released in English as *The Dark Side of the Copa Libertadores*.

It was a Tuesday afternoon. Dark, brooding clouds dropped lashings of rain on to the streets of Buenos Aires. As those who have walked the city in wet weather will know, loose paving slabs lurk underfoot, ready to slosh warm, dirty water into your shoe at any moment. I was meeting Luciano in upmarket Belgrano and just one block from the café, I received the dreaded bootful.

The anguish of my wet foot was offset by the pleasant surprise that Luciano had arrived at the café on time. This had never happened to me in Argentina before. People usually arrive at least 20 minutes after a meeting time and often much more. Early in the conversation Luciano revealed his German heritage, and while I don't like to indulge national stereotypes, it did feel like something of an explanation.

Before our coffees had even arrived, facts and anecdotes were spilling from Luciano like water from a *porteño* paving slab. Some were in Spanish but most were in English, as he revelled in the chance to show off his language skills and knowledge of British culture.

'Do you still have Lillywhites in England?' His beady eyes were full of hope and excitement. 'The sports shop? Yeah I think so.' He banged his palm on the table. 'Well, did you know that James Lillywhite, the founder, invented the size-five football! Because at the time, football was the fifth-biggest sport in the UK!' I have found nothing that corroborates this improbable fact, but I enjoyed the spirit in which it was offered.

Battling to get on to the subject of the Libertadores as Luciano embarked on tales of visiting Dundee United in the early 90s, I asked him if the *Copa*'s wild side had a long-standing history. 'Oh yes, it's always been this way,' he said. 'From the 1960s when the tournament began, playing away games in places like Montevideo and Asunción was like playing in hell. Fans used to bring huge vats of rotten oranges to throw at opposition players and fans. It was horrible.'

On the morning of the day we met, news reports from Belo Horizonte showed Atlético Mineiro fans brutally assaulting River supporters in the street before their Libertadores semi-final. Ahead of the other semi, footage from Rio showed the local police firing tear gas and rubber bullets into groups of Peñarol fans who had travelled from Uruguay. As Eduardo had mentioned, it was all a bit more dangerous than rotten oranges.

'Things are getting worse, especially in Brazil,' Luciano said. 'It's strange because when you go to places like Rio for a holiday, everyone in the street is friendly to you, whether you are from Argentina or any other country. But when the

Libertadores arrives and they go to the stadium, a switch goes and they become warriors – not people.'

Violent scenes during the tournament are not limited to the streets. In 1971, just 11 years after the Libertadores was introduced as a uniting force for the continent (its name honours the liberators who fought for independence across South America), an almighty mid-game brawl between Boca Juniors and Sporting Cristal from Peru saw 19 players sent off. Many of them spent the night in hospital or prison.

With the score at 2-2, a heavy tackle sparked war on the pitch. As punches and kicks rained in from both teams, Boca captain Rubén Suñé attacked opponent Alberto Gallardo with a corner flag. He received a flying kick from Gallardo in return, which left him needing seven stitches to the head. Fallen bodies were being kicked on the turf like footballs. Sporting Cristal's Orlando de la Torre fought off three Boca players alone. Tragically, it was all too much for his mother back in Peru, who died of a heart attack after watching the brutality unfold live on television.

'There is something morbid about the spectacle of the Copa Libertadores,' Luciano said. 'People sit back wanting to see the fights and the riots, whereas people watch the Champions League just for the football. The national rivalries have stayed strong between clubs in South America because there are fewer foreign players in each team. In Europe you had even more conflict in the past, when you think Real Madrid from Fascist Spain played Spartak Moscow from Communist Russia. But now every team is full of foreign nationals and the rivalries are diluted.'

We discussed the tactics used to disrupt visiting teams in the Libertadores. Luciano went through some well-worn classics, like setting off fireworks outside a team hotel the night before a game and switching off the water supply to the away dressing room. But there were more left-field tactics that I had not heard before. 'In the past, it was very common to plant hookers in the opposition's team hotel.

They pretended they were normal guests then chatted up the players and slept with them, so they didn't rest the night before a game and lost energy,' he said, in an oddly matter-of-fact way.

Traps may be waiting for players at their destinations, but sometimes just getting there is an ordeal – especially if budgets are tight. Before chartered jets were flying Ángel Di María around Europe for Champions League matches, he was making less-orthodox journeys across South America with Rosario Central, where he started his professional career and returned in 2025.

'I will never forget when we had to play a Libertadores game in Colombia against Nacional,' he told football website The Players' Tribune. 'You know the planes with the big ramp in the back that they use to ship cars and stuff? Well, that was our plane. They had to give us those huge military headphones to block out the noise. We climbed on to the platform and there were a few seats and some mattresses for us to lie on. For eight hours. To a Libertadores match. They closed the ramp and it got super dark. The plane starts to take off and we go sliding down the ramp, all the way to the back of the plane, and one of my team-mates shouts, "Nobody touch the big red button! If that door opens, we're all going to shit!" It was incredible. If you didn't live it, you wouldn't believe it.'

Atlético Tucumán's trip to Quito in 2017 was even more eventful. The small club from northern Argentina were playing El Nacional in their first-ever Copa Libertadores. The home match of their two-legged tie to qualify for the group stage had ended in a disappointing 2-2 draw. With the altitude of Quito awaiting the unfancied Argentinians in the second leg, the odds of getting through the biggest game of their history were almost as thin as the air at the Estadio Olímpico Atahualpa.

To break up the long journey north, the squad spent a day in the Ecuadorian city of Guayaquil, where another flight would take them to Quito on matchday. But just hours before kick-off, paperwork complications left the Atlético squad stranded on the runway, unable to take off. As the hours ticked by, rumours spread of an El Nacional plot to prevent the Argentinians from playing and secure a bye to the group stage.

Agonisingly for the Atlético fans already at the stadium, it became clear their team would miss kick-off. But Conmebol rules stated that the game could still go ahead if the team arrived no later than 45 minutes after the scheduled start. With kick-off officially at 7.15pm, the 30-minute flight from Guayaquil only took off at 7pm. The Argentinians needed a miracle, but they had a chance. The race was on.

The 24-hour news stations in Argentina were now tracking the saga live. I remember tuning in from the UK via YouTube and seeing the big red timer in the corner of the screen counting down the minutes Atlético had left to reach the stadium. With El Nacional's manager confirming that his team planned to claim the win without kicking a ball, the Argentinian ambassador in Ecuador, Luis Juez, decided to step into the chaos and help his countrymen.

Juez got himself on the team bus waiting for the Atlético players in Quito and negotiated a police escort to speed up the journey. Just 50 minutes remained to avoid the forfeit when the players finally arrived. The bus journey to the ground would usually take one hour.

With all of Argentina cheering on the Tucumános back home, the team bus sped down the Quito motorway at an astonishing 130kmh. I howled with laughter at the live footage. It was like watching a real-life segment of *Grand Theft Auto*, the bus slaloming through traffic at breakneck speed with police lights flashing behind. Nobody knew whether a game of football would be played but it was already pure Libertadores.

Juez, meanwhile, was taking centre stage from the bus, haranguing Conmebol officials on the phone and fighting the Atlético cause on live radio. 'Stop busting our balls with the ruling!' he shouted over the airwaves in his strong Cordobes accent. 'Just wait for us for an extra 15 minutes!'

Only nine minutes were left on the timer when the team bus flew through the stadium gates. The game seemed to be on, but the drama wasn't over. Amid the travel confusion, Atlético realised their kit had been left behind. They didn't even have boots. Just as the reality of another crisis set in, it came to light that Argentina's under-20 side had played in the same stadium just days before and all of their kit was available. Some of the shirts didn't fit and the names of other players were on the back, but it didn't matter. Atlético could represent the country on foreign turf and retain their normal sky blue and white colours in the process.

The players entered the pitch just in time to play the game of their lives. Despite their tumultuous preparation and the head-spinning altitude, the Tucumános battled bravely. With the score at 0-0 after an hour, Atlético striker Fernando Zampedri stunned the Ecuadorians with a looping header for a 1-0 lead, a momentous goal that would be enough to take them through.

Zampedri ran across the running track to the delirious knot of away fans, celebrating their precious reward for a 5,000km journey. On Zampredi's back was 'L. MARTÍNEZ' – the star striker of Argentina's under-20s, Lautauro, who would go on to play for the national side and Inter Milan. *El Decano* held on for an historic win. Their exhausted, jubilant players in second-hand Argentina shirts made iconic images for the back pages the following day.

* * *

Just over a year later, I found myself wearing the same Argentina shirt, standing alongside 1,000 or so Tucumán fans in another far-flung away end. We were at Atlético Nacional in Colombia.

During my brief stint living in Medellín, Atlético Tucumán had again qualified for the Libertadores. This time they reached the last 16 where they faced Colombia's biggest and most decorated club. The Quito saga had left me with a soft spot for *El Decano*. With Nacional's Estadio Girardot just a 30-minute walk away from my flat, I couldn't resist pulling on the Argentina shirt like the Atlético players in Ecuador and witnessing their latest Libertadores adventure.

Colombian football culture, which leans heavily on the influence of Argentina and its *hinchadas*, never fully pulled me in. But I did enjoy regular visits to the Estadio Girardot to watch both Nacional and city rivals Deportivo Independiente Medellín. The long, bar-lined street of La 70 guided me to the stadium and was always packed with fans letting off crackers and slinging back shots of *aguardiente* before kick-off. The Libertadores had just as tight a grip on the Colombians as I'd seen in Argentina. The streets of Medellín were a reggaeton and salsa party whenever Nacional had a date with *La Copa*.

I looked around the away end of the Estadio Girardot and wondered how many of these hardy souls had made the famous trek to Quito. I hoped that Medellín had made their latest journey worthwhile – and suspected it had. It was a typically balmy evening in the 'city of eternal spring'. As the sun set behind the dramatic mountainous landscape surrounding the stadium, the lights of a thousand homes began to twinkle on the horizon. It looked like a perfect starry sky had been lowered down to earth and draped across the hills.

The travelling Tucumános, separated from their heroes by another running track, watched a 1-0 defeat on the night, but a 2-1 aggregate win secured an historic qualification to the quarter-finals. They were crushed by Grêmio in the next round, but their brave performance in Medellín took the club to the highest point in its history, surpassing the heroics of Quito.

When the full-time whistle blew, a Tucumáno beside me collapsed to the floor and lay flat on the concrete terrace, hands to his face. It was the most Argentinian expression of joy you could hope to witness and neatly illustrated the emotions generated by the Libertadores.

Having already delivered a classic underdog story, the *Copa* showed more of its romantic side after the final whistle. Groups of Nacional fans approached the line of police dividing the supporters, but there were no missiles exchanged – just shirts. The Colombians handed over their green and white Nacional stripes and gladly received Tucumáno mementos in return. If the visitors had been from the big, brash fanbases of Boca or River, who tend to attract trouble wherever they go, such displays of harmony would be difficult to imagine. But the hardy travellers from lesser lights like Tucumán often receive a much warmer reception.

Outside the stadium, the goodwill continued. The *Decano* fans bounced around their drummer, singing about how *clásico* neighbours San Martín de Tucumán would be watching from home while they soaked up the adventure of a lifetime. Nacional supporters entered the crowd, magnanimously offering handshakes and hugs. Congratulations were passed on in the thick *paisa* accents of Medellín, a style of Spanish so different to the Tucumáno *castellano* that I wondered if anyone was really understanding each other. Either way, the sentiment was clear and the pan-American unity was heartwarming.

As Luciano's book points out, the Copa Libertadores has a dark side. But when certain teams meet in certain cities, there is plenty of light to be found too.

'We don't have much to celebrate in our societies,' said Luciano, when I asked him why the tournament meant so much to people. 'Football is the one thing we can enjoy and celebrate.' The ecstatic Tucumános were an unwitting case study. They would be returning to one of the poorest parts of a country suffering yet another economic crisis. Some would be travelling for days, already broke from the cost of travel.

But on that night in Medellín, they were heroes and *campeónes*. Their triumphant Libertadores expedition had pushed any problems to one side. In the cruelty and complexity of life, the little joys brought by football can go a long way. Proof, if ever it was needed, was in the Tucumáno at my feet at full time, totally overwhelmed by happiness.

As Fito Páez wrote in the song that South American *hinchas* continue to adopt on the terraces:

And give joy, joy to my heart
It's the only thing I'm asking, at least today
And give joy, joy to my heart
Sadness and pain will go away

Chapter 15

Bring on the Brazilians

Esta es tu banda descontrolada	This is your crazy gang
Siempre te alentó	That's always supported you
Y nunca pidió nada	And never asked for anything
La que está re loca por esa copa	The one who is crazy to win that cup
Para que nos chupen bien las pelotas	So that they can suck our balls
River y Boca	River and Boca

THE SAN Lorenzo I first encountered was a club on the rise. Two decades after its opening, the Nuevo Gasómetro felt like a home, if not *the* home. On the pitch, the club had won its first continental titles with the Copa Mercosur in 2001 and the expanded Copa Sudamericana in 2002 – each broadly an equivalent to the Europa League. Domestically, the club was winning league titles at a faster rate than previous decades, as the drought-ending *campeonato* of 1995 was followed by titles in 2001, 2007 and 2013.

But there was something missing. 'Club Atlético *Sin Libertadores de América*'went the joke. 'San Lorenzo de Almagro' swapped for 'Without the Libertadores de América'. Almost every major club in the continent had won the Copa Libertadores – apart from San Lorenzo.

Each of the other *cinco grandes* had raised the hefty silver trophy at least once in their history, with Independiente leading the way on seven, earning them the nickname *Rey de Copas* ('King of Cups'). Even smaller city neighbours Vélez

Sarsfield and Argentinos Juniors had a Libertadores each, while Estudiantes just down the road in La Plata had racked up an impressive four. The failure to win the most important competition in South America was a source of lingering shame for San Lorenzo.

The 2014 competition gave *El Ciclón* another precious opportunity to break the curse. But faithful to the club's turbulent history, the journey to this point had been anything but smooth. Just 18 months before winning the league, San Lorenzo had been preoccupied with the opposite end of the table – caught in a nerve-shredding relegation battle.

There was a moment when a second humiliating drop to the B Nacional seemed certain. On a grey day in May 2012, San Lorenzo trailed Newell's Old Boys 2-0 at half-time and were deep inside the relegation zone. Friends who were at the game say some *cuervos* were already in tears, resigned to their fate. But after a remarkable second-half comeback, the tears of sadness became sobs of joy.

With the score at 2-2, the boyhood *cuervo* and legendary number ten Leandro *Pipi* Romagnoli danced around two defenders and crossed for Emmanuel Gigliotti to head home the winner. Romagnoli fell to his knees, then collapsed face down to the floor, overcome with emotion. Footage from the *popular* shows the blind supporter Walter Lo Votrico crying and wailing with relief, white cane aloft. His T-shirt, custom-made in dedication to his beloved club, reads '*No te veo, te siento*'– 'I don't see you, I feel you.'

The full-time celebrations of eccentric San Lorenzo manager Ricardo Caruso Lombardi may not have been quite so poignant, but they were just as memorable, highlighting the hyper-superstitious nature of Argentinian football culture. With his thick black mane now slightly dishevelled and a gold medallion poking through his shirt, Lombardi was photographed holding a ginger-haired ball boy aloft like a trophy. The manager had sent the boy to sit behind the Newell's goal in the second half, hoping the aura of his ginger hair would act as a *mufa* – a force of bad luck – against the visitors. With three season-changing goals entering the Newell's net, the *mufa* had worked and Lombardi was hailed a genius. It's safe to say that superstition is usually a more powerful force than political correctness in Argentina.

Like many of his 26 (and counting) managerial jobs, Lombardi was brought in as a firefighter and sacked soon after, so it was the grizzled, greasy-haired Juan Antonio Pizzi who led San Lorenzo to a shock title win the following year. But the managerial merry-go-round waits for no one in Argentina and Pizzi's success earned him a move to Valencia in Spain, leaving San Lorenzo in search of a new head coach for their 2014 Libertadores campaign.

Step forward, Edgardo 'Bigfoot' Bauza. There was an obvious reason why *El Patón* had been chosen for the job and it wasn't just his imposing presence in the dressing room. When it came to the *Copa*, he had history. In 2008, Bauza defied all the odds to make LDU Quito the first side from Ecuador to win a Libertadores. Now he just had to repeat the trick in Buenos Aires, by any means necessary.

* * *

I flicked on the old box TV in the kitchen of my Buenos Aires flat. I was now a couple of months into my first six-month sojourn in Buenos Aires and was ready to find a new place to stay. The Spanish school had placed me in an old, crumbling apartment in the central *barrio* of Monserrat. I liked the high ceilings, the tall wooden doors with brass knobs, and the large front windows with wrought-iron railings. I was less keen on the creaking floorboards, the rats burrowing through the walls at night, and the kitchen roof which let in a steady stream of water whenever it rained.

On the fuzzy TV screen, Edgardo Bauza was taking his place in the dugout while his players limbered up on the pitch in Quito, Ecuador. It was the penultimate round of the group stage in the Copa Libertadores and San Lorenzo desperately needed a result at Independiente del Valle to boost their chances of reaching the knockout stage. For the first time, I was feeling a little nervous about a San Lorenzo match. As my visits to the Nuevo Gasómetro became increasingly frequent, I was beginning to feel invested in the team – in particular their struggle to finally win a Copa Libertadores.

As I sat on the hard kitchen chair staring intently at the screen, the two Dutch girls living at the flat asked why I was so transfixed on this strange match. It was a fair question. The stadium in Quito was oddly dark, half of the stands were empty and there was a gargantuan running track around the pitch. None of us were good enough at Spanish to know what the commentator was excitedly talking about. I didn't know how to answer their question without going into the trials and tribulations of the group stage and all the permutations going into the final fixtures, so I just shrugged and smiled.

Over my shoulder, our American flatmate was breakdancing in the corridor. He did this every day. His trainers clattered and squeaked against the tiled floor as he grunted his way through each routine. When a move didn't come off, which seemed to be quite often, he swore at the top of his voice. Part of me needed San Lorenzo to stay in the cup just to have more reasons to get out of the flat.

In Quito, *El Ciclón* took a second-half lead and clung on to their advantage until the 95th minute when, in sickening fashion, the hosts won a penalty and equalised with the last kick of the game. San Lorenzo's players were incensed. Had it been a penalty? Without question. Emmanuel Mas had completely wiped out the Ecuadorian forward without touching the ball. But this is the *Copa*. The locals are conspiring against you from the moment you enter their country. A penalty given so late in the game was surely part of a dastardly plot. With a misplaced sense of injustice, San Lorenzo's squad surrounded the officials. Of course, like almost all post-match remonstrations it would soon fizzle out. All that was needed were some cool heads to diffuse the tension.

But the Ecuadorian police had other ideas. Within seconds, a squad in full riot gear charged at the melee and began windmilling into the Argentines. Batons swung and shields slammed into bodies. Surprisingly, this didn't calm things down. The San Lorenzo players went into combat mode, raising their fists and throwing punches like *barra brava* on the streets. Curly haired defender Fabricio Fontanini led the fightback and received a hefty blow for his troubles. Outnumbered by the police, the besieged squad retreated down the tunnel. A handful of players now had injury to add to the insult of the late equaliser.

I switched off the TV. With the frantic commentary suddenly silenced, only the drip of the leaking roof could be heard in the kitchen. For the first time, I felt genuine despondency related to San Lorenzo – which, in a way, made me feel closer to them. Was this some sort of test on the way to becoming a fan? You can walk away from a defeat, feel nothing, and maintain your sanity. Or, you can dwell on the defeat, embrace the pain, crave redemption and start emotionally investing in a cause which, ultimately, has nothing to do with you. Something inside me was being drawn to the latter option.

* * *

From those first months in Buenos Aires, I was mesmerised by the city. It pulsed with energy, all day and all night, like nowhere else I had ever visited. Every day my senses were in overdrive – for better or worse. The constant hum of traffic and close humidity could feel overwhelming, but the elegant tree-lined avenues, grand colonial buildings and blood orange sunsets were reliable sources of beauty. Infectious cumbia escaped from car windows and pounding reggaeton vibrated through the streets at night. Buses coughed exhaust fumes into the air. The smell of barbecued meat wafted through the *barrio* on Sundays. Birds twittered in the trees and dogs left shit all over the pavements.

Life in the city came with a constant undercurrent of chaos, which seemed to act as a motor for its frenetic rhythm. The unpredictability of life – from whether your bus will arrive in the morning to whether the country's entire economy will collapse overnight – put society on edge. People seemed ready to boil over at any moment, be it in anger, joy, love or despair.

More than once, I saw raging drivers abandon their cars in the middle of the road to square up to each other. Wherever you looked, interlocked couples were revelling in public displays of affection. The streets felt safe to me, but everyone seemed to have a story of being mugged. A teacher from the Spanish school popped into the pharmacy on her lunch break and was threatened at gunpoint by armed robbers.

As Eduardo, my good *cuervo* friend, once said, 'When you walk down the street in Buenos Aires you never know if you're about to hook up with the hottest girl in the world or get shot in the face.' I kind of knew what he meant.

I was falling for the city and its intriguing energy, but I still felt like an outsider. Unable to speak the language fluently, my involvement in *porteño* life felt passive. I observed more than I participated. Meeting locals was restricted to conversations with taxi drivers, who gave encouraging nods in the rear-view mirror as I stumbled through my staccato Spanish, but were gone once I left the car. My friendships had all been made at the language school, so they offered little access to the inner-workings of Argentinian life, which I was now craving.

My peek behind the curtain came at San Lorenzo. No foreigners ventured anywhere near Bajo Flores (apart from the ones I dragged to games), and squeezing through the turnstiles on matchday, shoulder to shoulder with throngs of *cuervos*, I was part of an Argentinian ritual. When San

Lorenzo scored, people hugged me. When the opposition scored, we shook our heads and rolled our eyes in the body language of football – in which I was already fluent. Every other week, for two or three hours, it felt like I'd been let into an inner circle of Buenos Aires.

But all of this was becoming contingent on San Lorenzo staying in the Copa Libertadores. The short league season was petering out for Bauza's side and in a couple of months I would be flying home. As my experience of Buenos Aires became increasingly intertwined with the club, the final group stage match against Botafogo was the last chance for San Lorenzo to save their season, and in some ways, my trip.

El Ciclón were bottom of the group so the task was daunting. They would be at home to Botafogo, who outplayed them in the previous meeting and only needed a draw to progress. Even if San Lorenzo won, they also needed Independiente del Valle to either lose or draw at Unión Española in Chile. If the away side won, San Lorenzo would need to better the Ecuadorians' victory by two goals or be knocked out on goal difference.

With an obligation to win and win well, Bauza's men flew out of the traps. Joined by some friends from the Spanish school, I had taken a now customary position at the edge of the Platea Sur on the side of the pitch, to be as close as possible to La Gloriosa behind the goal. Rowdy days in the *popular* would come later, but tonight, even the *platea* was on its feet. A symbiotic energy seemed to pulse through the players and the fans, as the song of the moment rang out. 'Show some balls San Lorenzo, step up – your supporters are here, your people are here.'

The players responded. Young *Tito* Villalba, the boy from Villa 1-11-14, let fly from 20 yards. The ball took a wicked deflection and the *popular* sucked it into the bottom corner; 1-0. The stadium exploded and now there was belief in the air. Botofogo, so slick and confident at the Maracanã on matchday one, were a shadow of their former selves. Their small band of travelling fans looked on from their corner, stunned and helpless as their team wilted in the Nuevo Gasómetro's cauldron. The Brazilian players tried to shout instructions at each other, but they looked disorientated; the messages weren't getting through.

'At San Lorenzo, we used to do training sessions in silence because when we entered the pitch we couldn't hear anything through the noise of the fans,' former *cuervo* Sebastián Méndez once claimed. The Botafogo players were not prepared for this.

At half-time, we found out that Unión and Independiente were drawing 1-1. Ideal. As it stood, San Lorenzo were sneaking through, but the rollercoaster had barely got out of first gear. Across the two games, nine second-half goals were about to play havoc with the emotions of everyone following Group 2.

In the second half, San Lorenzo continued where they left off and pinned back Botafogo. But what was happening in Chile? Internet signal was patchy inside the stadium, so news from the other game came sporadically and rippled through the stands in waves. The first update of the half brought bad news: Independiente del Valle had gone 2-1 up, meaning San Lorenzo had slipped out of the two qualifying spots and needed another goal. Right on cue, menacing winger Nacho Piatti picked up the ball on the edge of the box and rifled it into the bottom corner; 2-0.

But the delirium was cut short by more news from Chile. It was now 3-1 to Independiente del Valle. If it stayed that way, San Lorenzo would need an unlikely 4-0 win. How was this happening? Unión Española had been flying at the top of the group; could they not manage a draw to help us out?

The Chileans would have cared little about the exasperated Argentines 1,000km away, but they too needed a result to qualify. Sure enough they fought back, cutting the deficit to 3-2 with 60 minutes on the clock. Five minutes later, another update reached us in the Platea Sur. The Chileans had scored again. It was 3-3.

Celebrations broke out as San Lorenzo returned to the qualifying spots, but there was more to come. *'Cuatro-tres! Cuatro-tres!'* came the cry from a fan in front of us, staring at his phone in disbelief. Unión Española had pulled off a remarkable comeback and were now leading 4-3 with just 20 minutes left. The Nuevo Gasometro returned to full party mode, with the *hinchada* bouncing en masse from side to side, swinging from the *tirantes* and belting out songs in euphoria.

Ludicrously, it didn't stop there. The *cuervos* with internet signal were looking pensively at their phones again. It was now 4-4 in Chile. These Ecuadorians would not give up. One more goal would put them through at our expense.

Within minutes, the talk was of 5-4. '5-4?! Which way?' To the Ecuadorians. It sounded like a wind-up. Some fans took it as such. Seven goals in less than half an hour? This couldn't be right. But the grim news was confirmed and San Lorenzo were going out by the finest of margins. Level on points with Independiente del Valle, level on goal difference too, but one behind on goals scored.

Hearts had sunk and minds were scrambled, but once the latest goal had been processed, the parameters were clear again. A 3-0 win for San Lorenzo would do it. Just one more goal was needed. It was time to get out of 'game management' mode and return to the fire and fury of the first half. Bauza made some changes – not just to add attacking energy – but so the substitutes could pass on the message that the team had to score again.

San Lorenzo were tiring below us and time was running out. With 88 minutes on the clock, the moment for patient football had well and truly passed. Torrico thumped a hopeful long ball into the Botafogo half, where it was met by the head of Mauro Matos – nicknamed *Abuelo*, 'grandfather', for his large bald patch and ageing features. The glancing connection was perfect, allowing Piatti to take the ball in his stride and break past the last defender. Suddenly he was clean through with just the keeper to beat. Time slowed down as Piatti approached the edge of the box, dead centre of the goal. It had all come down to this, the game-defining simplicity of the moment summed up in the Fox Sports commentary that gave me goosebumps when I watched the highlights later that night.

'*Piatti, Piatti … ¿Sí o no? Piatti … GOOOOOOLLLLL!*'

The cool side-footed finish made a mockery of the pressure. The ball kissed the underside of the bar on its way in and 40,000 *cuervos* lost their minds. I shook my watching friends and fell into the rapturous embraces of fans around me. The celebrations continued even as play resumed. Lit by the floodlights, *cuervo* faces were switching from ecstasy to disbelief and back again.

Injury time was played out to thunderous noise before the referee called time on a 3-0 triumph. All that was needed now was the final whistle in Chile, with no more nasty surprises. When the players started jumping in their huddle on the pitch, the fans knew it was over. San Lorenzo were through.

The singing cranked up for one final chorus, '*Este sentimiento es verdadero, Ciclón te amo, sin vos me muero.*' – 'This feeling is true, I love you *Ciclón*, without you I'd die.' Given what everyone had been through that night the opposite seemed true, but I wasn't about to argue with them.

* * *

The sheer drama of the group qualification made it feel like a tournament had already been won, but there was a long way to go if San Lorenzo were serious about lifting their first Libertadores. Personally, I was just happy to have more big games to attend. Going to the league fixtures was enjoyable, but everything felt geared towards the *Copa* now. Players were being rested and it felt like the fans were too. The Nuevo Gasómetro wasn't as full and boisterous as the

Copa nights. We were all just passing time, waiting for the next Libertadores match to come around.

When the knockout stages arrived, the opponents in the last 16 were one of the favourites for the tournament: Grêmio, from Porto Alegre in southern Brazil. With about 15 minutes until kick-off, I took the same spot behind the corner flag in Platea Sur; pitch to my left, *popular* to my right. The song that had pulled the players through the final minutes of the Botafogo match had spilled into the *recibimiento* for Grêmio. 'Your *hinchada* is here, your people are here,' the players were reminded. Based on 'Tres Marías' by *rock nacional* star Andrés Calamaro, the chant had become the terrace hit of the Libertadores campaign.

Fireworks exploded behind the *popular.* Bright red trails lit up the fresh night sky and faded into smoke, adding the faint smell of gunpowder to the mix of cigarette and cannabis fumes in the air. The goalless first half offered little in the way of action, but the second period brought a shift in energy. No team wants to go away to Brazil needing a win and San Lorenzo were now attacking like a side in a hurry. Just eight minutes into the half, their adventure was rewarded.

Ángel Correa – San Lorenzo's great promise – was the hero, firing the ball home and wheeling away with his familiar beaming smile. In a country where goals are often celebrated with anger, Ángelito's glowing grin always lit up the *cancha*. Not that we could see it in the terraces, where manic celebrations had broken out. The *cuervos* were smelling Brazilian blood again. Grêmio's response was spirited but fruitless and San Lorenzo closed out a 1-0 win. Bauza's side would go to Porto Alegre with a precious lead to defend.

By the time the away leg came around, I had another friend to indoctrinate into the cult of *El Cuervo*. Simon, soon to undergo a subtle rebranding to *Simón* by the locals, was a football fanatic and one of my best friends since university.

In a glorious coincidence, he had been relocated to Buenos Aires for his job so I now had a true friend in the city. His presence not only made my daily life more enjoyable, but it helped break new ground socially – particularly on a night out. Simon is tall, with fair hair and blue eyes, which immediately turns heads in Buenos Aires. My dark features, coupled with ropey Spanish and a paler complexion, meant I was simply a poorer version of what the Argentines had already. But Simon was an instant hit and the locals were keen to chat when he was around. Even more importantly, he enthusiastically jumped aboard the San Lorenzo train on his arrival. *Los Santos* – The Saints – is one of the club's many nicknames and is shared by his beloved Southampton FC, so it wasn't a difficult sell.

Watching the second leg over bottles of Quilmes would be the first of many nights out we shared in Buenos Aires. Not yet aware of the better spots to catch a game in the city, we plumped for a venue in Recoleta called Locos x Fútbol – 'Crazy for Football'. Its name and the wall of TV screens inside at least offered reassurance that it would show the match.

As kick-off approached, I gave Simon a rapid briefing about the importance of the Copa Libertadores to San Lorenzo and the delicate balance of this last-16 tie. The ref's whistle blasted through the bar's speakers, followed by the roar of the home crowd in Porto Alegre. Playing most of their game in their own half, *El Ciclón* clung on to their 1-0 aggregate lead until the 83rd minute, when a close-range header levelled the tie. Like Unión Española at home and Independiente del Valle away, San Lorenzo had blown a lead late in the game. Extra time passed without a goal and a place in the quarter-finals would be decided on penalties.

Swiftly moving through rounds of Quilmes with Simon, I felt more nervous for the shoot-out than I expected, but the same couldn't be said for Patón Bauza over in Brazil. Once the penalty takers were decided, he casually strolled off the pitch and down the tunnel. A cameraman caught him as walked towards the dressing room.

'Are you not going to watch the penalties?' he called out. Bauza's response would enter San Lorenzo folklore.

'Why would I, if we've already won?'

With a smile and an elaborate shrug of the shoulders, Bauza disappeared down the corridor. The shoot-out ended 4-2 to San Lorenzo. Toricco did it again, saving two penalties. The players danced below the travelling supporters in the Arena do Grêmio, while Simon and I toasted the Libertadores below the big screen in Recoleta. The show rolled on.

* * *

'To knock us out of this cup, they're going to have to kill us.'

Patón Bauza's quotes were reflecting the growing sense of belief in the San Lorenzo camp, but the fixtures weren't getting any easier. As an Argentinian club, it's received wisdom that you'll need to beat at least one strong Brazilian team if you have serious aspirations of lifting the trophy. You don't normally expect to face three in succession, but that was the reality facing Bauza and his side with Campeonato Brasileiro Série A champions Cruzeiro awaiting in the last eight.

As another *cuervo* friend, Tirman (everyone uses his surname), later told me, 'We couldn't believe it. Normally once you're drawn with a Brazilian side for the second time, that's it, you're in the oven.' *Estás al horno*, as Tirman put it, means 'you're screwed' or 'you're in trouble', but some Argentinian translations are best left in their original form. 'It was pure suffering, the Brazilians just kept coming,' he said.

Tirman admits that playing clubs from Argentina's old football enemy gave San Lorenzo's *Copa* streak an added edge. 'When you meet a Brazilian side in the cup, everyone is so up for it. It's almost like playing a *clásico* and everyone wants to go to the game. It's very different to playing a team from Chile or Paraguay or wherever. With the Brazilians there is always extra spice.'

On this occasion, however, the Argentina-Brazil rivalry was unlikely to get out of hand, thanks to an unlikely friendship between the *hinchadas* of San Lorenzo and Cruzeiro. When the two teams met in the Copa Mercosur in 1998, the leader of the Cruzeiro *barra brava*, or *torcida*, was so taken by San Lorenzo's support that he got a *cuervo* tattoo and struck up a relationship with his opposite numbers in La Butteler. The bond was strengthened a few years later when a group of San Lorenzo supporters founded an amateur football team in a favela of Belo Horizonte, the home of Cruzeiro. Cruzeiro shirts can often be seen at San Lorenzo matches and vice-versa, while hospitality is laid on for travelling fans if the teams ever have fixtures in each other's city.

But as Simon and I shuffled into our position in the Platea Sur before kick-off in the first leg, it didn't feel like a meet-up between friends. A reassuring amount of abuse rained down on the Cruzeiro players as they finished their warm-up and disappeared down the tunnel. Twenty minutes later, the ball boys on the pitch started to wave their arms frantically, indicating to the stands that now was the time to trigger the *recibimiento*. Streamers, ticker tape and fireworks filled the air. The concrete around us shook.

The decisive moment of the encounter came with 30 minutes remaining. With the whole of the Platea Sur on its feet, Simon and I had the perfect angle of a deep, in-swinging free kick from Néstor *Gordo* Ortigoza, which drifted invitingly towards the far corner of the Cruzeiro goal. It was one of those crosses that make you twitch your neck muscles in the stands, mimicking the flicked header that's required. Santiago Gentiletti obliged, the ball nestled in the corner, and the Nuevo Gasómetro exploded. San Lorenzo had a 1-0 lead to defend in Brazil.

For the second leg, Simon and I looked to upgrade Locos x Fútbol in Recoleta for something a little more refined, and a little more San Lorenzo. We ended up at a location as *cuervo* as they come, in a bar just metres from the intersection of avenues San Juan and Boedo in the heart of the famous *barrio*.

Win or lose, I knew it would be the last Libertadores fixture I would watch in Buenos Aires that year. My flight home was booked for the following month, so if they progressed, San Lorenzo's Libertadores journey would have to continue without me. Although I had no plans to return to Argentina at that stage, there was already a voice in the back of my head complaining that just six months in this city was not enough. Every time I watched San Lorenzo, the voice became louder.

We weren't in the ground but watching San Lorenzo in Boedo is the next best thing. Dozens of nervous faces peered up at the screen as Matos fed Piatti inside the box with nine minutes gone. Piatti dropped his right shoulder, surged on to his left foot, and cracked an unstoppable shot into the roof of the net. *¡Golazo!* Chairs toppled as we celebrated in the bar. San Lorenzo had a foot in the semi-final. With the away-goals rule in play, Cruzeiro now needed three to rescue the tie.

On another night they may have done it. The home side attacked in waves but time and again their luck was out. To sum up their plight, Cruzeiro's Marcelo Moreno hooked a volley towards goal on the stroke of half-time which struck the foot of the post, rolled across the line, then struck the foot of the other. A San Lorenzo player gratefully hacked it to safety. Moreno pulled his blue shirt over his head in disbelief. The *cuervos* in Boedo allowed themselves a chuckle as Fox Sports showed the replay on a loop during half-time.

The Brazilians did pull a goal back with 20 minutes left to make it 2-1 on aggregate, but it was in vain. When the referee blew for full time, San Lorenzo fans of all generations fell into hugs around us. In the street, cars beeped their horns. The boys from Boedo had made the semi-final of the Copa Libertadores and the *barrio* rejoiced.

Chapter 16

You can look but you can't touch

Yo te voy a alentar　　　　I'll cheer you on
Como todos los años　　　　Just like every year
Esta es mi ilusión　　　　This is my dream
Quiero verte campeón, Ciclón　　To see us be champions, *Ciclón*
Dale San Lore, queremos la copa　Come on San Lore, we want the cup

EVERY TIME San Lorenzo survived a close shave in their Libertadores run, the same memes appeared online. Their message was clear. Pope Francis was using his holy powers to swing matches in favour of his boyhood club and lift the Libertadores curse on Boedo. According to the crudely edited images, an apparition of the Pontiff had slotted the ball into the top corner against Botafogo, saved two penalties against Grêmio and cleared the ball off the line at Cruzeiro.

In a Catholic country steeped in superstition, where fate is constantly attributed to forces beyond human control, having a *cuervo* in the Vatican was no small thing. Of course, most people were just having fun with the idea that the Pope might be pulling the strings on the pitch, but for those who believed his presence could genuinely help the club, the signs were beginning to stack up.

Jorge Mario Bergoglio was elected pope on 13 March 2013, becoming 'Papa Francisco' in the Spanish-speaking world. Argentines have a great way of grounding you with a nickname, and many in his home country referred to him as *Pancho* – the diminutive of 'Francisco'. A *pancho* is also a cheap hotdog you can buy on the street in Argentina, which only adds to its merit as a nickname for the global head of the Catholic Church.

In the same month that *Pancho* entered the Vatican, San Lorenzo's goalkeeper Pablo Migliore entered prison. He had been accused of helping a member of Boca's *barra brava* cover up a homicide and was arrested at the Nuevo Gasómetro after playing in the team's loss to Newell's Old Boys. His replacement was the quiet man from Mendoza, Sebastián Torrico, who would become known as 'Saint' Torrico for his otherworldly heroics in goal.

Already 33 years old and warming the bench for Godoy Cruz, Torrico arrived with minimal fanfare. His initial contract ran for just two months, ideally leaving enough time for Migliore's legal case to be sorted. But by the end of the year, Torrico had solved the team's leaky defence, saved a late Riquelme penalty in a vital win against Boca, and produced a last-minute miracle save to win the title at Vélez. To *cuervos*, he seemed like a gift from above. One of their own had begun his papacy in Rome just a few months ago and now this was happening. San Lorenzo had gone from relegation candidates to the champions of Argentina.

A club delegation flew to the Vatican to greet the Pope with the league trophy and presumably thank him for recent interventions. Six months on, the favours were mounting. Not only had the team come through some hairy moments to reach the semi-final of the Libertadores, they now had an unusually kind draw for the rest of the tournament. Club Bolívar from La Paz were the opponents, while two more beatable teams met in the other tie: Club Nacional from Paraguay and Defensor Sporting of Uruguay. Not one of the final four had ever won a Libertadores, and of these hopefuls, San Lorenzo were now the favourites.

My personal Libertadores run had come to an end, but back in the UK I was counting down the days to stream the big match with Bolívar. In between the quarter-finals and the semis of the Libertadores came the World Cup in Brazil, and England's abject performance only increased my hunger for the return of club football. Argentina fared considerably better but lost the final to Germany. Sports channel TyC had based its keenly anticipated World Cup commercial around Papa Francisco supporting the team from the Vatican. It ended with a message to the squad, 'The Pope is with you.'

Pancho couldn't quite get *La Selección* over the line, but San Lorenzo fans hoped he was keeping something back for the Libertadores. However great the joy of a World Cup win is for the average Argentine, seeing your club win the Libertadores is generally considered the greatest of all joys. Even before the country's momentous triumph at Qatar 2022, I had never, ever met a *cuervo* who wanted Argentina to win a World Cup more than San Lorenzo a Libertadores.

***

More than two months had passed since the quarter-final against Cruzeiro, but on 23 July 2014, it was finally time for the semi-finals. San Lorenzo's lowly seeding for the knockout rounds – 15th out of 16 teams – meant the crucial second leg would once again be away from home. With Bolívar, that meant playing in the altitude of the world's highest capital city for a place in the final. Bauza's men had no choice but to win in Buenos Aires and take a healthy aggregate lead to Bolivia.

I hadn't yet moved into my flat-share in London, so I watched the game in the kitchen of my parents' house – the furthest room from where they were sleeping – to minimise the disturbance caused by possible goal celebrations. Kick-off in the UK was at 11.45pm. Over the years, this was the kind of logistical planning I would get used to when streaming San Lorenzo matches late at night.

But I soon discovered that no amount of planning could prevent me from being exhausted in the morning. I was in the process of freelancing at offices in London in a bid to win full-time work, and was increasingly aware that these late nights with San Lorenzo were not doing my job hunt any favours. The mornings were manageable, especially if there was a win the night before. A victory buzz could help sustain you until lunch time. But the afternoon crashes were inevitable, no matter how much coffee – and now yerba mate – I glugged into my system. Some years later, I experimented with 'the Libertadores nap' for the particularly late kick-offs. I would go to bed at around 10pm, set an alarm for kick-off at 1am or 2am, then go back to bed after the match. The adrenaline of an exciting game could keep me awake for an hour or so after full-time, so their effectiveness was limited.

Having sipped cans of lager on my own to pass the time before kick-off in La Paz, I felt suitably charged up by the time play began, and paced around the kitchen. San Lorenzo were similarly energised and immediately pinned Bolívar into their half. After just five minutes, a free kick for the home side was floated into the area where Matos inexplicably found himself unmarked on the penalty spot. His straightforward header hit the back of the net, and through my laptop speakers came a magnificent, interminable '*Goooooooooooooool*' from commentator Mariano Closs.

And that was just the beginning. In a match that exceeded the wildest dreams of every *cuervo* during the long two-month wait, *El Ciclón* ripped through the sorry Bolivians, leaving a devastating 5-0 scoreline in their wake. Emmanuel Mas added a header before half-time, then Pichi Mercier, Julio Buffarini and another header for the left-back Mas completed a surreal 90-minute rout. The Libertadores had offered a hint of its signature madness and San Lorenzo had taken full advantage.

When it comes to the second leg of a semi-final, nothing removes the jeopardy quite like a five-goal lead. The ghosts of altitude had too much work on their hands to give Bolívar any kind of chance. Bauza's side held firm at 0-0 until injury time, when the home side registered a consolation goal. It all looked very straightforward for San Lorenzo, but according to *Tito* Villalba, the reality on the pitch was very different.

'The coaching staff drove us crazy about the altitude and how we were going to run out of air, but I was feeling great when we warmed up,' he told TyC Sports. 'I was running back and forth and I didn't feel anything. But at the end of the game they threw me on as a sub, and if you watch the replay, I turned purple! I was desperate, I couldn't get any air at all. Bauza and Di Leo [his assistant] just started laughing at me from the bench.'

Given the drama of previous rounds, the semi-final had been overcome with an almost unnerving sense of ease. It wasn't meant to be like this, but San Lorenzo had cruised to their first Copa Libertadores Final and the biggest fixture in the club's 106-year history. Their opponents would be Club Nacional of Paraguay, who also found themselves in uncharted territory.

Before defeating Defensor Sporting in the semis, Nacional had disposed of two Argentinian opponents in Vélez Sarsfield and Arsenal de Sarandí. Both would have been viewed as tricky ties, but avoiding the cauldrons of the *cinco grandes* – of which San Lorenzo had been the only qualifier for the 2014 *Copa* – made life easier for the Paraguayans.

As fate would have it, San Lorenzo would play the second leg at home for the first time in the knockout stages. Just when it mattered most. *El Ciclón* may have been seeded 15th, but Nacional were 16th. They too finished the group stage with eight points, but registered an inferior goal difference.

Before getting to know South American football, I would have been horrified by the idea of a two-legged final – the format used in the Libertadores until the switch to a one-off match in 2019. But it worked. The size of the continent and lack of affordable flights makes travel between countries extremely difficult. The vast majority of fans simply don't have the money or time to make the journey to the host venue. In two-legged finals, every team had the chance to play club football's biggest game football in their home *barrio*, complete with *previas* in the street, the *recibimiento* of a lifetime, and 90 minutes of vociferous home support. Conmebol wanted to imitate the one-off spectacle of the Champions League Final, but the compactness and more developed infrastructure of Europe does not exist in South America, and the Libertadores is poorer for the change.

Curiously, Club Nacional were denied the chance to play a final in their home stadium five years before the format was even changed. In a stark illustration of the club's modest stature, their Estadio Arsenio Erico home had a capacity of just 7,000, so the first leg was moved across Asunción to the 42,000-capacity Estadio Defensores del Chaco, which usually hosts the Paraguayan national team.

Before the first leg, the club did a fine job of drumming up additional support to fill out the ground. Under the banner of *Causa Nacional* – 'National Cause' – the wider public was encouraged to get behind the team and show their support at the stadium. They duly responded, selling out the area and creating a famous night for Paraguayan football. As well as Nacional colours, plenty of Paraguay shirts could be spotted in the crowd as the locals unleashed a *recibimiento* worthy of any major club on the continent.

Back in my parents' kitchen staring nervously at my laptop, I could only admire the cascade of ticker tape and streamers that filled the air as the Nacional players entered the pitch. They had surely never experienced such an atmosphere. The camera cut to the tunnel where San Lorenzo's squad was in a huddle, still metres from the steps leading up to the pitch. But even here they could not escape the raucous *recibimiento*, as streamers blew down the tunnel and fluttered around the players as Ortigoza shouted in vain to have his pep-talk heard.

It was an intimidating reception, but the men in blue-and-red were backed by 4,000 away fans making as much noise as the 40,000 locals. The famous songs of La Gloriosa could be heard inside and outside the ground, as 10,000 *cuervos* had travelled despite the limited allocation. Having waited a lifetime for a night like this, many simply had to be there, regardless of whether they had a ticket or not.

If another long, solitary session of pre-match cans wasn't enough to get me in the mood, then San Lorenzo's performance certainly was. Paton Bauza's side rose to the occasion and controlled the game from kick-off. Stubborn defending from the Paraguayans kept the score at 0-0 until 65 minutes, but the breakthrough was worth the wait.

As a patient move gradually funnelled the ball over to Villalba on the right wing, a booming chorus of '*Soooooy de Boedo!*' could be heard from the away end, as if they were priming the *barrio* for celebrations back home. Villalba's cross dipped on to the right foot of Matos, who hooked a clean volley across the keeper into the bottom left corner. *Golazo. Abuelo* was mobbed by team-mates on the touchline as I celebrated wildly but silently in the kitchen, like a deranged mime artist.

San Lorenzo managed the remaining 25 minutes in comfortable fashion, but received an almighty gut punch in the 93rd minute, just 20 seconds before the full-time whistle. A long ball into the box was flicked on to Julio Santa Cruz – brother of former Blackburn Rovers and Manchester City striker Roque – who prodded the ball into the roof of the net in front of a distraught away end.

A 1-1 draw was by no means a bad result away from home, but the manner of the equaliser was crushing. Despite 90 minutes of superiority, San Lorenzo would head back to

Argentina without an advantage as there was no away goals rule in play. The final remained wide open.

* * *

With tickets for the return leg put on sale the following morning, there was no time for *cuervos* to dwell on the late equaliser. For some, it was a case of switching off the TV at full time and heading straight to Boedo to set up camp outside the ticket office. 'I've been here in the cold since three in the morning so I hope they don't leave me without a ticket!' one *cuerva* told the press from the queue. Thankfully, she got her hands on the precious ticket at 4pm. Even those arriving in the middle of the night had an 11-hour wait, as the queues snaked through ten blocks of Boedo.

My good friend Marko, a San Lorenzo sympathiser who I met the following year, was one of the tens of thousands queuing on that crisp winter day in Buenos Aires. He remembers people coming and going with supplies, sharing pastries, sandwiches and yerba mates with fellow fans. But when darkness fell after more than 12 hours of queuing, the sense of camaraderie was replaced by fear, then anger, then resignation.

First, gunshots were heard from a nearby vehicle and hundreds of people instantly dropped to the pavement. Shortly after that scare, a member of staff emerged from the ticket office with bad news. The game was sold out. No more tickets left. After an initial outburst of remonstrations, there was nothing left for Marko and thousands of *cuervos* to do other than turn around and head home empty-handed.

For the lucky 45,000 or so, eagerness and anxiety was all-consuming on the big day. Kick-off wasn't until 9.15pm, but the stands were filling up some four to five hours before kick-off. As darkness fell, so did the temperature. Even Buenos Aires is capable of single-digit temperatures during winter and a chilly breeze whistled through Bajo Flores. Thirty minutes before kick-off, a rudimentary stage was laid on the pitch and on came Colombian reggaeton singer J Balvin for the pre-match show.

Poor old Balvin was a beaten man before he could sing a note. It was still some three years before he became a global star, and predictably the San Lorenzo fans had little interest in watching a relative unknown just minutes before the game of their lives. Some local cumbia may have done the trick – like the legendary Los Palmeras show before fellow Santa Fe natives Colón played the 2019 Copa Sudamericana final – but reggaeton gets a mixed reception in Buenos Aires at the best of times. When the DJ fired up the first track, Balvin was immediately drowned out by the *popular*, who doubled down on their pre-match singing throughout the ten-minute show.

Kick-off time in the UK was 1.15am. The pre-match wait seemed to go on forever. It was August, so Charlton's season was only just whirring into life and results were not yet life-or-death. As such, all of my football-based emotional energy had been poured into San Lorenzo's final. I longed to be in Buenos Aires to experience the tension and excitement, but I was also aware of how new on the scene I was. Barely a year had passed since I first started following the club. True *cuervos* had waited a lifetime for this. My pre-match nerves were for them as much as the 11 players in blue and red.

In a moment of neat symmetry, I sat down to watch the action from a hard kitchen chair, just as I had for the very first game of the cup run back in Buenos Aires. Club legend and boyhood fan Leandro *Pipi* Romagnoli led the teams out the tunnel. It was impossible not to be struck by the enormity of the occasion for everyone packed into the *cancha*. A community of supporters that had been through it all, from eviction and homelessness to relegation and ridicule, now had the chance to put history in its place. A club founded by local children and a priest in a small Buenos Aires *barrio* could reach the summit of South American football.

The *recibimiento* was worthy of the occasion. A brilliant white haze of ticker tape and streamers filled the air. Blue-and-red balloons flowed down the terraces, bobbing through the blur of tape. Ear-splitting fireworks lit the sky red. Flares released shocks of light then faded into soft glowing orbs on the dark terraces. As the smoke subsided, the cameras panned to a mosaic of blue-and-red panels across my old stomping ground of the Platea Sur. 'GLORIA' was spelt out by the giant letters.

'*Ciclóooon! Dale San Loreeee, queremos la coooopa!*' the fans screamed. 'Come on San Lore, we want the cup.' Like the mosaic, the message was simple. The volume and desperation of their voices came through my laptop speakers. Would it inspire or overawe the players limbering up underneath the floodlights?

In truth, the answer was closer to the latter. The authority and fluidity of San Lorenzo's performance in Asunción was entirely absent throughout the first half. On the other hand, Nacional showed the kind of fortitude that bigger clubs had not been able to muster at a hostile Nuevo Gasómetro during the tournament. The Paraguayans wrestled control of the occasion and looked more dangerous than their hosts.

But, thankfully, football matches don't always follow a logical pattern. Interrupting a period of Nacional dominance on 34 minutes, San Lorenzo swung in a corner which bounced around the box. As Cauteruccio hooked a hopeful ball over his head, a Nacional defender flung his arm aloft and blocked it with his hand. '*Mano, penal! Mano, penal! Penal para San Lorenzo!*' I could feel a tightness in my chest.

Gordo Ortigoza placed the ball on the spot. In the *barrio* as a boy, *Gordo* played in 'football for cash' penalty shoot-outs during the night to earn some money. Here, he mastered his trademark penalty: a long, straight run-up, before opening or closing the ankle in the last second to direct the ball to either corner. 'They never saved my penalties,' he claimed.

The technique worked on the streets and it worked in the final of the Copa Libertadores. Ortigoza calmly dispatched the biggest kick in the club's history like he was back in the *barrio* and the Nuevo Gasómetro celebrated like never before. The roar echoed through Bajo Flores, Boedo and beyond. Ecstasy and relief gushed from the terraces. Despite a nightmare start to the game, San Lorenzo were in front, leading 2-1 on aggregate.

Going into the second half, *El Ciclón* had a hand hovering over the trophy. But as the old chant goes, '*La Copa, La Copa, se mira y no se toca.*' – 'The cup, the cup, you look but you can't touch.' In another example of Argentina's rampant superstition, it's a mantra that's taken very seriously. Nobody is allowed to touch the trophy as they enter the pitch at the beginning of either half, unless they wish to curse the team's chances. Besides, there was still a job to be done in the Nuevo Gasómetro. Bauza's men had been burned in Asunción and weren't going to let it happen again.

The second half was scrappy and disjointed. San Lorenzo were still below par, but at least they had stemmed the tide. Nacional were no longer finding space in their half. They were no longer creating chances.

Time ticked down slowly. Back in the kitchen, my eyes darted up to the timer in the corner of the screen every time play slowed for even a second. It was agonising, but the final whistle was edging closer. Minute by minute. Second by second.

Injury time arrived and the five minutes were added. The crowd was on its feet, lost in a trance. The only thing to do with the unbearable nervous energy was to sing, shout, gesticulate and hope the referee would end it all. After one final throw-in from the home side, he obliged – and it had happened.

'*¡Señoras y señores!*' commentator Mariano Closs announced. '*San Lorenzo campeón de América! San Lorenzo campeón de la Libertadores!*'

* * *

Given the excitement I felt as a humble newcomer, it was hard to imagine what lifelong *cuervos* were going through after the final whistle. At the time, I had nobody to share the experience with, so I took to my San Lorenzo English Facebook page that I had set up a few months before. Tired and tipsy, with the time approaching 3.30am, I looked at *Pipi* Romagnoli giving his interview on the pitch. The San Lorenzo captain broke down in tears, and to my surprise I welled up with him.

'This club has come to represent a lot of different things from the most enjoyable period of my life,' I wrote from the page, 'and maybe that's why, slightly ridiculously, I've started crying here at home.'

For me, the emotion came from witnessing the intense happiness of others, contemplating my life-changing six months in Argentina, and also being quite pissed. But for those who had spent their lives with San Lorenzo, the moment was altogether more intense.

A year later, my *cuervo* friend Gonza showed me footage of the final whistle which he captured from his GoPro in the Platea Sur. Watching it back, I was struck by the relative lack of cheering and joy from those around him. Everybody appeared to have their hands over their face or their heads buried into the shoulder of a fellow fan. More audible than singing was the sound of crying. Everyone looked totally overwhelmed by what had happened.

'I think it's the most difficult feeling to explain in my life as a fan,' Gonza told me. 'I remember that I could only sit down and cry. It left me paralysed, I couldn't react. It was like a short-circuit of happiness. I wanted to explode with emotion, but my body simply froze. Clearly it was more happiness than my mind and body could process at that moment.'

He then encapsulated what makes being a football supporter so special. Increasingly, the message from society is that all of our pursuits must have some sort of value – be it financial, educational or for our health. Football stubbornly offers none of these things, but can give you the most intense emotional experiences of your life.

'The truly magical thing is that winning the Copa is something that serves absolutely no purpose to you,' he said. 'It makes no sense at all. That's magic.'

Chapter 17

The invasion of Marrakesh

<table>
<tr><td>Se acabaron las entradas</td><td>All the tickets have sold out</td></tr>
<tr><td>Los hoteles no dan más</td><td>There are no hotels left</td></tr>
<tr><td>Nos vinimos a Marruecos</td><td>We've all come to Morocco</td></tr>
<tr><td>Para ser campeón mundial</td><td>To be champions of the world</td></tr>
</table>

FOUR MONTHS after his short-circuit of happiness at the Copa Libertadores Final, Gonza was on the roof terrace of a small hotel in Marrakesh, Morocco, enjoying a pre-match drink with fellow *cuervos*. San Lorenzo had crossed the planet to play in the FIFA Club World Cup and he wasn't going to miss out. An hour or so into the *previa*, he found himself in an unexpected encounter. Four distinctly non-Latin men had arrived on the terrace. They were speaking English to each other and, inexplicably, they were all wearing San Lorenzo shirts.

I was one of those unlikely *cuervos*, joined by my brother Ben and our two friends Matt and Oli. This was how Gonza and I first met – the beginning of a friendship that lasts to this day.

'None of this makes sense!' he kept saying, as we explained our trip from London to North Africa to support San Lorenzo. He shook his head with a dazed smile as these blue-and-red-clad Brits recited short bursts of San Lorenzo songs, even though three of them could barely speak a word of Spanish. Luckily, Gonza spoke perfect English and introduced us to the other *cuervos* on the terrace, parading us around like an excited chaperone. The episode was typical of our memorable trip to Marrakesh, where San Lorenzo fans greeted us with a mixture of bewilderment and delight wherever we went.

Morocco was announced as the tournament's host nation just as I was leaving Buenos Aires. San Lorenzo had only just qualified for the semi-finals of the Libertadores, but it gave me the precious hope that I may be able to see them again without having to fly 12 hours back to Argentina. Flights from London to Marrakesh are accessible, so as soon as the team clinched the *Copa* in August I began scouring the pages of easyJet and Ryanair.

I can still remember the confused reaction of my Tottenham- and West Ham-supporting friends at work when I punched the air at my desk having just secured tickets for the tournament. The Club World Cup has never caught the imagination of northern European fans. On the other side of the world though, it's a very different story. Since the days of the Intercontinental Cup in the 1960s, South American clubs have relished the chance to take on European giants and compete for the chance to call themselves 'world champions'. Indeed, a key motivation for the creators of the Copa Libertadores was to produce a team to take on the winners of the European Cup. The Club World Cup, in whatever guise, remains a highly significant event on South America's football calendar.

Undoubtedly, issues beyond the pitch have contributed to their eagerness to get one over on teams from the so-called 'Old Continent'. From Europe's dark colonial legacy in the region to the Falklands/Malvinas War of 1982, there are painful chapters which still linger in the South American psyche, particularly among older generations. Younger people may be more sympathetic to Western culture, but of the many Latino migrants I have met in Europe, nearly all have experienced some form of discrimination during their time in the continent.

On the pitch, an uneasy relationship between the regions was apparent from the very first editions of the World Cup. Many European nations, including England, refused to travel to Uruguay and participate in the inaugural competition in 1930. France did enter, but found themselves in an on-pitch brawl with Argentina during a controversial group-stage match. Mounted police had to enter the pitch to break up the skirmish. In 1954, near-constant fighting between Brazil and Hungary saw their World Cup clash in Switzerland nicknamed the 'Battle of Berne', while Chile's brutal contest with Italy in 1962 became known as the 'Battle of Santiago'.

If Conmebol and UEFA thought the Intercontinental Cup – played between the winners of the Libertadores and the European Cup – would offer a more sportsmanlike and peaceful contest, they were badly mistaken. By the end of its first decade, violence was already a habitual feature, and, just like those early World Cup meetings, finals were being remembered as 'battles' instead of matches. The brutality of Racing versus Celtic in 1967 was infamous, culminating in the 'Battle of Montevideo' play-off decider, where six red cards were brandished in a 1-0 win for the Argentinians.

In the following two Intercontinental Cup finals, double Libertadores champions Estudiantes meted out even dirtier tactics to Manchester United and AC Milan. In the latter tie, Milan's Néstor Combin was carried off the pitch on a stretcher with his kit soaked in blood. If that wasn't enough, the Argentine-born striker was bundled into a car after the game and imprisoned by local police on account of a draft-dodging accusation. Only an intervention from Argentina President Juan Carlos Onganía ensured he could board the plane back to Milan the following afternoon. Onganía described the game as a 'lamentable spectacle which breached the most basic sporting ethics' and ordered that Estudiantes' worst offenders were sent to jail. Three players spent 30 days behind bars.

Despite the ugly circumstances of their finals, Estudiantes and Racing continue to celebrate the Intercontinental triumphs with great pride. One of the first things I noticed when visiting Racing's impressive old stadium in Avellaneda – named after Juan Domingo Perón but commonly known as *El Cilindro* due to its distinctive cylindrical shape – was the huge 'CAMPEÓN DEL MUNDO 1967' lettering emblazoned the hoardings of the upper tier.

As the Intercontinental Cup became the ultimate source of glory for South American clubs, the Europeans wondered whether it was worth the bother and the bloodshed. European Cup winners began to withdraw from the competition during the 1970s and its reputation never fully recovered in the continent – especially in countries like England.

Indeed, when our group left Gatwick Airport for Marrakesh on a cold December morning in 2014, nobody in the departure lounge would have guessed we were travelling for a football tournament that might culminate in a final against Real Madrid. But just outside Buenos Aires, Ezeiza International Airport was bedlam. San Lorenzo fans turned up in their thousands to send the team off with drums, flags and flares, while those lucky enough to travel began their 9,000km journey to Morocco.

Earlier in the year, Argentina had defaulted on a US$29bn debt to the International Monetary Fund. The population was once again suffering hardship from the nation's economic woes. But neither a lack of funds nor the outbreak of ebola in Africa were going to stop San Lorenzo fans with a Club World Cup dream. Desperate to make the trip of a lifetime, some *cuervos* signed up to travel packages which would take three whole years to pay off in instalments.

Given the marathon journey and difficult circumstances, I told my brother and friends that as many as 3,000 fans would probably travel. But I had underestimated the *cuervo* community. In a monumental pilgrimage from Buenos Aires to Marrakesh, the final number of travelling supporters was estimated to be a staggering 12,000.

* * *

'*Ya vaaan a veeer, la fiesta de San Lorenzo en Marrakesh!*' The chant drifted through the souk. 'And now you'll see the San Lorenzo party in Marrakesh!'

The day after we arrived, some 48 hours before the semi-final with Auckland City, San Lorenzo fans began to appear on almost every bustling street of the city. It was the most incongruous cultural crossover I have ever seen. The narrow alleys were already flooded with slaloming motorbikes, performing monkeys and waiters pulling you inside for their tagine. Now, packs of disorientated Argentines were entering the mix, clinging on to their yerba mate and thermal flasks amid the chaos.

I have never been to a World Cup, but I imagine it is this collision of cultures which makes a host city such fun during the tournament. But in Marrakesh, there were no fan parks to contain the hordes and many locals were unaware that the cup was even being played in their city. The environment made for an organic and disorderly meeting of worlds, which was entertaining to observe as we sipped Maghrebi mint tea at street-side cafés. From language and religion to culture and customs, there is little shared ground between your typical Argentine and Moroccan. Apart from football, that is.

The trite concept of 'football uniting the people' evokes the kind of nauseating speech you might hear from Gianni Infantino at a FIFA sportswashing jamboree, but the game's very real power to bond strangers was on full display in the Jemaa el-Fnaa central square. The night before San

Lorenzo's match against Auckland, the touring *cuervos* congregated in the square for a *banderazo* – a noisy gathering to inspire the team before a big match. La Gloriosa was out in force and their songs echoed between the buildings.

The Moroccans were in raptures. Old women smiled and clapped from the side, young men tried to sing along and were enthusiastically welcomed into the mob of *cuervos*. Entire stretches of the square were now cloaked in *trapos*, with fans hanging from the top of buildings and bouncing around the plaza below. It must have felt like an invasion for the locals, but there was nothing but goodwill from both sides.

After the *banderazo*, we found a bar that served alcohol – which isn't always easy in Marrakesh. A large group of Argentines next to us began to sing San Lorenzo songs and the volume rose steadily. Unlike those in the square, the smartly dressed bar staff looked a little irritated and gestured for them to keep the noise down. With a blissful light-headedness caused by lager and shisha, I briefly became part of the problem and joined in with a couple of the songs.

When we struck up conversation with the *cuervos* and told them about our trip, the familiar reaction of surprise and joy followed. 'You came here for San Lorenzo?!' Soon, the table was calling for me to start the next song and our corner of the bar fell quiet. Two of them had their phones out, ready to film the *cuervo inglés*.

Having mixed with very few San Lorenzo fans in my first year of following the club, I was only too happy to be their performing monkey – much like the poor creatures performing tricks in the street. I wasn't thrown any Moroccan dirham for my efforts, but I did receive an item of clothing. An excited *cuervo* removed the San Lorenzo hoodie he was wearing and demanded that I keep it. 'I'd give you a shirt but this is all I have!' he said, almost apologising.

As I looked at my gift surrounded by the group, I suddenly felt quite touched. On the front of the hoodie was an outline of the Viejo Gasómetro in Boedo, with a Gloriosa lyric printed underneath. '*Te juro que no voy a parar hasta volver a Boedo.*' – 'I swear I will not stop until we return to Boedo.'

* * *

The semi-final against Auckland City was a bizarre contest. San Lorenzo treated it as a practice match for the probable final against Real Madrid, ready to sit deep and defend against Cristiano Ronaldo, Karim Benzema and Gareth Bale at the weekend. But their opponents were an amateur club of part-time players. Auckland City had qualified for the tournament by beating a team from Tahiti in the final of the Oceania Champions League in front of just 3,000 people. This was not a serious outfit, yet San Lorenzo lined up, quite literally, as if they were playing the most successful team in the history of football.

It made for a tight and nervous game. *El Ciclón* went ahead but Auckland found a shock equaliser in the second half. Becoming increasingly nervous, my brother and I were exchanging the same 'here we go' eye-rolls of the countless doomed Charlton games we'd watched over the years. That horrible feeling of a match slipping from your grasp. If we were on edge, you can only wonder how the *cuervos* who'd dug into their life savings for the trip were beginning to feel. Thankfully, Mauro Matos saved the day in the first half of extra time with a crisp finish to put San Lorenzo back ahead. Relief rushed through our stand. It finished 2-1. Blushes were spared and a place in the final was secured. Just.

* * *

Three days later, Morocco's winter sun dazzled in the clear blue sky as we stepped on to the roof terrace in the souk. A friendly *cuervo* we'd met in a bar told us that he would be drinking here with friends before the final against Real Madrid. Sure enough, there was a hum of *castellano* and San

Lorenzo colours on display when we arrived, but we couldn't see our contact. In fact, we never saw him again, but the invitation was meant to be. It led us to Gonza, who spotted our arrival and hauled us into the *previa*.

Despite the language barrier, the strangers on the terrace treated us like lifelong friends. We were passed the famous Argentinian *viajero* – the large, cut-off plastic bottle filled with booze and shared within a group. Usually these serve the national favourite of fernet and coke, but this particular *viajero* was a free-for-all, containing beer, lashings of rum and who-knows-what-else.

A short, hyperactive *cuervo* called Gastón was pouring, sipping and circulating the *viajero* at an increasing pace. After a while, he removed his T-shirt and jeans and changed into a full San Lorenzo tracksuit, as if he was part of the matchday squad. It seemed to give him an extra lease of life as he climbed on to the edge of the terrace and serenaded the streets below with a selection of chants. He was desperately looking for a Spaniard to insult but, given Real Madrid's relatively small following for the tournament, no white-shirted fans were available below. His songs were therefore directed at the more modest enemy of Huracán – with a touch of Boca thrown in for good measure.

'We took on Huracán and they all ran,' he sang, 'now we'll go after Boca 'cause they're pussies!' At that moment, somebody's glass smashed and shattered on to the tiled floor, which, for some reason, launched the whole terrace into a raucous rendition of the chorus that followed.

'Una gitana hermosa tiró las cartas, me dijo que San Lorenzo va a ser campeón,' we sang. 'A beautiful gypsy laid down her cards, she told me San Lorenzo would be champions.' Chairs, tables and balustrades all had people clambering on top of them, as drinks sloshed and shirts swung above our heads.

The songs continued as our *previa* moved from the terrace to the busy main square of Jemaa el-Fnaa. *Cuervos* seemed to be everywhere, weaving between kebab grills and herb stalls, singing in groups and swarming towards the taxi rank on the perimeter. Gastón led our group's charge towards the taxis but they were quickly oversubscribed. Then he spotted the tuk-tuks.

You could hardly pick a more suitable matchday vehicle for an overexcited *hincha*. As we squeezed into the backwards-facing carriage behind the driver, Gastón clung on to the rear with most of his body hanging precariously off the edge. Just a small slip would have seen him tumble into motorway traffic, but Gastón was in his element, bouncing, singing and orchestrating traffic all the way to the ground.

As the Grande Stade de Marrakesh came into view, everything around it seemed to disappear. Like a football oasis in the desert, the rectangular arena stood alone on the vast barren planes of the city's outskirts. Despite being a modern build – it was opened in 2011 – the design was strikingly unique. The four two-tiered stands which met at each corner imitated the red sandstone colour of the buildings which give Marrakesh its nickname of 'The Red City'. Wide, clay-like pillars lined the exterior, while towering, rectangular floodlights on each corner added to the distinctive look.

When we scrambled out of the tuk-tuk to walk the final stretch to the stadium, you could tell that the San Lorenzo contingent had swelled by a few thousand fans since the semi-final. The locals, meanwhile, were thrilled to have Real Madrid in town and had hoovered up all the remaining tickets. With around 12,000 *cuervos* and 3,000 *madridistas* in attendance, the Moroccans filled two-thirds of the ground – and the vast majority were rooting for the European champions.

More specifically, they were rooting for Cristiano Ronaldo. Even in countries deprived of star names, I've always found the idolisation of individual players slightly childish and off-putting. So I wasn't a huge fan of the giant Ronaldo-themed flag unfurled by the Moroccans around ten minutes before kick-off. I hoped someone in blue-and-red could leave a few heavy challenges on the Portuguese when the action began – much like Charlton's Radostin Kishishev at The Valley in 2003.

The flag got a few whistles from the San Lorenzo side of the stadium, but the focus was on our own *recibimiento*. Years of dreaming and days of travel had all come down to this match. *El Ciclón* had arrived at the pinnacle of club football and the travelling fans were going to give everything they had in the stands, no matter what the players could realistically achieve on the pitch. The *hinchada* seemed to inhabit their space more boisterously than the Auckland match. It was busier, louder and somehow messier, much more like the terraces in Bajo Flores.

Bags of ticker tape were passed around, along with blue-and-red inflatables. For us, the pressing challenge was maintaining our balance and a view of the pitch rather than blowing up balloons. Brits aren't used to battling for space in the bedlam of a *popular*. As Gonza, Gastón and the rest of the Argentines discovered gaps or perched on railings, we found ourselves packed tightly into the end of a row. Four of us stood across less than two seats' worth of room, with *tirantes* pulled over our heads and shoulders. It wasn't comfortable, but it was impressive how the Argentines had transformed a modern arena with FIFA-organised ticketing into just another *cancha*. A heaving mass of bodies in a blue-and-red den.

As soon as the captains Juan Mercier and Iker Casillas appeared from the tunnel, we were consumed in a tornado of confetti and balloons. The PA system blasted out the FIFA anthem, forcing the San Lorenzo fans to strain every last vocal cord to make their racket heard.

On and off the pitch, the 90 minutes panned out as expected. The *cuervos* gave a masterclass in *aguante*, but it was never going to put Carlo Ancelotti's Champions League winners off their stride. As 'Gordo' Ortigoza and co. chased shadows, endless passes were exchanged between the polished Madrid players in their pristine white kits. A free header for Sergio Ramos gave them a first-half lead, before a weak shot from Gareth Bale squirmed past Torrico in the second half to finish the contest.

Just as the fans' ecstasy of scoring against Auckland City had taken me aback, the depression that briefly engulfed our end after Bale's goal surprised me too. What did everyone expect? I supposed that it was another sign of what the tournament meant to people. Gonza was crestfallen. He may be a rational thinker on football, but the fantasy of seeing San Lorenzo crowned *campeón del mundo* led him to believe they had a chance, however small, of beating an imperious Real Madrid side. Having lost star men Ángel Correa and Nacho Piatti since the Copa Libertadores triumph, Bauza's weakened side never had a prayer. The gap between South America and Europe was already wide enough.

After five or ten minutes of processing the impending defeat, the *hinchada* clicked back into gear with renewed energy, determined to leave their mark on the big stage. The reaction of Casillas at full time suggested they had done so. According to San Lorenzo's right-back Julio Buffarini, Casillas approached him at full time and gestured up to the 12,000 *cuervos*, who were still singing their hearts out. 'Are they like this every game?!,' he asked.

The Moroccans outside the ground were similarly impressed. Mistaking me for an Argentine, a man offered his congratulations for the atmosphere San Lorenzo had created. It didn't feel like my compliment to take, so I explained that I was a foreign outsider – a mere observer – who'd only recently begun following the team.

But when another person repeated the same words of praise a few minutes later, I decided to accept it and smile along. I had now seen San Lorenzo play in three different stadiums across two different continents. I had entered the *hinchada* and made *cuervo* friends along the way. San Lorenzo was beginning to feel like 'us' rather than 'them'.

Chapter 18

Battle of the *barrios*

Ya sabemos que naciste vigilante	We know that you were born snitches
Ya sabemos que aguante no tenés	We know that you've got no balls
Y también sé	And I also know
Que las patas no te dan para correr	That you haven't got the legs to run
Cuando ves	When you see
Que se acerca la Gloriosa Butteler	The Gloriosa Butteler coming your way

WHEN I returned from Morocco, 2015 was approaching – and with it, a new season for San Lorenzo. Six months had passed since my Argentina stay, where I'd had the fortune of going to games in the Primera División and the Copa Libertadores. Following the team to the Club World Cup after coming back was a glorious, unexpected bonus. I suspected that an away trip to Africa would tide me over for the foreseeable future, and perhaps even offer closure to a period of supporting San Lorenzo in person.

But the effect was quite the opposite. It left me craving more – more games, more *previas*, more parties in the stands – and the new season was about to bring something I had not yet experienced: the *clásico* with Huracán. By January, I was plotting a return to Argentina. My head told me to save the money for visiting a place I had never been, but my heart was already on the plane in Buenos Aires.

Since returning to London, I had developed a habit of derailing conversations at the pub by harping on about Argentina and its football culture, so my friend 'Welsh Tom' (a name used here to distinguish him from another incoming Tom) was keen to see what all the fuss was about. I duly welcomed him on to my budget-conscious, *clásico*-focused holiday planning committee, which now numbered two.

Handily, our old friend Simon – who had carried on watching San Lorenzo since our time together in Buenos Aires – offered us to stay in his studio apartment. Yes, it was small. Yes, his new Argentine girlfriend had practically moved in. Yes, another friend of ours – 'Kiwi Tom' – had begun an indefinite period sleeping on a lilo on his balcony. But two more people could apparently be accommodated somewhere on the floor, and that was good enough for us.

When the fixtures were released, Huracán's visit to the Nuevo Gasómetro was scheduled for March. A holiday request was quickly submitted at work and our flights to Buenos Aires were booked. I remember being so excited that I shut myself in the office toilets so I could punch the air and celebrate without anyone seeing me. It was easier that way. Explaining the Club World Cup-based holiday to colleagues had been tiresome for all parties. Nobody needed to hear about the Huracán *clásico* by the coffee machine.

* * *

Derbies, or *clásicos*, have been fundamental to shaping football culture across the world. The club identities that give the game its richness and colour are constructed not only by a sense of who the club is, but also who it isn't. Clubs need rivals.

If Argentinian football is famous for anything, it's the rivalries. The *Superclásico* between Boca and River is firmly embedded in the collective consciousness of football fans across the world but, thanks to social media and the globalisation of the game, there is an increasing awareness other *clásicos* like Rosario Central versus Newell's Old Boys and Racing Club versus Independiente. These two rivalries may determine who is the king of the city – be it Rosario or Avellaneda – but the broader evolution of Argentinian *clásicos* owes more to the localised disputes between small neighbourhoods, separated by nothing more than a street. Without *barrios*, there are no *clásicos*.

In Europe, the divides within cities long pre-dated the birth of football and contributed to the growth of derbies when the sport became popular. Society imprinted itself on football. But in many ways, Argentina was the opposite. When football arrived, the republic was young and the cities were only just beginning to develop as urban centres. The lower classes' infatuation with the game meant local teams and their *clásicos* began to shape *barrios*, rather than the other way round. Football imprinted itself on society.

'Football, as a practice and trend among young people from working-class sectors, pre-dated the appearance of *barrios* in Buenos Aires,' affirms the sociologist Julio Frydenberg, in *Society, City and Football in Buenos Aires*. The values of the sport 'spread through the communities thanks to these young people, who quickly learned the meanings of rivalry, enemies, and fan culture'.

Frydenberg argues that 'neighbourhood-based identities were built upon pre-existing football traditions', adding that club founders considered themselves the 'true and only representatives' of the *barrio* who must 'defend the honour of their area'.

This heavily localised sense of identity and rivalry does not exist in many other South American countries. Whenever I am in Colombia, for example, I notice that far more hostility is directed at teams from other cities than local rivals. I was stunned when a Deportivo Independiente Medellín fan told me that he'd much rather DIM beat a team from Bogotá or Cali than Medellín rivals Atlético Nacional. He even said he was happy when Nacional won the Copa Libertadores in 2016.

My football fan instincts made me recoil inside, but his argument stayed with me. How could he be angry when the city he adored was basking in glory? Medellín's informal economy boomed when the final came to town and he cashed in by burning CDs of Nacional songs and selling them to drivers as they waited in traffic jams. When Nacional won, members of his own family celebrated in the street and the city's feel-good factor lingered for weeks. He said he would rather the fans who weren't part of his life – like followers of Millonarios and Santa Fe in 'cold and unfriendly' Bogotá – were on the losing side than his fellow *paisas*.

It was difficult to argue with the logic. Given the tangible differences in culture and values that often exist between people from different regions, longer-distance rivalries theoretically make more sense than local disputes with people who are generally more like you. Why was I conditioned to hate thy neighbour? Why did growing up surrounded by Crystal Palace fans turn me against their club, rather than lead me to view them sympathetically? It didn't make sense, but I couldn't shake how I felt.

Fortunately for me, Argentine fans are fully entrenched in the tribalist spirit of wanting the worst for your neighbours. In fact, they are probably its greatest exponents. It is often said that defeat for your *clásico* rival is just as sweet, if not sweeter, than victory for your own team.

San Lorenzo versus Huracán may not be Argentina's most high-profile derby, but it is perhaps the most traditional. In a nation where *clásicos* owe so much to the history and culture of *barrios*, San Lorenzo and Huracán is known as *el clásico de barrio más grande del mundo* – 'the biggest neighbourhood derby in the world' – and *el clásico porteño* – 'the Buenos Aires derby'. It's Boedo versus Parque Patricios; two working-class neighbourhoods of industry, tango and football, side by side and forever at odds. Just a dozen blocks separate the site of the Viejo Gasómetro from the central park in Parque Patricios which gives the *barrio* its name.

Given the close proximity, you would expect a loose 'border' in terms of fans crossing into each other's territory. Surely people wear San Lorenzo shirts in Parque Patricios and vice-versa? I came to learn that is not the case. One day, when picking up a retro San Lorenzo shirt from a shop between the two *barrio*s, I slipped the top over my T-shirt to save carrying it around. The shop owner looked alarmed. 'That's a bad idea, take it off,' he said. I was far too close to Huracán territory to take such a risk, he explained, handing me a bag to hide the colours.

But the short distance between the clubs has its advantages too. As we chatted about the *clásico* over coffee, Gallego, the former member of La Butteler, fondly remembered the days of travelling to Huracán away on foot. 'There were a thousand of us!' he said, recalling the marches from one *barrio* to another with a nostalgic smile. 'We collected the tickets in the afternoon and all walked to the game together. There was always some trouble on the way but when the group is that big there's not much other people can do.'

Without the travelling army, Parque Patricios is a no-go area for the likes of Gallego. It may only be a mile and a half from his home, but the risk of walking through enemy territory was too great – whether or not he was wearing San Lorenzo colours, he said. In the relatively small *barrio* communities, faces are remembered.

* * *

When it comes to claiming superiority over your *clásico* rival in Argentina, there are three key weapons at your disposal. The first two – the trophy count and the *historial* – draw on cold, hard football facts. The third – *cargadas* – is all about evoking myths and legends of the past to insult your rival, whether or not it has anything to do with football.

Citing the trophy count is a self-explanatory attack, but is deployed in a particularly fastidious manner. Whenever a trophy is won, it is added to the entire history of your club's titles, from obscure local trophies in the 1900s to one-off Supercopas (equivalent to the Community Shield) in the modern day. If the tally is outstripping your rivals, that number will be celebrated loudly and visibly.

In a surreal pre-match parade some years ago, I remember watching Boca Juniors captain Fernando Gago carry a giant star around the pitch with the number 66 on it. A drone was circling above him, dangling another star with 66 in the air. All around the stadium, you could not escape the 66 and the stars. With River trailing Boca by a handful of trophies at the time, you sensed the grandiose display was for their old rivals watching at home more than those who were actually in the Bombonera.

The *historial* also pays close attention to numbers by carefully counting the head-to-head record between two rival clubs. If you have won more *clásicos* than your rival, you become the aforementioned *papá* (father), and they your *hijo* (son). Unlike the trophy counts, which often have questionable value due to stars collected in the amateur era, I do admire how the Argentinian game keeps track of the *historial*. All head-to-head records – not just those with the local rival – are cited before two teams meet, bringing some welcome historical context to a fixture. During my time as a San Lorenzo fan, the club has always been within two or three games of Racing in the *historial*, which adds significance and edge to a game that has taken place repeatedly for over 100 years. In the endless cycle of football, the *historial* adds meaning.

It can also throw up interesting quirks, such as San Lorenzo being the only club in Argentina to lead their *historial* over Boca. *El Xeneize* may have more trophies than San Lorenzo, but they remain their *hijos* and are constantly reminded of the fact. Each time they enter the field at the

Nuevo Gasómetro, you can expect to hear the same warm greeting from the home end: *'Hola qué tal Boca, cómo te va? Bostero hijo de puta, te saluda tu papá!'* – 'Hello Boca, how's it going? *Bostero* son of a bitch, your dad is saying hello!'

In that chant, the *historial* is being used as a *cargada*, or insult. But *cargadas* often call upon off-field matters – *bostero* being one such example. La Bombonera was once famous for the bad smells around the ground due to the proximity of a factory which used horse manure, or *bosta*, to make bricks. This gave birth to the *bostero* insult, but it has since been reclaimed by Boca fans who now use the name with pride.

Cargadas are most useful for teams who cannot compete on trophies or head-to-head records. Huracán, for example, must find a way of claiming the upper hand against San Lorenzo, a club with nine more trophies and a lead of nearly 40 matches in the *historial* – the biggest gap between any derby rivals in Argentina.

And so, San Lorenzo losing the Viejo Gasómetro and no longer playing in Boedo is a source of endless *cargadas* for *El Globo*. When *El Ciclón* visit the impressive, art deco-inspired Estadio Tomás Adolfo Ducó, the whole stadium enters a jumping frenzy with the gleeful chant, 'You have to jump, you have to jump, because they're never returning to Boedo.' Another popular *cargada* is recalling the day that Huracán's *barra brava* stole the prize San Lorenzo flags from La Butteler. Scraping the barrel, perhaps, but when your players don't help you in the *clásico* debates, you need to get creative.

That isn't to say that *cuervos* have been above such pettiness in the past. In 1972, San Lorenzo gave their supporters a precious *cargada* by winning the league title one game before an away game at Huracán, meaning they could enjoy a victory lap with the trophy – a highly symbolic act in Argentina – in Parque Patricios. Huracán rescued some pride by winning the match 3-0, but the images of San

Lorenzo's players celebrating in the faces of their great rival instantly became part of *clásico porteño* folklore.

The following season, Huracán had the chance of cancelling out their humiliation within a year. The famous team of César Luis Menotti (who won the World Cup as Argentina manager in 1978) was closing in on the league title and the fixture list suggested their lap of honour was likely to be away at San Lorenzo. Desperate to avoid the eventuality, groups of *cuervos* threw bottles on to the pitch during a match with Boca to try and receive a stadium ban and get the fixture out of Boedo.

It nearly worked. The AFA ordered San Lorenzo to play its next home fixtures at Atlanta's ground, but the ban ended earlier than expected and the Gasómetro was reopened the week after Huracán clinched the title. *El Globo* were all set for sweet payback in Boedo, but the *cuervos* had another trick up their sleeve. Just days before the game, a group of supporters broke into the Gasómetro overnight, dug up the turf and even hid the goalposts. The pitch was unplayable and the AFA moved the match to Vélez Sarsfield.

San Lorenzo won 1-0 in the Estadio José Amalfitani but, far more importantly, Huracán could not perform the *vuelta olímpica* in front of the *cuervos* in Boedo. *El Globo* have not won a league title since and San Lorenzo fans proudly claim that no club ever performed the victory lap after facing them at the Viejo Gasómetro.

* * *

As we walked through the blue-and-red-splashed streets of Boedo before the long-awaited *clásico* of March 2015, the warm air crackled with anticipation. Huracán's four-year stint down in *La B* had given *cuervos* and *quemeros* (Huracán fans) plenty of time to work up a renewed appetite for the derby. The wait was finally over.

We had arrived in Buenos Aires two days earlier and the night before the game had been a full-blooded reintroduction to the city's bars and *boliches* – or nightclubs. It was good to be back. To restore energy, we devoured pizzas in the Ugi's chain on Avenida La Plata. For the incredibly cheap prices, you had to accept a toppings menu of either 'plain' or 'onion', and what can best be described as an austere dining environment. When I got up from my hard steel chair to collect the oregano, the shaker pinged out of my hand before I could sit back down. A thick metal chain was connecting it to the counter. Nobody was going to steal Ugi's oregano.

As we made our way from Boedo to Bajo Flores, Gonza was busy fashioning a *viajero* of fernet and coke, using his lighter to melt the plastic and smoothen the corners of the sawn-off bottle. It was the first time we'd reunited since Marrakesh, and being the only Argentine in a group of nationalities spanning England, Scotland, Wales, France and New Zealand, Gonza took it upon himself to add some *porteño* features to the *previa*.

Despite the absence of Huracán fans, the essence of the *clásico porteño* was still present on the streets. Front doors were opening up and down Boedo, with children, parents and even grandparents stepping out in blue-and-red stripes. While Argentina's ban on visiting supporters is a tragedy, I did wonder how many of these families would be happily strolling to the game if Huracán fans were around. There was no sense of nervousness or tension in the air, just excitement and celebration.

Seven years earlier, on one of *El Globo*'s last visits to San Lorenzo, the atmosphere was very different. At the same stage of the day, Gallego from La Butteler was carrying a wounded fan to the basketball courts of the club in Bajo Flores. Pandemonium had broken out after a clash between the *barras* escalated to a shoot-out, and a Huracán fan lost his life.

This year, the only attacks on *quemeros* were verbal. '*Qué te pasa quemero, todavía seguís esperando …*' sang the fans leaning out of bus windows, revelling in their rivals'

40-year trophy drought. 'What's up, *quemero*, you're still waiting …' The song is clear about where the blame lies for Huracán's years of failure, 'The years go by, as do players and even directors, but they don't realise, the fans are the real problem.'

The lack of away support did not relax the security measures around the ground and we must have passed at least three rows of riot police before we arrived at the turnstiles. I would be in the *popular* for only the second time, along with the rest of our group. We had all signed up to be club members the day before, gaining us access to the carnival behind the goal.

By the time we arrived at the front of the stand, only 20 minutes were left before kick-off. Many had grabbed their spot on the terrace two or three hours ago – as is so often the way in Argentina – so the *popular* was now a tightly packed, intimidating wall of 20,000 people looming above us. There seemed to be no way in, but Gonza ducked low and burrowed his way through some bodies. We followed him to a tiny patch of terrace space close to the *barra*.

Just as the sun dipped behind the terrace at the far end, the players entered the pitch. Rather than cheering on those in blue and red, the *recibimiento* song was aimed squarely at the visiting players and their small delegation of officials contained in the away stand.

'*Cada vez te falta menos, al Bajo vas a venir, cada vez te falta menos para morir.*' – 'Your time is running out, down to Bajo Flores you come, your time is running out before you're dead.'

When the crowd jumped, you had no choice but to jump with them. Stand still and a shoulder barge would send you toppling. I could not believe how much the concrete steps were moving below us. If you jumped out of sync with the masses, the floor juddered you off balance like a mistimed landing on a trampoline. I wondered if my mind had exaggerated the feeling under foot, but a year later the *popular* was temporarily closed to repair serious structural damage, including large cracks in the concrete. I hadn't imagined those shaking steps.

It was a baptism of fire for the two Toms in our group who were both experiencing their first match in Argentina. Kiwi Tom was briefly carried away in an *avalancha*. Welsh Tom clung on to an overhead *tirante* for dear life. He admitted after the game that he had a genuine fear that the terrace was going to give way beneath him. The *tirante* was his lifeline in the event of a collapse.

The first 15 minutes in the *popular* were so chaotic and exhilarating that I had barely noticed what was happening on the pitch. When I came up for air amid the bedlam, I saw Huracán's Patricio Torranzo approaching San Lorenzo's box at the far end and curling a beautiful strike into the corner for 1-0. The volume rose around us – the *hinchas* knew they needed to step up. Luckily, one of them was on the pitch.

Some 20 minutes later, boyhood *cuervo* and club legend Leandro *Pipi* Romagnoli was lurking on the edge of the area. Showing a burst of pace that belied his 34 years, *Pipi* collected a knock-down and raced into the box. As a defender approached, he dropped his shoulder and surged past him, before angling a perfect finish into the bottom corner just metres in front of us.

My feet left the ground as an *avalancha* rushed us forwards. The density of bodies kept me upright as the sweaty, red-faced *cuervos* celebrated with wild euphoria. I have never known a first-half equaliser to feel so much like a last-minute winner. Out of sight on the other side of the *trapo*-covered fencing, *Pipi* grabbed fistfuls of his shirt and manically kissed the San Lorenzo badge. The pent-up passion of four years without a *clásico* was fizzing through the stands and across the pitch.

After the equaliser, there was only ever going to be one winner. Time had run out for the *quemeros*, as they had been warned. San Lorenzo took the lead before the break and made it 3-1 after half-time, leaving nearly half an hour for the fans to revel in the demise of their old neighbours before the full-time whistle.

Few songs were sung as enthusiastically as '*Llegó la banda de Huracán*'. Packed with metaphors about the meagre support and relegation of San Lorenzo's 'son', it became the soundtrack to our two-week holiday in Argentina. I remember trying to teach the Toms the first verse:

> *Llegó la banda de Huracán*
> *Mirenlos que pocos son*
> *Vienen en un Fiat 600*
> *Y en un ciclomotor*
> *La justicia los condena*
> *Esto no se aguanta más*
> *San Lorenzo pierde un hijo*
> *Y la patria potestad*
> *Se fue a La B, se fue al descenso*

> Here come the Huracán fans
> Look how few they've brought
> They've arrived in a Fiat 600
> And on a moped
> The law has condemned them
> This can't go on anymore
> San Lorenzo has lost a son
> And the parental rights
> Down to *La B*, down they went

* * *

The following morning, we debriefed over coffee and *medialuna* ('half-moon') croissants in Palermo. Dappled sunlight covered the table as we flicked through the sports daily, *Olé*, while tourists and the city's upper classes wandered past.

We were a world away from Bajo Flores and it was difficult to imagine many of the passersby spending an afternoon in the *cancha*. Perhaps a nice *platea* seat at River Plate for some, but certainly not the *popular* at San Lorenzo. My legs and joints ached as if I had played 90 minutes of football the previous day, not watched from the stands. *El aguante* of supporting your team can take its toll.

Even in Argentina, where analysis of big games is always thorough, *Olé*'s coverage of the *clásico porteño* was almost comically extensive. Page after page after page (we counted 16) was dedicated to the game, with match reports, opinion pieces, player ratings and interviews covering every inch of San Lorenzo's fairly routine – and expected – 3-1 win.

But the reporting became more surreal when we noticed a small article at the very end of the coverage. A mere footnote, taking up less than a third of a page, was news that a San Lorenzo fan had fallen to his death from the back of the *popular* during the game. Worse still, he had somehow collided with another fan on the way down. We had been within metres of the fall and, like nearly everyone in the stadium, were none the wiser.

Pablo Giménez, a 24-year-old *cuervo*, had climbed on to a railing at the top of the stand and lost his balance. He plummeted 50 metres to where 33-year-old Esteban Otero was leaving the bathroom with his son in an otherwise empty concourse. The chances of the collision which compounded the tragic fall must have been less than one in a million. It was later confirmed that, while his son had survived, Otero was paralysed in all four limbs and consigned to a wheelchair. He passed away ten years later.

Our minds boggled as we read the brief report. Though some details had yet to emerge, this would surely have been the game's headline story if we were back home. How could such a horrific accident and the death of a fan come after 16 pages of trivial reaction to the match? Why wasn't this all over the news channels, too?

It seemed to speak of a national mindset which accepts that football and death can go hand in hand. Even without away fans and the fighting that killed hundreds of supporters over the years, the idea of someone dying at the football in Argentina still wasn't *that* shocking to people. Just like every game, the packed *popular,* with its avalanches and trembling concrete, did not have a single steward or police officer present during the *clásico.* When people grow used to seeing terraces sold beyond their capacity, free of security and full of feral support, you can understand why disaster is almost expected.

There is no doubt that the freedom fans have in the all-standing *popular* terraces of Argentina adds to the matchday experience. They are colourful, exuberant and virtually self-policed by supporters. Usually, they manage this effectively. On more than one occasion I have seen fans quickly circle around an injured or fainting supporter, summon paramedics on the other side of the fence and help transport them to safety. Behind the goal at San Lorenzo, you have the feeling that people are looking out for each other, and I hope the terraces remain broadly free of fastidious policing, which tends to bring conflict more than peace in Argentina.

However, it's hard not to think that the bar on basic safety provisions has to be raised. Nobody in the stands should be able to dangle from a sheer drop, 50 metres above a concrete floor. And nobody should lose their mobility, and ultimately their life, from walking along a stadium concourse with their son.

Chapter 19

Taking on the establishment

Vos sos así, vos sos gallina	It's how you are, you're a gallina
Junto con Boca	Together with Boca
Son la mierda de Argentina	You're the scum of Argentina
Yo soy así, nací en Boedo	I'm like this, born in Boedo
Si no lo sigo a San Lorenzo yo me muero	I'll die if I don't follow San Lorenzo

A WEEK after the Huracán match, I decided I would return to live in Buenos Aires. During our holiday, Welsh Tom and I had travelled to Iguazu to see the spectacular waterfalls straddling the border between Argentina and Brazil, where I was struck by an unlikely epiphany. We may have been standing on a UNESCO World Heritage site taking in a true wonder of the natural world, but I was still thinking about San Lorenzo and the *cancha*.

I took it as a sign. Despite my decent job and enjoyable life in London, I seemed to have unfinished business in Argentina. I wanted to progress from intermediate to fluent Spanish and discover more of Buenos Aires. But above all, I wanted more experiences with San Lorenzo – to go every other week as a *socio*.

I told Tom I would move back the following January and spend 2016 in Argentina. We'd only had 90 minutes of fitful sleep between a night out in Palermo and our flight to Iguazu that morning, so neither of us had the energy for a deep analysis of the idea. 'Sounds good,' he said. And that was pretty much that. A few months later, I had quit another job in London and booked another flight to Buenos Aires.

As 2015 came to a close, I pored over the fixture list for the upcoming season, eager to see what matches I could attend in Bajo Flores and beyond. The stadium ban on away fans was still disappointingly in place, but home-end 'infiltration' and cup competitions at neutral venues would allow me to see San Lorenzo in undiscovered *canchas*.

One such competition was the Torneo de Verano – the 'Summer Tournament' friendlies. Played in the country's biggest holiday destination – the seaside city of Mar del Plata – the tournament grouped *clásico* rivals together in mini competitions and allowed all fans to attend. The result was thousands of supporters heading to the coast each summer to enjoy almighty *previas* on the beach and pack out the 35,000-capacity Estadio José María Minella. With fervent crowds and pride at stake, the tournament staged the least friendly friendlies you could ever wish to see. To my delight, San Lorenzo would play Huracán in Mar del Plata just a few days after I landed in Argentina.

The 2016 Summer Tournament was proving faithful to its feisty reputation. In the Boca v River *Superclásico*, five players were sent off. In the *Clásico Platense* between Estudiantes v Gimnasia, the second half was delayed for ten minutes because Gimnasia fans unfurled a series of *trapos* they had stolen from their rivals, sparking outrage in the stands. In the second half, Estudiantes defender Álvaro *Palito* Pereira knocked an opponent unconscious with a flying tackle to the head and was sent off. Two more red cards followed in injury time when the match was abandoned due to a mass brawl. Whatever purpose these friendlies were meant to serve, gently easing players and fans into the new season was clearly not one of them.

With San Lorenzo's meeting Huracán on Saturday, we began the five-hour car journey to the coast on Friday evening. Gonza was driver and DJ, with myself, Simon and our French pal Clement sharing yerba mates as passengers. 'I'm going to give you all an education,' Gonza announced as he connected his phone to the car speaker. The humid city disappeared behind us, giving way to the endless flat planes of the Pampas.

Hours of Argentinian *rock nacional* followed: Soda Stereo, Divididos, Babasónicos. Then came punk, as Gonza explained the story of 'Ya No Sos Igual' by 2 Minutos. 'It's about a guy from Lanús who was always part of the gang – drinking, going out, fighting at the *cancha* every Sunday – but then he became a policeman and now everyone hates him. They have "a bullet waiting for him",' he said with a chuckle.

When Gonza cranked up the volume for the ska-infused songs of Los Fabulosos Cadillacs and Los Autenticos Decadentes, Clement switched the yerba mate for a bottle of cheap Malbec. From that point, our first night in the city known as *La Feliz* ('The Happy One') became something of a blur, until we emerged from a beachside *boliche* into the bright morning sun at six or seven in the morning. Grizzled *barra*-looking types in San Lorenzo jackets were already wandering the streets of Mar del Plata and I suddenly remembered why we were there. It was matchday – the first of the year – and it was time to get some sleep.

Given San Lorenzo's performance that evening, we probably should have stayed on the beach. Huracán ran out 3-1 winners, with *El Ciclón* picking up a late red card for good measure. Despite the worryingly loose performance under new coach Pablo Guede, who was trying to fill the literally and metaphorically large shoes of the departed Bigfoot Bauza – experiencing a *clásico* with two *hinchadas* was a treat.

The back-and-forth of chants was frenetic throughout. Insult followed by counter-insult. Instant jeers for any quiet moments at the opposite side of the ground. '*Ay, ay, ay, no tengas miedo, podés cantar!*' – 'Don't be scared, you're allowed to sing!' The Huracán end erupted into a full *fiesta* during the second half as they realised they would have bragging rights on the beach the next day, but the travelling *cuervos* were going to enjoy their night in Mar del Plata regardless. The drums of the *hinchada* rolled on and the scent of marijuana drifted through the warm evening air.

* * *

After the warm-up on the coast, it was time for competitive action and it wasn't hard to choose the fixtures I was most excited about. In my first few months back in Argentina, San Lorenzo had dates with the overlords of Argentinian football – the detested duo of Boca Juniors and River Plate.

As a follower of any other team, the power of Boca and River at the top of the hierarchy makes them easy to dislike. Their political manoeuvres inside and outside the AFA mean fixture scheduling, media coverage and referee selection are routinely massaged in their favour. Fans of the two clubs claim this is all part of the game, while those below cry foul and call it corruption. If these tactics aren't enough to gain the upper hand, Boca and River use their financial might to pick off the league's best players in each transfer window. Even as a fellow *grande*, San Lorenzo lose countless fan favourites to the big two. Many of these players are quickly tossed aside and sold on again, but it doesn't matter to Boca and River as weakening a rival team is, in itself, a successful endeavour.

Although I was an outsider, I was quickly irked by the big two's overwhelming presence in Argentinian culture and society, and the way they flaunted their status. Despite openly trying to control all elements of the Argentinian game, both clubs like to cast themselves as humble and authentic representatives of their local *barrios* – particularly in the case of Boca. When I visited La Bombonera as an *infiltrado* for a San Lorenzo match in 2014, this illusion was somewhat shattered.

Much of La Boca feels like a tourist trap, with tango-dancing couples and Boca-branded tat trying to extract as much money as possible from the daily tide of visitors. La Bombonera lived up to its billing in terms of the impressively compact architecture and lively atmosphere, but the heavy tourist presence was hard to ignore. From groups of gringos bussed in from the hostels to wide-eyed Argentines filming every second of a rare visit to the ground, the sense of community felt weaker at Boca than every other *cancha* I have visited. Of course, sitting in the pricier seats at one of the world's most popular clubs meant some of these impressions were inevitable. But even in the *popular*, the *hinchada* now sells packaged *barra brava* experiences to tourists, reinforcing the sense that the Boca phenomenon is increasingly something to be consumed, rather than felt.

Boca and River may both be despised by *cuervos*, but their existence is important – whether they admit it or not. As football fans, and maybe as people in general, we like the notion of the powerful enemy above. It gives shape to our struggles and a way to make sense of the world. Big clubs are a bit like corporations or governments: symbols of control and targets for our frustration. If we can challenge them, or just land the occasional blow, our own lives might be better. And if we can't, their presence can at least explain our defeats. When those with power contribute to the things that go wrong, we don't have to contemplate our own failings quite so much.

For the vast majority of San Lorenzo supporters, Boca are regarded as the bigger rivals. They are closer, both geographically and in the *historial*, and being the only club in the country with a superior head-to-head record against them has become a key part of *cuervo* identity. Every match is crucial to maintaining dominance over the *hijo*. As the song goes, 'You were born our sons, you will die our sons.' Just a few weeks after Mar del Plata, Simon, Gonza and

I were back on the road to see if the so-called 'paternity' would be cemented. San Lorenzo faced their biggest match since Morocco: the final of the Supercopa against Boca at the Estadio Mario Kempes in Córdoba, Argentina's second-largest city.

In theory, the Supercopa is the same as the Community Shield in England, but with one vital difference: it matters. Argentinian football's insatiable appetite for trophies and finals makes the Supercopa hotly contested on the pitch – but also in the stands, with both sets of fans allowed to attend. Boca had won both the *campeonato* and the Copa Argentina in 2015, allowing San Lorenzo to qualify for the final via their second-placed finish in the league. Adding incentive for the winner was fast-track qualification to the Copa Sudamericana, but the chance to beat the *bosteros* in a final was the only motivation San Lorenzo needed.

We decided to break up the long journey into central Argentina with a two-day stop in Rosario. Simon and I never need an excuse to visit Rosario. An onward bus took us to Córdoba, where we were joined by Gonza and around 20,000 *cuervos*. But wherever and whenever you play Boca and River, you will be outnumbered. With millions of supporters up and down the country, Boca had no issue selling out the remainder of the 57,000-capacity Mario Kempes. And on our way to the stadium, we became uncomfortably aware of the *bostero* majority that awaited us inside.

A local bus had left us stranded on a motorway a few kilometres from the stadium. Minibuses of Boca fans saw our colours and shouted abuse across the road. When a taxi finally stopped for us, the driver turned out to be a *bostero*. Rather than take us to the San Lorenzo side of the ground, he proceeded to drive us directly into a boisterous mass of yellow and blue. Some of the fans saw our San Lorenzo colours through the car windows and started banging on the glass. I was glad that the doors were locked. We sat in nervous silence, edging our way towards the San Lorenzo side via streets of Boca *previas*. According to Gonza, the *bostero* taxi driver had deliberately taken us the wrong way to put us on edge, while elongating the journey to get a few extra pesos on the metre.

With more fans in the stadium, Boca already had a slight edge in Córdoba, but the real advantage was the squad itself. *El Xeneize* would line up with Carlos Tevez, fresh from a 29-goal season for Juventus, former Real Madrid lynchpin Fernando Gago, and the likes of Dani Osvaldo, who had recently had spells in the Premier League and Serie A. Such talent is rarely within San Lorenzo's reach. Indeed, Boca have a habit of poaching Boedo's best players.

San Lorenzo had a respectable team, but its main weapon against Boca was intangible: history. A so-called 'paternity' over their opposition. Could such things really make a difference in the carefully engineered world of modern football? As a superstitious Argentine, Gonza certainly thought so. The day before the match, he opened *Olé* over lunch in Córdoba and saw that Boca were switching to a cautious back five for the final. 'Look, they're shitting themselves!' he announced. 'They always shit themselves when they have to play us!'

For Gonza, the defensive formation itself wasn't the key factor at play. It was the fact that their manager, Rodolfo Arruabarrena, had clearly overthought his tactics in the face of their bogey side. He was changing the entire system to accommodate a weaker opponent. Boca's inferiority complex with San Lorenzo had got into his head and the *bosteros* were already in retreat. Gonza closed *Olé* with a confident grin. Tomorrow, the Supercopa would be going back to Boedo, he said.

But even Gonza at his most optimistic could not have foreseen the 90 minutes that unfolded under the floodlights of the grand Estadio Mario Kempes. Fernando Belluschi, whose wispy mullet and extravagant flicks seemed to belong in another era of Argentinian football, was the first to strike. After controlling a fizzing cross on the edge of the box, Belluschi swivelled to rifle a stupendous left-foot strike into the top corner, right in front of our baying end. Every now and then, football offers the fan a moment of sheer perfection. An occasion, a piece of brilliance and your view from the stand all come together in glorious harmony. This was one of those moments. Our sweaty shirts were ripped off in the celebrations.

In the second half, Pablo *Pitu* Barrientos rifled San Lorenzo's second into the roof of the net from close range, then bent a stunning 30-yard free kick into the top corner with less than ten minutes remaining; 3-0. It was almost too much to take in. With the clock ticking down, every San Lorenzo pass was greeted with a huge, mocking *'ooolé!'* Tevez was visibly irate. His forlorn attempts to win back the ball in front of 30,000 disconsolate *bosteros* made each pass sweeter than the last. It was the humiliation you dream of dishing out to your rivals.

To cap it all off, another *'olé'* pass in the 90th minute sent Nico Blandi clear on goal. He mercilessly lashed the ball into the net against his former club. San Lorenzo 4 Boca Juniors 0. Gonza collapsed into me and Simon, and down we went to the concrete, all three of us, locked in a delirious embrace.

'Que nacieron hijos nuestros, hijos nuestros moriraaan!' we bellowed at the Boca when we got back to our feet. 'You were born our sons, and our sons you will die!'

* * *

So what of River Plate? The pool of *cargadas* that San Lorenzo fans can use is far smaller than for their blue-and-yellow *hijo*. Only the most painful memories for *las gallinas* will serve the *cuervo* looking to get a rise, such as the last-16 Copa Libertadore tie between the teams in 2008. This wasn't just a miraculous nine-man comeback for San

Lorenzo on the pitch – it was the night of the 'appalling silence' in the Monumental.

In the first leg, San Lorenzo beat Diego Simeone's River 2-1 at the Nuevo Gasómetro. A young Radamel Falcao cancelled out San Lorenzo's lead in the first half, but a late penalty gave *El Ciclón* an aggregate lead to defend in Núñez. However, River levelled the tie after just 11 minutes of the second leg, before two San Lorenzo players were sent off either side of half-time.

With an hour gone, River scored again to lead 2-0 on the night and 3-2 on aggregate. San Lorenzo were down by one goal and two players. They were surely dead and buried. Simeone pumped his fists on the touchline.

But the night was far from over. Gonzalo Bergessio cracked home a shock equaliser ten minutes later to throw the tie back into the balance. Rather than play for penalties, the nine men of San Lorenzo – managed by River Plate legend Ramón Díaz and featuring another *gallina* hero in Andrés D'Alessandro – had the audacity to keep attacking. With 15 minutes left, they won a corner and Bergessio flicked a near-post header past the keeper in front of a disbelieving away end. 2-2. The comeback was complete and San Lorenzo won 4-3 on aggregate.

Gonza was there to witness it all. 'It was the best match of my life,' he tells me. 'The only one that truly made me lose it – I started wrecking things when we equalised. For no reason at all, I devolved into a caveman for half an hour.'

On the River side of the police cordon, things were a lot more subdued. Dumbfounded by San Lorenzo's fightback, the home sections fell quiet. So quiet that River midfielder Oscar Ahumada later described it as an '*un silencio atroz*' – 'an appalling silence' during an interview. The lack of support made it difficult to mount a response, he complained. The phrase instantly became folklore for San Lorenzo (and Boca) fans. It was the perfect insult for a fanbase they always accused of being cold and dispassionate, and it had been served up by their own player.

Eight years later, and some four months after Boca were put to the sword in Córdoba, I stood in a tightly packed *popular* for River's visit to the Nuevo Gasómetro. *Las gallinas* were still being reminded of that night in 2008.

'It was a special night, I will never forget it, the appalling silence of The Monumental,' went the chant before kick-off.

In a hostile Bajo Flores, the modern-day River played as if haunted by the ghosts of Simeone's chokers. San Lorenzo harassed, bullied and teased them. A back-heeled *caño*, or nutmeg, from Ezequiel Cerutti on River legend Leonardo Ponzio sent the crowd wild. Soon after, Blandi went close to scoring when a ball flashed across the goalmouth, causing me to release a premature, curtailed cry of '*gol?!*' It absolutely infuriated a *cuervo* next to us on the terraces.

'*Los goles no se gritan antes!*' He shouted at me. 'Never celebrate goals before they go in!' I'd broken a golden rule of the terraces. Now, at least partly, it was my fault Blandi hadn't scored. I had been a *mufa* at a vital moment.

Just as I began to worry about the apologies I owed if San Lorenzo failed to win, Blandi came to the rescue. Two sharp close-range finishes put the game beyond the *gallina*, who could only manage a late consolation goal. The 2-1 win was priceless for San Lorenzo, but playing River is not just about trying to win. It's about showing their fans – spoilt on success throughout their club's history – what real support looks like. As we made our way out of the ground at full time, an epic of La Gloriosa was being sung to the tune of '*Cuervo, Mi Buen Amigo*':

River, you're a *gallina*
You only turn up when you're winning or playing at home
Today San Lorenzo's going to show
All the feelings that football can give you

The joys and the heartbreaks
Of living for a passion
Something that River fans
Don't carry in their hearts

The song moved into its second verse. The *cuervos* were enjoying their sermon.

That's why I want to explain to you
That the beauty of football is the passion
If winning was all that mattered
You might as well watch it on TV
While you're installing seats
All over your standing section
You'll never be able to match
The San Lorenzo party

The final verse, which references the military junta's remodelling of River's stadium in the 1970s, is always sung with particular enthusiasm. The two clubs had very different experiences under the dictatorship, which, in the eyes of *cuervos*, cemented the contrasting identities of the two *grandes*. As we walked away from the *popular*, the words echoed off the towering concrete above us.

We are just so different
You're the *platea*, we're the *popular*
You can tell from the fans
That we just don't think in the same way
This *hinchada* built their own stadium
And it will never be forgotten
That the military government
Were the ones who built yours

Chapter 20

If we don't suffer, it doesn't count

Yo era cuervo desde que estaba en la cuna   I've been a *cuervo* since I was in the crib
A San Lorenzo cada vez lo quiero mas   And I love San Lorenzo more every day
De la mano de la hinchada de este año   This year, guided by the *hinchada*
El campeonato de Boedo no se va   The title will not leave Boedo

SODA STEREO are the best-selling Argentinian band of all time. I'm not a regular listener, but I have always been drawn to the lyrics written by Gustavo Cerati, their late frontman, who also had a successful solo career. The way he sings about Buenos Aires is particularly captivating. Though he references his home city in various songs, his most iconic tribute is the Soda Stereo track that gave the city its most famous and enduring nickname, *'En la Ciudad de la Furia'* – 'In the City of Fury'.

Because song lyrics are memorable, I liked using them as a means to study Spanish when I lived in Argentina. Of course, my main focus material were the songs I heard at the Nuevo Gasómetro, but I would supplement my learning by listening to *rock nacional* as I walked around Buenos Aires. There was so much to discover in this giant, atmospheric urban sprawl, and while it may be a cliche, songs like 'En La Ciudad de la Furia' were the perfect soundtrack to my morning, evening and night-time walks through its nocturnal streets. Hearing the first lines of the song always transport me back to the city.

Me verás volar
Por la ciudad de la furia
Donde nadie sabe de mí

You will see me fly
Through the city of fury
Where no one knows about me

'The City of Fury' is an apt descriptor for a place as intense and passionate as Buenos Aires, but the third line resonated almost as much – neatly capturing the liberating anonymity of walking through the city as an outsider. You could lose yourself and the world within its endless grid. At the same time, because Buenos Aires stayed alive all night, there was an ever-present sense of possibility as I walked those streets. Places were always open and, less constrained by diaries, people were always available. It was common to play football at 10pm. Have dinner at midnight. Go for a drink at 2am. A party at four. An after-party at 7. Though, to be honest, I never quite made the latter.

After a few weeks sleeping on Simon's floor, I moved into a flat in the central *barrio* of Almagro with Kiwi Tom and French Clement. I promptly fell in love with our new place. It had all the historic charm of my first apartment in Monserrat, but without the rats and the leaks. From the marble-tiled entrance and creaky lift with concertina doors, to the large open-plan living room full of wooden furniture, it had the rare combination of both space and character.

Almagro, meanwhile, quickly became my favourite *barrio* in Buenos Aires. Despite being so central, it had a surprisingly calm 'neighbourhood'-like feel, while still attracting plenty of locals to its bars and cafés. The cobbled streets near our flat played host to old-school, *porteño* institutions like El Banderín and El Boliche de Roberto, which buzzed with evening drinkers, while our location was almost equidistant from the nightlife of Palermo, the hum of downtown and, of course, the *cancha* of San Lorenzo.

Taking off like Cerati, I flew between all three. Sometimes alone and anonymous, but mainly with friends. Between my two spells living in the city, my old pal Simon had brought together a stellar rotating cast of five to ten friends from different countries. We met multiple times a week to share yerba mates in the park, fernets in a bar, or an hour on the football pitch. With representation from the UK, France, New Zealand, Colombia and Argentina, our five-a-side team was known as CALI: Club Atlético de Los Inmigrantes.

A popular spot for 'The Immigrants' was of course the *popular* at San Lorenzo. Despite the varying degrees of fandom in the group, nearly all of us were now club members. I enjoyed the rhythm of *socio* life. No longer did I have to plan for big fixtures, queue in the ticket office before games, or settle for a spot in the *platea*. With a *socio* card in my pocket and only £10 leaving my bank account each month, I could walk straight through the turnstiles of the *popular* and join the San Lorenzo party every other week.

Going to matches was now a routine rather than an event and it drew me even closer to the club. Attending the more mundane fixtures seemed to add to the overall experience. Who have we got this weekend? San Martín de San Juan. Sarmiento. Arsenal de Sarandí. It didn't matter, I was going. It also didn't matter how dull the games could be; the *hinchada* always delivered a rhythmic and energising few hours on the terrace. It was like going to a concert. There was simply no better way of spending the ample free time I had.

Our pre-match routine typically involved the 'austerity pizza' from Ugi's on Avenida La Plata, followed by a one-litre carton of red wine bought from a corner shop for the equivalent of 75p. That kind of value is very seductive when you're in your 20s. The Termidor *vino tinto* had a habit of inflicting half-time headaches, but it remained a fixture of our *previas* as we strolled down to Bajo Flores from Boedo. For the first half of the year, a San Lorenzo win to cap off the day seemed almost inevitable. They were flying high at the top of their 15-team mini-league in the Primera División. If they finished top, they would play a one-off final for the league title at El Monumental against the winner of the other group, which looked destined to be Lanús.

There is a well-coined phrase among San Lorenzo fans which was going against the grain of the season so far. *'Si no sufrimos, no vale.'* – 'If we don't suffer, it doesn't count.' But in the climax to the season, the club was faithful to its mantra. To qualify for the grand final, San Lorenzo needed to better the result of first-placed Godoy Cruz in the last round of fixtures. *El Tomba* travelled from Mendoza to San Juan to play the *Clásico de Cuyo* against San Martín. For San Lorenzo, it should have been a comfortable win at home to struggling Banfield, but they chose to suffer. Their fine form deserted them and it finished 1-1. But over in the mountainous Cuyo, Godoy Cruz seemed to be blowing it too, trailing 1-0 to San Martín in injury time. Our game in the Nuevo Gasómetro finished first and we prayed for confirmation of a Godoy Cruz defeat. Just one late goal would send them through to the final instead.

A few rows below us in the stands, someone was streaming the Godoy Cruz game on his phone. We joined the 20 or so people gathered together, craning our necks to catch a glimpse of the tiny screen. We couldn't see a thing, but sporadic commentary from those with a better view told us what we needed to know. Godoy Cruz had the ball. One minute of injury time left. Godoy Cruz attacked. Corner for Godoy Cruz. Cleared! Counterattack from San Martín. Chance for San Martín! *Gol de San Martín! Gol de San Martín!*

We erupted in our corner of the stand and the news quickly spread around the stadium. San Lorenzo had chosen the hard way but a place in the final was secured. I wondered if my move back to Argentina was going to be rewarded with a glorious league title.

* * *

A week later, a group of us were in Gonza's car. It was 6am and the sun was preparing to rise as we whizzed along the motorway. We'd been celebrating Clement's 30th birthday at one of the clubs on Buenos Aires's northern waterfront. Just as I was drifting into a fernet-induced sleep in the front seat, the giant Monumental stadium moved into view through the windscreen. In 12 hours we would be inside it, watching San Lorenzo and Lanús lock horns for the league. A little surge of adrenaline shook me back into life. '*Hoy ganamos, eh!*' Gonza shouted, banging his steering wheel. Like in Córdoba, he seemed confident of a win.

It proved to be another day of suffering. When we returned to Núñez later that Sunday, the rain was pouring down. The police had successfully separated the arrival of each *hinchada*, but it didn't stop some heavy-handed treatment outside the stadium. Lines of armed officers herded us into overcrowded queues. Riot shields buffeted us towards the turnstiles. Fathers shouted at the police to take it easy as they pulled their children close.

Recovering from the knocks and shoves of the Policia de la Ciudad, we took our place alongside 35,000 *cuervos* in the all-standing, upper-tier terrace of the Monumental. I looked across at the sea of blue-and-red balloons, their vibrancy contrasting against the leaden sky. There were no breaks in the cloud cover and no roof over our heads. The rain poured and so did the goals. For Lanús. By the second half, *El Granate* had raced into a 3-0 lead. The tiny *hinchas* at the other end of the stadium scuttled around their terrace, jumping up and down. *Trapos* blew in the wind and their maroon umbrellas bobbed under the rain.

In front of me, a young *cuervo* was clutching a small figure of Saint Expeditus – 'the patron saint of urgent causes'. Held aloft by the boy, Expeditus gazed out at the carnage unfolding below. The gaping holes in San Lorenzo's defence looked pretty urgent to me. As did the 3-0 scoreline with only 15 minutes left. But the tiny plastic saint looked on motionlessly as Lanús scored a fourth.

Resigned to defeat long ago, La Gloriosa was now revelling in the disaster. The rain, the 4-0 thrashing and the lost title combined to create a scene of perfect pathos.

'Since I was in the crib, I've carried you inside my heart,' went the melancholic song. 'You are my reason, nothing makes sense if there's a day without you.'

It had begun before Lanús scored their fourth and the volume rose as the final goal hit the back of the net.

'That's why I follow you in the good times and the bad. Win or lose, I don't care about that.'

Some 35,000 *cuervos* were now jumping in the rain and screaming the words, drowning out cheers from the Lanús end.

'Because despite everything that we've been through, my dear San Lorenzo, I'll always be at your side.'

* * *

The final at the Monumental made me realise that something had been missing from those first few months as a San Lorenzo *socio*. A distinct lack of suffering. Some disappointing losses had perversely drawn me closer to the club in the past, but being part of such a catastrophic loss on a big stage had raised the stakes.

The atmosphere in the San Lorenzo end at 4-0 down stayed with me. It was almost a celebration of defeat and suffering. By the end, each goal from Lanús and every fresh downpour unlocked another level of hysteria among the *cuervos*. Some people had told me before that this kind of behaviour was very 'San Lorenzo'. Losing their stadium and

The passion of *la popular*.

"Welcome to the Holy Land." Boedo, Buenos Aires.

'Pancho' with his
beloved *azulgrana*.

A *recibimiento* worthy of a final.

'We want players who feel the colours.'

Enter the *hinchada*.

Bobbing parasols –
a common sight in
the *cancha*.

The 'away *popular*' at the Nuevo Gasómetro.

Spectacular sunsets in Bajo Flores are a common occurrence.

The sun sets as San Lorenzo take on Boca Juniors.

'El abrazo de gol'
— the celebratory
post-goal hug.

Looking into *la popular* (left)
and looking out (right)

A *cuervo* watches on.

enduring a history of relative misfortune had turned the fans into connoisseurs of disappointment – so much so that each new disaster carried a strange, almost masochistic glory. I've heard similar things said about the long-suffering supporters of Racing, whose history holds far more lows than highs.

In his study of San Lorenzo and Boedo, anthropologist Matthew Hawkins argues that Argentinian football fans actively embrace suffering – not only through their team's fortunes, but through the physical experience of matchdays. He suggests that making long journeys to a match, being too hot or too cold, getting crushed in the crowd, harassed by police, and forced to stand for hours all constitute a kind of bodily sacrifice for the team. Enduring this discomfort becomes a source of pride. The fans' *aguante* – their stamina, their toughness – turns into a badge of honour.

Club football finally returned some three months after the league final. I couldn't say that I was actively seeking physical and mental suffering from the new season but, subconsciously, perhaps the rainy day at the Monumental inspired another level of commitment to the cause; to turn up whatever the day, whatever the weather and whether or not my friends were going. Curiously, when I did travel alone to games on dark, chilly nights, it gave me some of my best experiences as a *cuervo*.

One such occasion came in the Copa Argentina, which has become a fan favourite in the post-away ban era as games are played in neutral stadiums with both sets of fans present. San Lorenzo had reached the last 16 and Godoy Cruz were the adversaries once more. In their perpetual wisdom, the AFA decided that the 'neutral' venue should be the home of Lanús in the Buenos Aires province. The journey was 12km for San Lorenzo, while Godoy Cruz would travel 1,000km from Mendoza. *Cuervos* rightly see Boca and River as the privileged duo of Argentinian football, but they would do well to note the favours that still drip through for the other *cinco grandes*.

Our undertaking would not be a fraction of what the Mendocinas faced, but a 9.15pm kick-off in the deep, dark province was enough to deter everyone in my group. Locals advised me not to travel to somewhere like Lanús so late at night. The bus should also be avoided, especially as it would drop me off at the notorious Plaza Once at the end of the night. But I was desperate to experience another trip that resembled an away day, so embarked on the one-hour bus ride to the city where Diego Maradona was born.

Outside the stadium, there was a certain edge to the atmosphere. Perhaps it was the lack of street lamps and the near-pitch darkness. Maybe it was the sheer amount of *barra brava* patrolling the barbecue-lined street that led to the stadium. Inside, the 15,000 or so *cuervos* thought better than to goad the couple of hundred Godoy Cruz fans in the opposite end. The Estadio Ciudad de Lanús has a compact feel, so the empty spaces did not seem too big. I was stunned to find out the *cancha* can hold as many as 45,000 people, which goes to show the enormous capacity of Argentina's all-standing terraces. When two or three *hinchas* can cram into a spot usually reserved for a single seat, the numbers swell.

I was enjoying the solo experience of the *cancha*. Without the conversation, you find yourself being more observant of peripheral details on the pitch and particularly in the stands. I perched on a railing directly above the entrance to our terrace, giving me a perfect view of the *banda* entering below. I could see the cheeks of the trumpet players puffing and deflating, the Butteler branding on the rims of the bucket hats, the glazed eyes of young fans who had smoked their way through the *previa*.

It was the first time in Argentina that I'd watched from a stand with a roof, and the difference it made to the acoustics was striking. The travelling *cuervos* made an absolute din throughout the 90 minutes and the players responded with an electric, free-flowing performance. It ended 3-1 to San Lorenzo but the margin of victory could have been far greater.

Fernando Belluschi scored the third and was nothing short of masterful behind the forwards. Flitting between the lines and ghosting past challenges, he exhibited the traits of both the *potrero* street footballer and the graceful Argentine *enganche* – 'hooking' play between the midfield and attack. The next morning, *Olé* called for his return to the national squad.

As the papers were going to print, my long bus back to the city finally pulled into Plaza Once at 1am. People are right, Plaza Once isn't the sort of place you want to be at night, but I was on too much of a high from the *fiesta* in Lanús to worry. Instead of fleeing for Almagro in a taxi, I walked home slowly in the drizzle, feeling light and care-free. If they wanted, the plaza's pickpockets could take my old phone and the few pesos I had left in my Adidas joggers. They couldn't get their hands on La Gloriosa's songs ringing in my ears or Belluschi's nutmegs etched on to my mind.

* * *

The WhatsApp group had gone quiet again. Nobody seemed to fancy San Lorenzo's early round Copa Sudamericana match with Banfield. Whether it was the cold weather, the 7pm kick-off straight after work, or the usual anxiety about Bajo Flores at dark, my messages were going unanswered. Perhaps I was the problem? Either way, I decided to go alone. When the heavy front door of our apartment block clicked shut behind me, I was greeted by a sharp gust of wind. Suddenly, I was tempted to follow the advice of those who warned against a solo journey to Bajo Flores and settle back into our warm living room.

But I pressed on. Arriving at the *cancha* with just minutes to spare, the stands were as quiet as I had ever seen them. The unappetising conditions and the 2-0 defeat in the first leg meant only the hardcore had turned up. San

Lorenzo needed to start fast to overturn the deficit – and they certainly managed that: *El Ciclón* led 3-0 after just ten minutes. The comeback had been achieved in the blink of an eye. With enough space to run and jump around, the terrace was a jubilant frenzy. It didn't matter that I was standing alone; after the second and third goals I had hugged half the people in the *popular*.

'The moment of a goal can result in an immediate and dramatic embrace,' Matthew Hawkins comments in his behavioural analysis of the *cancha*. 'When experienced with strangers, it transforms the perception of the crowd as one defined by anonymity into a viscerally personal relationship, transgressing boundaries that are otherwise maintained in public.'

Normal social boundaries had indeed broken down in the *popular*. Wrapped in the arms of strangers, I was no longer the anonymous man in the City of Fury. I was with the tribe, feeling the visceral connection that Hawkins describes. In the aftermath of the third goal, an ecstatic *cuervo* climbed up the fencing that ran down the middle of the *popular* and I instinctively followed. Clinging on to the metal rails a metre or so apart, we gazed down on the bouncing *hinchada* below, swinging items of clothing in the air.

When Banfield pulled a goal back, Martín Cauteruccio responded by scoring a spectacular bicycle kick in front of our end; 4-1. Four explosions of joy and it wasn't even half-time.

The second period passed in calmer fashion, but with just two minutes left, Banfield won a penalty. *La concha de tu madre*. The country's favourite refrain echoed through the terrace. Score and Banfield were through on away goals. Some turned their back on the pitch. Others dropped to their haunches, heads buried in their hands.

But these are the moments that Sebastian Toricco lives for. The goalkeeper dived to his right and parried the penalty away. The save was celebrated like a goal. Within minutes, the referee blew the final whistle and San Lorenzo were in the next round. In the *popular*, we jumped up and down as one, the long *trapos* billowing dramatically in the wind above the *barra brava*. I was almost too exhausted to jump with them. But then I remembered: if you don't suffer, it doesn't count. I summoned the energy to bounce on the spot as we belted out our victory songs.

Chapter 21

The cup without a final

Yo soy del barrio de Boedo	I'm from the *barrio* of Boedo
Y siempre lo voy a seguir	And I'll follow you everywhere
Aunque juegues en cualquier cancha	No matter where you're playing
Contigo yo tengo que ir	With you I've got to be there

THE HISTORY of immigration in Latin America and the resulting ethnic mix never ceases to fascinate me. Every country in the region seems to host populations of a heritage you would never imagine.

Welsh communities in Argentina? A classic of the genre. Japanese in Peru? Absolutely. In fact, over 200,000 Peruvians are thought to have Japanese ancestry. The influence of *nikkei* cooking, which combines elements from both countries, helps to make Peruvian cuisine some of the best in the continent.

The most famous waves of European immigration to Argentina may have come from Italy and Spain, but the country also hosts around a quarter of a million people of Croatian descent. For their part, neighbour Brazil has the largest Lebanese diaspora in the entire world. The list goes on.

But what about Palestinians in Chile? Historic Arabic immigration is apparent across the continent, but I was surprised to discover that Chile had the largest Palestinian diaspora outside the Arab world, with an estimated 500,000

Chileans tracing their ancestry back to Palestine according to Turkish broadcaster TRT World. The community grew exponentially after the Nakba – the ethnic cleansing of Palestinian Arabs – in 1948, but it had already put down significant cultural roots in the country.

This included the formation of a football team – Club Deportivo Palestino – which emerged in Santiago in 1920. The club's stature is relatively modest compared to the city's leading lights of Colo-Colo, Universidad Católica and Universidad de Chile, but Palestino have picked up a respectable two league titles and three Copas de Chile in their history.

As I neared the end of my year living in Buenos Aires, San Lorenzo were still alive in the Copa Sudamericana and Palestino were their opponents in the quarter-finals. Seduced by the prospect of another away day and a relatively affordable airfare, I booked my flight to Santiago for the crucial second leg.

The Chilean capital was transitioning from spring to summer when the *cuervos* landed. It was prime time for the beautiful jacaranda trees which sent bright shocks of purple across the city's neat, well-maintained parks. The streets in the city centre were noticeably clean too. As I walked from my hostel to meet Eduardo, who was staying with a friend and would join me in the away end, it all felt a little more orderly than Buenos Aires.

The air was just as warm and thick as it had been in Argentina, and I was already perspiring underneath my San Lorenzo shirt. Palestino's relatively small and docile support meant we could enjoy a relaxed *previa* in town without fear of being attacked for wearing club colours. Having seen countless videos of Argentines being assaulted on their Copa Libertadores and Sudamericana away trips, it was a relief not to have that concern in Santiago. It could have been a different story had the opponents been one of the city's bigger, fiercer teams. The rivalry between Argentina and

Chile waxes and wanes, but in 2016 it was as tense as it had ever been.

The previous year, Chile made history by beating Argentina in the Copa América final on penalties, winning their first major trophy. Twelve months later, a special centenary Copa was played and Chile faced Argentina in the final once more. The Chileans had ended their hoodoo, now it was *La Albiceleste*'s moment. The perfect time to end a 23-year trophy drought. But history repeated itself. *¡Chile campeón!* Again, it had finished 0-0. Again, Chile had won on penalties.

The agonising sense of déjà vu against their traditionally inferior neighbour left Argentina traumatised. I was watching from a bar in Recoleta and can still hear those glasses smashing against the floor en masse when Chile scored their winning penalty. Simon and I allowed ourselves a smirk as the locals raged. Nobody was more distraught than Lionel Messi, who missed a penalty in the shoot-out and briefly entered international retirement after the game. Thankfully, that one didn't last long, but the finals had stoked – perhaps even created – a rivalry between the two nations.

I took my seat outside a bar and was soon joined by Eduardo and his friend Andy – an Argentine who had moved to Santiago. Andy was a River sympathiser but willing to be an honorary *cuervo* for the night. 'You're playing a Chilean team, I want you guys to win,' he said. His move to Chile was led by his job rather than his heart.

I had arrived in Santiago the day before and joined an eclectic mix of hostel dwellers for a night out. *Piscolas* – the brandy-like pisco spirit mixed with cola – were in perpetual circulation. I had only been able to face natural light and the outside world for a matter of hours before our *previa* and soon found myself explaining the 'hair of the dog' concept to Andy. We were interrupted by the waiter who asked for our orders and engaged in friendly chit-chat. I had now spent ten months in Argentina in addition to the six in 2014, and felt like I'd reached a certain level of fluency in Spanish. But I could barely understand a single word from the Chilean waiter. 'Don't worry,' said Eduardo, 'it's the craziest Spanish accent in the world. Even I only get like 50 per cent.'

Palestino's home ground, the Estadio Municipal La Cisterna, holds just 8,000 people, so the match was moved to a stadium more befitting the quarter-final of a major continental cup. Along with 1,500 travelling *cuervos*, we made our way to the 47,000-capacity home of Colo-Colo, also known as the Monumental.

As we passed Palestino fans in the streets, many were wearing patterned keffiyeh scarves. I had never seen them co-opted as football scarves before, and alongside the home colours reflecting the Palestinian flag, it gave the local support a distinctive and powerful visual identity. On the back of a replica shirt worn by one fan, the printed number 1 was shaped as a map of Palestine before Israel's creation. There is usually little fuss in Chile about the club's displays of Palestinian pride, but this particular shirt was banned from being worn in matches by the country's football federation in 2014.

San Lorenzo had won the first leg of the quarter-final 2-0, so a solid, professional display would surely be enough to book a place in the semi. The reassuring lead, balmy weather and beautiful mountainous landscape behind the Monumental set a pleasantly mild pre-match atmosphere.

As we approached the turnstiles, we could see that the Chilean police had not been swept up by the same mood. Batons were raised for their Argentine guests, with queues of *cuervos* intimidated and shoved despite their general compliance. The aggressive security only served to slow down the entrance of supporters, and as kick-off neared, hundreds of fans were in danger of missing the start of a match they had travelled nearly 1,000 miles to see.

Tempers were rising when I suddenly noticed a familiar face remonstrating with the police. To my shock, it was the San Lorenzo president, Matías Lammens, dressed in a scruffy T-shirt and jeans, right in the thick of the commotion. Every time he persuaded a policeman to lower his baton and step aside, he grabbed a few more fans and hauled them through, desperate to help them enter before kick-off. We had to admire his brave and proactive intervention. He could easily have been quaffing wine with suited officials in the hospitality boxes, but he was down in the thick of it with us. Lammens, himself a San Lorenzo fan, is now considered an enemy of the club. His administration left crippling debts and institutional chaos behind, somewhat marring the heroics we witnessed at the turnstiles.

We finally entered the away end some ten minutes after kick-off, but you could tell from the rhythm of the game that we hadn't missed much. San Lorenzo were sitting deep, ready to defend their 2-0 lead for the 90 minutes. The atmosphere in our stand was more akin to an away game in the UK, as we were relying purely on our voices to build the support. La Butteler was largely absent, and subsequently, so were the drums, trumpets and giant *trapos*. Perhaps Lammens had refused to pay for the *barras'* travel, as club executives often did for overseas away games.

I missed the presence of the band, but nobody around me seemed to care. You didn't need instruments to cheer on the team or insult a Chilean. *'Hay que saltar, hay que saltar, el que no salta, es un traidor!'* The entire away end jumped up and down for the chant. 'If they're not jumping, they're a traitor!' they claimed, referencing Chile's decision to support Britain rather than Argentina during the Falklands/ Malvinas War. The nations' rivalry doesn't just come from the football pitch.

I happily jumped along with my pack, but the rare moment of Anglo-Argentine kinship was short-lived. The chant was immediately followed with the old favourite, '*El que no salta, es un inglés!*' – 'If they're not jumping, they're English!' Eduardo and Andy were in fits of laughter and enjoyed telling everyone around us that I, the enemy within, was not allowed to jump.

An hour later, the mood was far more tense. Palestino had broken the deadlock with a superb free kick. It was 1-0 on the night, but still 2-1 to San Lorenzo on aggregate. Around 20,000 Palestino fans were spread across the shallow one-tier stands of the Monumental, and despite only half-filling the arena, they were making themselves heard – and seen. Moments after taking the lead, a giant Palestine flag was unfurled to cover nearly half of the *platea* to our right. I surreptitiously took an admiring photo and noticed a few other *cuervos* doing the same.

As time ticked down, Palestino launched an aerial bombardment on the San Lorenzo area, but almost every ball was met by the sizeable head of Fabricio Coloccini. The burly centre-back had returned to his beloved San Lorenzo during the winter and was having one of his best games since his arrival. One final flurry of Coloccini's curly locks cleared a dangerous Palestino cross and the final whistle was blown. San Lorenzo had qualified for the semi-finals and the players came over to salute their travelling army.

The next day, as my Buenos Aires-bound plane drifted over the snow-capped Andes mountains separating Santiago and Mendoza, I allowed myself to daydream about a Copa Sudamericana Final in another far-flung location. My hopes of seeing San Lorenzo lift a major trophy before I returned to the UK were still intact.

The full-time celebrations in Santiago would stay in the memory, but perhaps not as long as the powerful Palestinian symbols we had seen throughout the evening. The club's extremely visible commitment to their roots, nearly a century after they were founded, had taken me by surprise. I had expected a nod to the national colours and little more, but the club's community appeared to live and breathe their Palestinian identity.

From the keffiyeh scarves and the Gaza-based Bank of Palestine sponsor, to the flags, stickers and clothes shouting *'Palestina Libre'* – 'Free Palestine', everything to do with Club Deportivo Palestino felt a lot bigger than football. By reaching the latter stages of a major continental tournament, the team were achieving unprecedented things on the pitch, but it still felt secondary to the club's wider purpose. When the *telón* came down in the second half, it could have featured the club badge, the name of the *hinchada* or a message for the players, but they chose to unfurl the flag of the State of Palestine. In the face of such a cause, winning a football match was put into perspective.

* * *

It was sad to see the tournament lose a club like Palestino, but San Lorenzo were on a mission. A host of big clubs had now been knocked out, opening up the field for lesser lights such as Chapecoense of Brazil, who awaited San Lorenzo in the semi-finals.

As we took our place in the very back row of the *popular* for the first leg, you could feel a sense of confidence around the Nuevo Gasómetro and San Lorenzo took a 1-0 lead into half-time. But Chapecoense were determined not to leave Buenos Aires empty-handed. After all, they were playing the biggest match in their history. The club had only been founded in 1973 and had never won a national or international title. Desperate to make their mark and no doubt buoyed by beating fellow Argentinian *grande* Independiente in the last 16, the visitors asserted themselves in the second half and scored a deserved equaliser with half an hour left. It finished 1-1 and the Brazilians were well positioned to make a historic final.

When the second leg came around, I was lucky enough to be in Brazil, but not so lucky to be at the game. A group of us had booked a short trip to Rio de Janeiro and I thought better than suggesting a 1,000km detour to the state of Santa Catarina. From the beaches to the bars, Rio was full of distractions, but I could not get my mind off the crucial match taking place further south in Chapecó. We pitched up in a bar near Copacabana beach for the game, knowing San Lorenzo had to score. A 0-0 would take Chapecoense through to the final on away goals. *El Ciclón* controlled possession in Chapecó but lacked thrust, failing to carve out a clear-cut chance that might clinch the tie. That is, until the final 30 seconds of injury time.

San Lorenzo won a dangerous-looking free kick to the right of the Chapecoense box. The whole stadium was on its feet, knowing that the home side were in the final if they could just survive the set piece. Torrico left his goal to join the attack. The free kick was swung into the chaotic penalty area and the ball dropped to the feet of Marcos Angeleri on the edge of the six-yard box. This was the chance. He had little time to think, but a clean connection would surely be enough to beat the keeper and send San Lorenzo through. Angeleri struck it low, but the right foot of *Chape* stopper Danilo twitched just enough to deflect the ball clear. Somehow, it had stayed out. The referee blew for full time.

Nobody could possibly have imagined the consequences of that save. Had the ball been a few centimetres to the right of Danilo's foot, Chapecoense would not have been in the final against Atlético Nacional – and they would not have boarded LaMia Flight 2933 five days later, which crashed in Medellín. Of the 77 people on board, 71 were killed, including all but three of Chapecoense's players and staff.

I first got the news in a text from Gonza. It didn't seem real at first. You don't hear of plane crashes very often. How could that happen on the way to a major final? I felt queasy when the news apps on my phone confirmed the crash.

Shock and sadness kept returning in waves as the extent of the tragedy unfolded. It was hard to accept that so many people had perished because a plane didn't have enough fuel. Watching videos of the players getting ready for take-off ahead the match of their lives was stomach-churning. We had seen these young men in the flesh just three weeks earlier. I looked at the only photo I had taken from the first leg, which showed the 11 Chapeconese players lining up in their penalty box to defend a free kick. Only one person in the image – centre-back Hélio Hermito Zampier Neto – was still alive. Fellow survivors Alan Ruschel and Jakson Follmann were on the bench, out of shot.

It feels cruel and inappropriate to connect such a horrific accident to something that happened on a football pitch. But soon after, Marcos Angeleri spoke publicly about the tormenting consequences of his miss. 'When I heard about the accident, it was the first thing that came to mind. That missed opportunity,' he told Brazilian daily newspaper *Folha de S.Paulo*. 'I was upset in the dressing after the game because I'd had the chance to put our team in a final and give the fans something to celebrate. But what happened afterward goes so far beyond football. It's impossible not to think, "What if I had scored?"'

In football, we often say we are 'devastated' after a defeat. We allow the disappointment and pain to linger. I was guilty of moping after San Lorenzo's exit to Chapecoense. Having watched the team go so far in various competitions without the crowning glory, I felt like something had been snatched away from me. How trivial and self-indulgent those thoughts became. If ever there was a sequence of events to expose the emotions we tie to football and the absurdity of post-match despair, this was surely it. The highs and lows of football are part of what makes it so special, but when life itself is so fragile, defeats on the pitch do not deserve our mourning.

Atlético Nacional graciously awarded the final to their would-be opponents and Chapecoense were crowned winners of the 2016 Copa Sudamericana. A few days later, San Lorenzo entered the field for their away match at Olimpo wearing the green of *Chape* over their normal colours. The kits hadn't been bought for the tribute, but were the very shirts worn by the young Brazilian men in the semi-final – all but one playing their last game of football.

Chapter 22

The folklore fallacy

Buenas tardes bostero   Good afternoon *bostero*

Hace tiempo te estaba esperando   I've been waiting for you for a while

Buenas tardes bostero   Good afternoon *bostero*

Tu papá te está saludando   Your *papá* is saying hello

BETWEEN 2014 and 2016, I went to nearly 40 San Lorenzo matches. Over the next seven years it was down to just two. Moving back to London and the Covid-19 pandemic dramatically limited opportunities to return to Buenos Aires and the Nuevo Gasómetro. Since 2023, I have been trying to make up for lost time. Two trips and six more games have helped to satiate my appetite, but the call of the *cancha* always echoes in the background.

My desire to relive the glorious days on the terraces is charged by a powerful sense of nostalgia. Those 40-odd games, across ten cities and three different countries, came slap bang in the middle of my 20s. The only major concerns I had while living in Argentina were going out with friends and following San Lorenzo. It was a simple, carefree life. All bar one of my non-Argentine friends from Buenos Aires have since returned home, and all of them admit to daydreaming about the city in the halcyon days of the mid-2010s. Every trip back is a hit of the old drug, even if it's never quite the same. One friend aptly refers to Buenos Aires as 'Neverland'.

I may miss Argentina, but thanks to live streaming I don't miss many San Lorenzo games. The necessary channels are always ready on my laptop and phone, and have allowed me to watch San Lorenzo on buses, trains and planes, in the office, at the park, on a beach, in a nightclub, at a wedding, on a remote farm in Colombia, and many more places I have no doubt forgotten.

Social media, for all its ills, comes into its own for long-distance fandom. I can share pre-match nerves with the rest of the *cuervo* community, cheer with others as goals go in, and participate in the commiserations or celebrations after the game. I have a Cuervo Ingles account on X but rarely post opinions or analysis. I just use it to feel part of what's going on. After a win, I might post a photo of my laptop streaming the game, with an insightful caption like 'VAMOS' or 'GET IN'. Each time somebody drops a like, I feel like we've exchanged a little post-match hug or handshake in the *popular*.

Occasionally, our San Lorenzo *peña* (supporters' group) in London meets up for matches. Among them is my good *cuervo* friend Lucas, who has joined me on Charlton away trips all over England in a kind of football-based cultural exchange. One man's Bombonera is another man's Burton Albion. Lucas attends the annual meet-ups between San Lorenzo *peñas* across Europe and brought me back a T-shirt from one such event. On the back is a lyric from a terrace song written by Escuela de Tablones, which captures the feeling of the overseas *cuervo* and their club. '*Sé que no hay distancia que nos pueda separar,*' it reads. 'I know there's no distance that can separate us.'

In late 2023, nearly five years after my previous visit to the Nuevo Gasómetro, I returned for what is probably the most attractive fixture on the San Lorenzo calendar: Boca Juniors at home. Playing Boca doesn't require extra incentive, but the stakes were raised by San Lorenzo's hunt for a Copa Libertadores spot. It was a season of rare promise after seven years of steady decline for the club, which began soon after I left Argentina. Perhaps I was a lucky charm – the famous *cábala*? Maybe they needed me back in the *popular*?

I was only too happy to test the theory. Reuniting with Gonza on a balmy spring evening, I floated across Ciudad Deportiva on a cloud. The pre-match fernet and coke was like sipping water from an oasis in the desert. I didn't really care about the match, it was just a dream to be back.

This was the first time I had been to a San Lorenzo match with a video assistant referee and a spanner was about to enter the works. I loathe VAR deeply and was anxious that it would interfere with the pure and spontaneous Argentinian match experience that I had missed so much. My fears were realised. San Lorenzo cancelled out Boca's opener with 15 minutes remaining and attacked the goal in front of our baying terrace in search of a winner. When the clock hit 90 minutes, the 5ft 1in midfielder Nahuel *El Perrito* Barrios (the 'Little Dog') rifled a shot from the edge of the box into the roof of the net. The celebrations in the *popular* were as dramatic as I had ever witnessed and turned Gonza and me into a teary, euphoric mess.

Sometimes things are too good to be true. A full four minutes after the goal, the referee blew for an irrelevant, ultra-marginal offside in the build-up that not a single Boca player had appealed for. A five-year wait and a trip across the world had led to one of my greatest moments as a *cuervo*, but VAR had snatched it away.

Gonza and I left Bajo Flores debating whether we had truly experienced the Barrios goal. I felt as if we hadn't. It didn't exist now. 'But the ball went in and we went crazy,' Gonza argued. 'We celebrated for minutes – that all happened.' He was right. I had felt the ecstatic high and it lasted long enough to start sinking in. But the goal being ruled out did in some way alter reality and invalidate those emotions. VAR couldn't erase time and memory, but it could erase goals – and the afterglow of that indescribable joy that comes with them.

I was bruised by the VAR intervention, but it wasn't the only part of the day that left me feeling depressed. Like every *hinchada* in Argentina, San Lorenzo sing some politically incorrect and ugly songs. Over the previous years of going to games, these had only been heard fleetingly and were usually drowned out by La Gloriosa's more positive chants. But during the Boca game, a particularly offensive song had been chanted incessantly.

Also sung by River and Racing fans, the chant uses the trope that Boca's support includes a high number of 'lower-class' people of Bolivian or Paraguayan heritage (*Boliguayo* is often used as a catch-all xenophobic slur in Argentina). The chant says that the Bolivians from La Boca shit in the streets, clean themselves with their hands and take holidays at the dirty Riachuelo river. 'We've got to kill all the *bosteros*, mama,' it finishes.

La Boca is a traditionally poor area of Buenos Aires with a high amount of immigration. In the late 19th century and the first half of the 20th century, most of the city's immigrants came from European countries like Italy and Spain. In the second half of the century, those arriving from Latin American countries like Peru, Paraguay, and in particular Bolivia began to make up most of the immigrant population. The *barrio* of La Boca was historically stigmatised, known for the bad smells caused by the manure factory – key to its portrayal as a dirty and undesirable place. Some opposition players and fans still hold their nose as an insulting gesture when they enter La Bombonera. The history of the area and its immigrant population gave rise to classist and xenophobic chants, like the one sung on my return to the Nuevo Gasómetro.

Although Argentina's Bolivian-heritage population has grown significantly since the turn of the 21st century, pejoratively referring to Boca fans as *Bolivianos* has long been a depressing custom on the terraces. The Bolivian writer Edmundo Paz Soldán studied in Buenos Aires in the 1980s and fell in love with Boca – partly because of their talented Bolivian midfielder, Milton Melgar. In the literary blog El Boomeran, Soldán remembers taking his brother to watch the *Superclásico* at La Bombonera, thrilled to show him the colour and passion of Argentinian football. But his memories of what should have been a special day were forever tainted.

'The teams came out on to the pitch; I saw Melgar and felt moved,' he writes. 'Suddenly, the River supporters began chanting, *"Bolivianos, Bolivianos, Bolivianos!"* The reaction of the people around us struck me … For Boca fans, the worst insult someone could throw at them was *"Bolivianos"*. Luckily, my brother didn't understand what was happening; when he asked me why they were shouting *"Bolivianos"*, I told him – doing my best to hide my anger – that it was River's way of recognising Melgar's talent.'

Soldán's account is just one of the infinite examples of xenophobic chanting against Boca, but I find it particularly impactful. I have the privilege of not suffering or witnessing abuse related to my background, but every other part of Soldán's experience was familiar. I too had fallen for an Argentinian team as a foreigner and found a sense of belonging in the *cancha*. I too had taken my brother to games to show him this exciting new world, hoping he would enjoy it as much as me. The thought of standing on the terraces of the Nuevo Gasómetro and lying to him – to hide that San Lorenzo fans were disgusted at being seen as 'like us' – is heartbreaking.

Some *hinchas* stubbornly refuse to consider the wider social context of their chants on the terraces. They usually hide behind the fabled 'folklore' of the Argentinian game. According to this convenient doctrine, insulting opponents in all manner of ways has always existed within the walls of the *cancha*, and as a result, everyone is fair game and anything goes. The art of provocation matters more than the racist, classist or homophobic connotations of their language. If calling Boca fans 'Bolivian' winds them up, their job has been done.

I am not qualified to further the discussion around racism in Argentina and the debate is rarely constructive anyway. The same narratives – 'It's an inherently racist nation!' versus 'Racism has never existed here, we don't even have black people!' – go round in circles and neither tell an especially accurate story. Picking apart the complex realities that lie between those extremes would probably require a book of its own. But if you celebrate the creativity of Argentinian football songs and terrace culture, you have to acknowledge its uglier moments too.

After hearing the anti-Bolivian chants at San Lorenzo, I was keen to hear from someone close to the issue. Pablo Fernandez Rojas is a Bolivian writer and San Lorenzo fanatic who grew up in Villa 1-11-14. Tellingly, it took a great deal of searching online to find a *cuervo* with Pablo's kind of background and perspective. I would love to have met him in person on my visit to the 1-11-14 but, as mentioned in that chapter, I could not find anyone like him at the time. 'The fact that you already found it hard to find foreign San Lorenzo fans from the *villa* is a symptom in itself, no?' he proffered. Outside the broad church fanbases of the big two, it seems that football fandom and inclusivity do not go hand in hand in Argentina.

I asked Pablo how he feels when he hears the chants. 'The main feeling is one of defeat – a defeat tied to a fracture in the world. I'm ashamed of myself. Not because of my Bolivian identity, but because of how normalised this situation has become. I take for granted that San Lorenzo, the thing I love, carries a certain kind of misery. Being a San Lorenzo fan is part of my identity, and I understand that embracing that comes with a burden of xenophobia and a kind of Buenos Aires chauvinism. The fact that it no longer surprises me feels increasingly damaging. A song is just a song, but knowing that this is the world I live in ... sometimes it's crushing.'

Like any football fan in Argentina, Pablo values the famous *cargadas* exchanged between fans, but he despairs at the insults used by fellow *cuervos* when it comes to Boca. 'Mocking or belittling the opponent is a fundamental part of football. It's strange that San Lorenzo, the only club in Argentina with concrete grounds for claiming superiority over Boca, doesn't just rely on that fact to attack them, and instead does so from a racial or national perspective. It's something that cruelly reflects reality – San Lorenzo's reality, more than Boca's.'

* * *

Just eight months after the Boca match, the debate around Argentina and racism flared up on a global scale. Following the national team's Copa América Final victory against Colombia, Chelsea midfielder Enzo Fernández filmed himself singing the racist chant created by Argentina fans against the France squad. It adapts a controversial Nueva Chicago song (originally aimed at rivals Almirante Brown) to question the nationality of France's players with African heritage. A common defence in Argentina was that the song merely pointed out a concrete fact – some of the players *did* have parents born in African countries.

Rather than acknowledge Fernández's mistake (just as the player himself did), Argentina's vice-president Victoria Villarruel defended the song and tried to frame her response as an anti-colonialist stance.

'Argentina is a sovereign and free country. We have never had colonies or second-class citizens,' she wrote on social media, citing the ethnic mix of the population which built the country. 'No colonialist country is going to intimidate us over a football chant or for speaking truths others refuse to admit. Enough with the feigned outrage, hypocrites.'

The Afro-Argentine political scientist Federico Pita described Villarruel's response as cynical. 'Denying them [France's players] their citizenship is not a critique of a colonial empire's hypocrisy, but rather rubbing salt into the wounds of the victims of colonialism,' he wrote in daily newspaper *Página 12*. Questioning Villarruel's apparent concern for those who suffer discrimination, he added that she is 'part of a government that, through its public policies, manufactures second-class citizens by the millions' and 'hails the closure of INADI as a victory for freedom of expression'.

INADI was the National Institute Against Discrimination, Xenophobia and Racism in Argentina. Set up in 1995, it ran education programmes to raise awareness around all forms of discrimination and provided practical support to victims. Its free-to-call nationwide phone service received a record 12,087 inquiries in 2021. Javier Milei's government waged a war on the organisation and finally managed to close it in 2024.

Pita, who praised Fernández's quick and unequivocal apology, said understanding must improve among everyday Argentines to curb discriminatory chanting in football. France and Chelsea defender Wesley Fofana called Fernández's video 'uninhibited racism' when it surfaced, but later acknowledged that his team-mate 'did not understand when singing it'. Fofana added, 'I trust him, because I know him. I know Enzo. He is not racist ... We need to educate [people] about this because cultures are different. We don't have the same education, for good or bad. But we need to educate everybody if we don't want this to happen again.'

The education that the likes of Pita and Fofana call for was carried out by INADI programmes – not just in everyday life, but specifically in sport. The organisation set up the Commission on Discrimination in Sports and ran several football-specific campaigns with the AFA to crack down on prejudice in the game. By closing INADI down in the name of 'free speech', the Argentinian government has at best hampered progress, and at worst empowered discrimination.

Campaigners like Pita hope that the football community – with or without support from the government – can come together to tackle discrimination in the game. 'We want the AFA to take this as an opportunity to shift from a defensive posture to an offensive strategy against racism in Argentina,' Pita said after the Fernández scandal. 'Not through punishment or cancellation, but through action, repair, and prevention. Let's move from saying "No to racism" to saying "Yes to anti-racism". Let apologies be only the beginning.'

Whether an organisation as questionable as the AFA will be the specific instrument for change seems unlikely. But the power and influence of the football community can undoubtedly have a positive impact on society if harnessed in the right way. It wouldn't be the first time. During Covid, scores of Argentinian clubs allowed their premises to be used as vaccination centres. Others went the extra mile and opened soup kitchens too. In 2025, *barra brava* groups of all colours marched alongside pensioners who were protesting against the government's austerity policies. In the same month, clubs were raising vital funds for the victims of the floods which hit Bahia Blanca in the Buenos Aires province. And these are just examples from recent times.

'I believe everything in life has some kind of political, social, and emotional impact on the world – especially a passion like football,' said Pablo. 'As a force, it's far too powerful to be reduced to a business, or a vehicle for showing the worst parts of who we are. I want to believe that football is one of the best tools we have to change something.'

Chapter 23

The one not jumping
is an Englishman

Y ya lo ve	And now you see
Y ya lo ve	And now you see
El que no salta	The one not jumping
Es un inglés	Is an Englishman

IT WAS a Monday afternoon during the Buenos Aires spring of 2024. The previous day had been spent with Gonza, Eduardo and the Cuervos de San Martin for San Lorenzo's 1-0 win against Barracas Central. I was still on a high from the raucous minibus journey to the game – and the precious three points secured in Bajo Flores.

Having recently switched to working freelance, I had the freedom to enjoy a full month back in Buenos Aires. The Barracas game was one of four San Lorenzo fixtures in the diary, but with 18 other grounds in the city and many more in the province, I was keen to take in some previously unseen *canchas* too. Perhaps some lower league spots where San Lorenzo were unlikely to ever take me.

Letting this idea slip to Eduardo opened the floodgates. Using his deep knowledge of *ascenso* football, he began to fire all manner of teams, stadiums and fixtures over to me. I was trying to use the afternoon to get some work done, but my buzzing phone and the prospect of Monday night football had suddenly diverted my focus.

'Excursionistas. Playing tonight. Probably 4K fans there. In Belgrano – nice area.' My phone buzzed again. 'Deportivo Español. Also playing tonight. Primera C. Lots of history, but they are truly shit.' My phone buzzed once more. 'All Boys. Big game in Primera B. They're like a smaller Vélez. Probably 10K fans there.' This one had piqued my interest. 'They're playing a tiny club called Agropecuario. Nobody will mistake you for an *infiltrado*.'

Only Buenos Aires, the land of football, could offer so much choice on a Monday night. I opted for All Boys. On the journey from Caballito, my bus passed the Estadio Diego Armando Maradona of Argentinos Juniors – the club where Diego's career began. He made his debut here aged just 15 years old, pulling off an audacious nutmeg within minutes of entering as a substitute. He would go on to play 167 games for *El Bicho* – 'The Bug'. Murals of Diego are all over the surrounding streets, creating a kind of Maradona *barrio*. Twenty minutes later, I hopped off the bus in Floresta, the home of All Boys.

For a fairly nondescript part of the city, I was surprised by how busy the streets were on this humid Monday night. It felt like everyone had come out for All Boys. The club must lean heavily on its neighbours in Floresta to keep it going as local competition is fierce. Argentinos Juniors are just 20 blocks away – a historic club with a Copa Libertadores title. Twenty blocks the other way are Vélez Sarsfield: another Copa Libertadores winner. San Lorenzo, Nueva Chicago, Ferro Carril Oeste and Atlanta are all within 7km, and that's before you even consider that the continental behemoths River and Boca inhabit the same city.

But none of these teams felt relevant on the streets of Floresta. The All Boys club facilities were a hive of activity. Parents collected their children from sports practice and the gym was packed. Outside, fans sipped cans of beer in their black-and-white All Boys bucket hats. Behind them was the 20,000-capacity stadium, neatly enclosed within the residential grid of the *barrio*. The faint sound of drumming echoed from a nearby *previa*. It was the traditional, member-owned, Argentinian club in full swing. Perhaps a mini version of San Lorenzo's old social hub in Boedo that Adolfo Res and so many others had described to me.

A mural beside the gym paid homage to four All Boys *socios* who had been part of this club before they were 'disappeared by the military dictatorship', as the lettering read. It featured the club badge and pictures of the swimming pool and basketball court that would have been a part of their daily lives. Below the spray-painted pictures of 'Samuel, Susana, Carlos and Daniel' were the words 'AQUÍ FUERON FELICES'. 'They were happy here'.

It was time to enter the Estadio Islas Malvinas. References to the islands are everywhere in Argentinian football and there is another stadium with practically the same name in Mendoza (Estadio Malvinas Argentinas). I couldn't imagine a team playing at a 'Falklands Stadium' back home. The name of the ground offered a patriotic counterweight to the very English name of the club. In 1913, the founders had apparently wanted a name that represented *todos los muchachos* – 'all the boys' who became the first members. As the fashion of the time was to use English names, they adopted a literal translation as the name of their club, All Boys. These days, fans often shorten it to 'Albo'.

I found myself on a large all-standing terrace on the side of the pitch. As it filled up for kick-off, I could still hear the *banda* in the streets outside. The noise of the drums and trumpets worked its way around the block, with sporadic bursts of fireworks coming closer and closer. But the local *barra brava*, known as La Peste Blanca – 'The White Plague' – still hadn't arrived on the terraces when the match kicked off. An Albo fan next to me explained that the *barra* had fallen out with the club and weren't currently entering the stadium. They continued supporting from the street outside with all their songs and instruments, but without watching any of the actual game. Given how little attention most *barras* pay to the match up on the *paravalanchas*, I supposed it didn't make much difference.

But the White Plague members who did enjoy watching their team missed a great start. All Boys took the lead inside 30 seconds. Their muscular striker bustled into the box and crashed home a low drive. It was a goal scored through willpower and thrust – the sort of attributes that don't quite give you an edge at elite level, but are crucial in the early stages of a feisty Primera B tie in Buenos Aires. Bone-crunching tackles flew in all night. Players careered off the pitch and into the metal wiring below our stand. All Boys added a 20-yard *golazo* before half-time and a third late on. The win secured play-off qualification and Floresta enjoyed a Monday night carnival.

As the fans celebrated, I noticed an interesting lyric in one of their songs. '*Yo que nací en Floresta, en Floresta moriré,*' it began. 'I who was born in Floresta, in Floresta I will die.' Nothing remarkable so far. But then, '*Yo quiero ir a las Malvinas a matar un inglés.*' Did I hear that right? As the song got louder, I realised I wasn't mistaken. 'I want to go to the Malvinas to kill an Englishman.' The words were bellowed across the terraces.

Had I not spent so much time in Argentina over the previous ten years, I may have felt uneasy. There I was, alone on a terrace of the 'Malvinas Stadium', far from the tourist-friendly parts of Buenos Aires, surrounded by a baying mob expressing their desire to kill an Englishman. Outside the only exit available to me were a group of football hooligan-cum-local gangsters setting off fireworks. But I found the scene amusing. If anything, it added something to the evening.

To me, this kind of *cancha* bravado sums up what remains of anti-Englishness in Argentina. Patriotic football chants are now one of the only manifestations of a fading hostility.

They may be aggressive in both content and delivery, but they don't feel too different to the English terrace songs about 'getting your father's gun' and 'shooting the [insert team name here] scum' to the tune of 'Que Será, Será'.

Having attended dozens of matches across 18 different stadiums in Argentina, nobody has ever made me feel remotely unwelcome on the terraces. While I'm sure there are some nationalistic *barra* types you could rub up the wrong way as an Englishman, from my experience the locals are thrilled to have you in their *barrios* and their *canchas*. I had already enjoyed a couple of friendly chats in Floresta that night and was confident that none of these All Boys fans actually wanted to kill me.

In the 1980s, it would have been a lot more uncomfortable. Even before the Falklands/Malvinas War, Great Britain was an unpopular country in Argentina and viewed as an imperialist bully. Many were glad when the historically British institutions were nationalised under Juan Perón. When Margaret Thatcher's government sent troops to confront Argentina's military advance in 1982, its public mission was to defend British territory and a population who wanted to remain under its rule. But for Argentina, *los ingleses* were reviving their colonial legacy on a land they always saw as theirs; just 480km from Argentinian mainland and 12,700km from the UK. The two-month war claimed the lives of 649 Argentines and 255 Brits, as well as three Falkland Islanders. Hundreds more were wounded, and the mental scars were just as deep. The Argentinian government estimates that between 350 and 454 war veterans committed suicide in the following years.

'I believe it would have been impossible for an Englishman to remain in Argentina at the time,' legendary midfielder Ossie Ardiles told Jonathan Wilson in his seminal book, *Angels with Dirty Faces*. Ardiles, an Argentina international, was playing for Tottenham Hotspur when the war began. Of course, the conflict was a major event in Britain and generally united people across the political divide. But Ardiles described being an Argentine in London as only 'a minimal thing' at the time. He may have been reassured by a banner held up by Spurs fans at White Hart Lane, which read 'ARGENTINA CAN KEEP THE FALKLANDS, WE'LL KEEP OSSIE'.

In the end, they kept both. Ardiles stayed at Tottenham for a further six years and the Falklands remained under British rule following a military victory for Thatcher. During the intervening period, Argentina famously took revenge on the football pitch. How? 'A little with the head of Maradona and a little with the hand of God.' That was the verdict of Diego himself after the 2-1 win against England at the 1986 World Cup. His unforgettable handball had an unforgettable name.

'We, in some way, blamed the English players for everything that had happened [in the war], for everything the Argentine people had suffered,' Maradona later reflected in *Yo Soy El Diego*. 'I know it sounds crazy, absurd, but that really was how we felt. It was bigger than us: we were defending our flag, the boys who died, the survivors … It was like beating a country, not a football team. Even though we said before the match that football had nothing to do with the war, we knew that many Argentine boys had died over there, that they'd been killed like little birds.'

Within a decade of 'stealing the wallet of the English' – another quote from Diego about the Hand of God – and following it up with the 'goal of the century', as the Argentines call his extraordinary second goal in that quarter-final, Maradona seemed to have made his peace with the old enemy. In 1995 he accepted an invitation to speak at the prestigious Oxford Union debating society, where he stated that 'time heals all wounds'. With a stark blonde streak in his hair, Diego still had the look of a rebellious forward ready to pick your pocket, but he was widely praised for his gracious and thoughtful speech.

'It's been very emotional,' he said afterwards. 'It's not often a football player can face so many people so rich in culture and education.' The man who knocked England out of the World Cup, tore apart their old ideals of fair play, and claimed revenge for the Falklands, received a standing ovation on English soil.

* * *

Anti-English hostility has been blissfully absent since my very first day in Argentina, but the Falklands/Malvinas loom much larger than I ever expected. When I arrived in 2014, I studied the newspapers almost every day to try and understand more Spanish. Bizarrely, the islands seemed to be a near constant topic of discussion, with government officials regularly announcing 'progress' in their plans to redeem them. The Kirchner administration must have been going through a tough time, as pretending to have a fresh Malvinas strategy is a go-to government tactic to boost morale when the chips are down.

When I wasn't seeing the islands in the newspapers or on TV, they were appearing on graffiti, road signs, posters and people's clothing. Even grocery stores bore its name. Would the neighbours say to each other that they were 'popping to The Malvinas to pick up some carrots'?

On my last visit, I noticed a picture of the islands on the side of a bus, with the national slogan 'Las Malvinas Son Argentinas' – 'The Malvinas Are Argentine'. As drivers like to customise various parts of their *bondi* in Buenos Aires, I assumed these were just patriotic stickers added on a whim. But no, this was the law. 'All public passenger transportation vehicles of national origin are required to display in a visible and prominent place within their units the phrase "The Malvinas Islands are Argentine",' states the 2022 resolution from Argentina's Ministry of Transport.

But away from football chants, this obsession with the islands does not translate into ill-feeling towards their current rulers. Like me, none of my English friends have had any issues from Argentines on the subject. I wondered if my social circles had just been lucky, so I asked Gonza if he was surprised by our experiences.

'No, no, that's completely logical. Like me, 99 per cent of our population had nothing to do with that war. Everything the military dictatorship did at the time was political propaganda. So unless someone's a fanatic, actually fought in the war, or knows someone who did, nobody's ever going to say anything to you.'

Nevertheless, there have been occasions in the past where I have erred on the side of caution. Sometimes a quick risk assessment results in deploying 'the Irish card' – and overplaying the heritage I proudly get from my Irish grandmother. One such instance came at a rowdy cumbia party in 2016. The crowd was predominantly male and the air was thick with testosterone. Curiously, everyone looked like they were in a *barra brava*: long sports jackets, baseball caps and puffing cigarettes. Smoking inside clubs was still common at the time.

Before we left, I went to search for my coat, which had got lost in a pile of strangers' clothes. A tall, wide-shouldered man with a neck tattoo – perhaps a *barra brava capo* in the making – tapped me on the shoulder and asked what I was doing. When I nervously explained the situation of my elusive jacket, he noticed my foreign accent and asked me where I was from in a tone that was firmer than I'd have liked. I paused. '*Irlanda*' was my response. His stern face lit up and he pulled me in for a hug so tight it almost winded me. 'I'm glad you said this, man!' he said, switching to English for the first time and shouting in my ear over the music. 'Because England is a shit!' I laughed and nodded, hoping he wouldn't see the fear in my eyes or request some form of ID. 'Yes, England *is* a shit!' I repeated.

But for every damning verdict on my home nation, there are a hundred examples of gushing praise. Somewhat paradoxically, Argentina is full of Anglophiles. Football is unsurprisingly an area where this takes form, and the English Premier League is wildly popular. But they also admire the stadiums and tradition throughout the football pyramid and it's not uncommon for an Argentine to follow an English team. Middle-aged football fans seem to love Paul Gascoigne, who still gets mentioned a lot. I think they see some of Diego in both Gazza the player and Gazza the man.

But their Anglophilia comes through most strongly in the arts and literature – particularly music. They obsess over British bands. Taxi drivers always seem to listen to Aspen FM, which is dominated by the likes of Led Zeppelin, Pink Floyd, the Cure and the Smiths. The Rolling Stones are an institution and inspired an entire subculture known as *rolinga*. The *cuervos* in Escuela de Tablones adapt songs by the Beatles and Oasis into stadium chants. In his home *barrio* of Castelar, my friend Lucas is known as 'the Who' (pronounced '*Th'oo*') because of his intense love of the band. I once went to a Buenos Aires cinema for a 1am screening of an entire Arctic Monkeys gig that had taken place nine years earlier. Lesser bands who almost disappeared in the UK – like Travis or Keane – still sell out big venues in the country. I'd go as far as saying that Argentines are more passionate about British rock and indie than we are.

It is often said that the Argentine psyche is complex and contradictory. Their relationship with Britain – or 'England', as they tend to refer to the UK as a whole – is a good example.

Particularly among the lower-middle and working classes, fierce political rejection coexists with a deep cultural appreciation. In crude terms, 'We don't much like the colonialism or Thatcher, but we do like your music.'

The *cancha* is a place where this paradox is particularly visible. Anti-English chants are heard at every Argentina match, and across club stadiums during the week of

Malvinas Day in April each year. That night in Santiago was not the only time I have stood sheepishly on the terraces while everyone around me jumps up and down to '*El que no salta, es un inglés!*' But in the very same space, Rolling Stones logos are co-opted on flags, chants are sung to the tune of English songs, and the fans shout English words like 'corner!' and 'offside!' as they appeal to the officials during the game.

When a video went viral of a grizzled Almirante Brown fan regaling people in the street about a fight that (apparently) took place during the 1998 World Cup in France, I was struck by how deftly it managed to capture various different threads of Argentina's anti-Englishness. The story was of underdog fans from small *descenso* teams like Almirante, who came together to rescue a group of Boca supporters being chased down by English hooligans. Evoking some kind of military victory, the plucky Argentines captured the flags of the English, which boasted the names of national giants like Manchester United. He ends the story with an emphatic cry of '*¡Viva Perón!*'

In the anecdote, Argentina is fighting a winnable war in the streets, not the battlefields of the Falklands/Malvinas where inferior resources, equipment and expertise are brutally exposed. Their underdog spirit and nationalistic unity defeats a powerful enemy. A triumph for Peronism and the common man.

In the comments, the poster of the video is called a hypocrite for celebrating the story but having a social media profile full of references to the Rolling Stones. 'The day you show me a member of the Rolling Stones murdering Argentinians on our islands is when I'll respond to you about apparent hypocrisy,' he writes in response. 'Decent Argentines have never had a problem with the English people. The problem is with the British crown.'

Hidden beneath the cloak of social media triviality is a neat encapsulation of Argentina's supposed anti-Englishness.

To me, it always feels more like a pro-Argentina sentiment than an intrinsically anti-England one. It is an expression of the working-class patriotism espoused by Perón, who wanted to convince his nation that it no longer needed to be subservient to old imperial powers.

Margaret Thatcher, someone who romanticised the British Empire and waged war on sections of her own country's working class, was the antithesis of this Argentinian patriotism. The military machine that carried out her orders on the Falklands/Malvinas was more than an adversary in a conflict, it represented an ideological enemy. Argentina's callous military government no doubt recognised this propaganda opportunity, and rallied a nation behind a cruel, unwinnable war.

For the Argentines who still sing about *Las Malvinas* in football stadiums, there is no shame in their military defeat to a greater power. The ideals of Peronism do not stigmatise material weakness. The idea of having less but showing courage and determination is something that's celebrated in Argentina's terrace culture. There is a chant sung by fans of numerous clubs which goes, *'No tengo un mango y voy igual, de visitante o de local.'* – 'I don't have a penny but I'll go anyway, home or away.'

Having become so used to an English fan culture which uses poverty as an insult – with chants like 'we pay your benefits' and 'feed the Scousers' being depressingly common – I find the sentiment of the Argentinian *hincha* refreshing. It creates an atmosphere of economic inclusivity, that nobody should be left behind if they wish to support their club.

These beliefs have no doubt helped to sustain the member-owned model of Argentinian clubs which keeps ticket prices low for *socios* to this day. Meanwhile, as we English hurl abuse at opposition fans about being poor, our privately owned clubs raise ticket prices every season, pricing more and more people out of following their teams. There is something in Argentina's patriotic, pro-working class fandom that seems to protect the interest of the *socios* – and that should be admired. If a byproduct of this culture is the occasional chant calling for my death as an Englishman, I'll just have to take that on the chin.

Chapter 24

A place to call home

Pero hay un sueño   But there is a dream
Que aún me queda por lograr That I'm still yet to achieve
Ya falta menos nada me puede parar Nearly there, nothing can stop me now
Yo te prometo que muy pronto volveremos I promise you that we'll be there very soon
A levantar los escalones en Boedo To build the stands in Boedo

ONE LAST wall was all that remained. Only recently, the surrounding rubble had formed a vast, imposing structure – held firm by a multibillion-dollar global empire. Its foundations had been laid on Argentinian soil by enterprising Europeans some 40 years earlier, but now its time was up.

One last wall, and down it came. Crashing to the ground in a cloud of dust. Finally, on 30 January 2025, no more walls stood between San Lorenzo and their return home. The demolition of the Carrefour supermarket was complete, leaving a perfect vacant rectangle at 1700 Avenida La Plata in Boedo, Buenos Aires.

'Seeing that video of the bulldozers was beautiful. It was pure joy. Now there are no traces of the past. Just the open land, as it was when they first decided to build the Viejo Gasómetro.' Martín Cutino – the actor, writer and *cuervo* who always speaks so evocatively about Boedo and his beloved San Lorenzo – peers through my screen, misty-eyed. I wanted to get a sense of the mood among *cuervos* since the Carrefour demolition was completed. It's a chilly night in London and I'm wrapped in a fleece as I hunch over my laptop in a dark room. Only four months have passed since my last trip to Argentina, but with sunshine pouring into the garden behind Martín, it feels like a world away.

'Recovering that land is an epic feat. People said it was impossible. In these times of capitalism, with what a giant supermarket chain like that represents, it *was* impossible. But here we are.'

San Lorenzo have not won a trophy – or even come particularly close – since I travelled to Córdoba to see them win the Supercopa against Boca in early 2016. But Cutino says that passing milestones in La Vuelta a Boedo more than compensates for a lack of silverware.

'These are like small championships that we're winning. In football, the trophies can cover up its essence and everything gets reduced to that one form of success. But for those of us who fought for La Vuelta, every step, every little thing that's achieved is a triumph. And it's emotional, because it means that the struggle of so many years, of so many fans from all over the world, is bearing fruit.'

As I write, a timeline to start building the new stadium is conspicuous by its absence. Crippling debts and boardroom chaos continue to undermine San Lorenzo on and off the pitch. But with the land cleared, La Vuelta has never been closer and Martín has no doubts that destiny will be fulfilled.

'San Lorenzo was founded by nine kids between 12 and 16 years old. And after just 12 or 13 years, they built the biggest stadium in South America. So when you dream and work tirelessly for something, it can be achieved. It's only a matter of time. San Lorenzo fans are not going to give this up. It might happen during this administration, it might be the next one, but the stadium is going to be built.'

At one stage of our chat, Martín picks up his laptop and I lurch through his house as the camera swings from floor to ceiling. When it resettles, He is standing by a cabinet with a little block of wood in his hand and a big grin on his face. The block, tied in a tiny blue-and-red bow, is a piece of the original terracing at the 75,000-capacity Viejo Gasómetro. Martín puts the block back inside the cabinet and picks up the item lying next to it – a leather booklet with a passport-style photograph and hand-written details inside. It's the San Lorenzo *socio* card which belonged to Martín's grandfather, from 1968. Side by side, the items neatly illustrated the power and symbolism of the Gasómetro among *cuervos*. It connects generations and carries the spirit of loved ones who have passed. The struggle to return is the struggle to keep their memory alive.

'Thousands of souls gathered in that place for years and left their trace. Many of them are no longer with us, but they're spiritually there,' Martín said in his husky voice, as if delivering a line from one of his plays. 'It's a force you have to believe in. Beyond the religious, [the club founder] Lorenzo Massa always believed in man rising above the factual and connecting with the spiritual, with the sacred. I think there's some of that in Boedo. The souls of the *barrio* are asking for San Lorenzo to return.'

Many *cuervos* believe the soil in Boedo carries some kind of energy that inspires all who wear the blue-and-red stripes. In 2016, San Lorenzo opened the Roberto Pando Sports Complex on the land where the Viejo Gasómetro once stood, and the venue became home to the club's popular basketball and futsal teams. Success was instant. San Lorenzo had never been champions of the Liga Nacional de Básquetbol since its reorganisation in 1985, but from the year the team started playing in Boedo, it won the title for five consecutive seasons. The futsal side, on a 12-year trophy drought, won two tournaments within two years of returning to the *barrio*. Then in 2021, it made history by becoming the first Argentinian club to ever win the Copa Libertadores de Futsal. On the sacred ground of their spiritual home, San Lorenzo teams were suddenly being lifted to glory.

* * *

From an outsider's perspective, sports like basketball and futsal may seem like an unusual and unnecessary sideshow to a club's main offering of professional football. But these additional teams, which run through all ages and ability levels, are a crucial part of what differentiates member-owned Argentinian clubs from the privatised entities across most of the world.

By offering myriad sports, recreational activities, cultural programmes and educational classes, clubs are designed to bring people in as participants, not customers. Their affordable membership models, which allow you to walk into the gym on a Wednesday morning or into the *popular* on matchday with the same card, create an accessible environment for both supporters and the wider community.

As Frydenberg and other sociologists have detailed, football clubs have been a focal point of the *barrio* and a vital part of everyday life for more than a century. They forge friendships and sometimes create families too. I once spoke to a *cuervo* who met his wife at San Lorenzo, and now his teenage children have boyfriends and girlfriends who they met through playing sports at Ciudad Deportiva. The clubs also offer valuable space beyond the four walls of an apartment and refuge from the insecurity of the streets. I often think about Christian from La Butteler sleeping within the club when things weren't easy at home.

When you boil La Vuelta a Boedo down to its simplest form – moving a football stadium 20 blocks up the road – the decades of campaigning and depth of feeling around the movement make no sense at all. But it is driven by the powerful human desire for a home beyond home. A familiar place which puts you at ease and gives you a sense of belonging. People need more than places to consume entertainment. They need places where they can connect with an area, a community, their ancestors and their past.

However, as Argentina pursues the libertarian doctrine of privatisation, the community-driven, member-owned football clubs – and the 'homes' they offer – are under threat. In December 2024, president Javier Milei issued an 'urgent decree' aimed at legalising the conversion of football clubs into private businesses, known as a *sociedad anónima deportiva* – or SAD.

'No more poverty socialism in football,' Milei proclaimed on social media, while criticising the AFA's opposition to his bill. Privately owned clubs 'have the best players' and 'results matter', he said. A few months later when the bill was put forward, he stated, 'Argentina is a hotbed of football talent and viewed as a business, there are lots of opportunities.'

And therein lies the rub. When clubs are only 'viewed as a business', there is little room for the affordable activities and extracurricular programmes currently on offer. They don't make enough money. And when a club becomes an enterprise, there is certainly no place for the leadership elections which are held at football clubs. The owner will be the one calling the shots, and they will only move on when they decide to, not when the *socios* vote them out.

The likes of Milei are absolutely correct in identifying the need to address the alarming decline of Argentina's domestic leagues and the ability of clubs to retain talent for longer. A better place to start might be an overhaul of the AFA, whose chaos and cronyism is devaluing the Primera División's product every season. If those offers for privatisation do come in, fans will be faced with a series of dilemmas. Will supporting a team with more power in the transfer market justify losing low-cost access to club facilities, and a democratic say in how the club is run? Will lifelong *socios* carrying the baton of their ancestors be happy to become customers rather than members? Should they give away their club to improve chances of winning a Libertadores?

'The day clubs are privatised, that's it. They cease to exist,' Martín argues. 'They become businesses, and when a business fails, it shuts down. But when a club is in trouble, it doesn't shut down. Even if it goes bankrupt, even if it loses everything – it carries on.'

The latter point is not lost on *cuervos*, who had to drag their club through the perilous circumstances of bankruptcy, homelessness and relegation in the 1980s. By the turn of the century, San Lorenzo had a home but were still not free from financial concern. Spotting an opportunity, a Swiss firm called ISL planned to circumvent Argentinian laws to make an investment in the club.

Supporters were fearful and furious in equal measure. On 30 November 2000, protests against the investment at Ciudad Deportiva led to violent clashes with the police. '*San Lorenzo no se vende!*' – 'San Lorenzo is not for sale!' – was the message and ISL's interest soon cooled. Since then, 30 November has been the official San Lorenzo Supporters' Day. Every year I receive messages from fellow *cuervos* on WhatsApp. '*Feliz Día del Hincha!*' they'll say. It feels like Christmas or a birthday.

In the *cancha*, some songs still reference the ISL episode. '*Pasaron cien años, que late este sentimiento, quisieron privatizarte, pero yo a vos no te vendo.*' – 'A hundred years have passed, with this feeling beating on, they tried to privatise you, but I will not sell you.'

* * *

As I follow Argentinian football from afar, there are two off-the-pitch struggles I will be watching with close interest. The Vuelta a Boedo campaign captured my heart from the very beginning and I cannot wait to see the day that San Lorenzo finally return home, just as my dear Charlton Athletic did in 1992. I was too young to witness the emotional return to The Valley in person, but I hope to be present for San Lorenzo's first match back in Boedo, whenever that may be. I will look down at the square metre of pitch I bought a decade ago and no doubt shed a tear.

But it's not just San Lorenzo who are fighting for their home. The second struggle looks set to play out across Argentinian football, with every supporter and *socio* due to have their clubs – their second homes – affected by the privatising forces circling over the game. External investment isn't inherently bad. Often it is necessary. But in the UK we have seen first-hand how the over-commercialisation of football can damage the sense of belonging and community at a club. I have lost count of the number of friends who have drifted away from their teams – particularly those in the Premier League – where supporters are converted into consumers, or simply replaced by them. In an increasingly atomised and lonely society, that's a worrying trend. More than ever, we need spaces that bring different people together, unite them in shared experiences, and create precious bonds.

San Lorenzo was exactly that kind of space for me. Without the club, my experience of living abroad would have been infinitely poorer. I would not have connected with Argentines in the same way – a people I had been told were my enemies, especially inside a football stadium. We would not have stood shoulder to shoulder, talking together, singing together, and embracing each other in moments of ecstasy. San Lorenzo connected me to their beautiful homeland, too. Following *El Cuervo* gave me a reason to discover new places – on and off the beaten track – from Rosario, Córdoba and Mar del Plata to Lanús, Avellaneda and Sarandí. It took me beyond Argentina's borders to countries I had never seen, like Chile and Morocco. The club even helped me speak a new language. Studying the words to the best chants in the world and talking about San Lorenzo built up my confidence and conversation skills. Spanish had been a struggle for so long, but suddenly the words began to flow.

Above all, I know that without the communal space of the stadium and the shared purpose of following a football team, I would have missed out on some special, lasting friendships. Conversations that began on the terraces now continue around dinner tables. You may go to a country for its culture, but you stay for its people. San Lorenzo opened the door to a new world and gave me a home, when I was so far away from my own.

Acknowledgements

THANK YOU, LILI, and all my family, for your support over the years – especially as I kept flying back to Argentina, which didn't always seem like the most sensible life choice.

Gracias a Rosalba Rodríguez por la cama, la comida y la gran compañía durante esos hermosos meses en la Esquina de San Pedro. El proceso de escribir este libro no habría sido posible sin su hospitalidad.

Jenny Douch and Marcus Haydon have brains as big as their hearts (both massive) and I am eternally grateful for their help. Their enthusiasm and generosity helped me at every stage of this project and the book benefitted no end from their sharpness, sensitivity and deep knowledge. Thank you for a priceless contribution that I will never forget.

Chris Hylland is a fantastic writer and I'm lucky to be able to call him a friend. His encouragement and advice now spans several years, and beginning this book owed a lot to his positivity and wise words. Thank you.

I have appreciated the interest – feigned or otherwise – from all my wonderful mates. Special thanks to those who offered their thoughts, skills or contacts in some way, including Chhaya, Eduardo, Gonza, Gav, Lucas, Marko and Martín Tirman.

Gracias de corazón a los siguientes que compartieron su tiempo, conocimiento y buena onda conmigo: Guido Gallo, Martín Cutino, Gallego, Mariano de la Fuente, Pablo Fernández Rojas,

Christian Evangelista, Adolfo Res, Luciano Wernicke, Jenny y Andrea del Club Atlético Madre del Pueblo, Jorge y Los Cuervos de San Martín.

También estoy muy agradecido por el hermoso trabajo y la generosidad de Facundo González Trejo y Jorge Osuna. Muchas gracias.

Y gracias eternas a la familia azulgrana por haberme aceptado como un cuervo más a lo largo de los años.

Finally, thank you to everyone who has picked up this book and read it. Your curiosity and support is appreciated.

Un abrazo azulgrana.

Selected bibliography

Albarces, P., *Fútbol y Patria* (Prometeo, 2003)

Armus, D., & Rinke, S., *Del football al fútbol / futebol historias argentinas, brasileras y uruguayas en el siglo XX* (Vervuert Verlagsgesellschaft, 2014)

Bryce, B., *Immigration, Communities, and Neighborhoods in Buenos Aires, 1880–1930* (globalurbanhistory.com, 2018)

Campomar, A., *¡Golazo! A History of Latin American Football* (Quercus, 2014)

Frydenberg, J., *Society, City and Football in the Buenos Aires of 1920–1930* (Vervuert Verlagsgesellschaft, 2014)

Gallo, G., & Rezzónico, J.M. *La Hinchada que Hace Cantar Al Mundo* (Buenos Aires, 2023)

Goldblatt, D., *The Ball is Round: A Global History of Football* (Penguin, 2007)

Hawkins, M., '*This is Boedo' Stories of a Lost Football Stadium, a Buenos Aires Barrio, and How the Hinchas of San Lorenzo Fought to Return* (Carleton University, 2017)

Hylland, C., *Tears at La Bombonera* (Pitch Publishing, 2021)

Nouzeilles, G., & Montaldo, G., *The Argentina Reader: History, Culture, Politics* (Duke University Press, 2002)

Wilson, J., *Angels with Dirty Faces: The Footballing History of Argentina* (Orion, 2015)